8. 22

S0-ARF-250

FREE COPY

The
Least
You
Should
Know
about
English

FREE COPY

FREE COPY

FORM C
Fourth Edition

The Least You Should Know about English
Writing Skills

TERESA FERSTER GLAZIER

HOLT, RINEHART AND WINSTON, INC.

Fort Worth   Chicago   San Francisco   Philadelphia
Montreal   Toronto   London   Sydney   Tokyo

This text is available in Form A, Form B, and Form C so that a different form may be used in various semesters. The three forms are essentially the same except that they have different exercises, writing assignments, and essays.

Library of Congress Cataloging-in-Publication Data

Glazier, Teresa Ferster.
    The least you should know about English : writing skills : form C
/ Teresa Ferster Glazier.—4th ed.
        p.   cm.
    Includes index.
    ISBN 0-03-047034-X (soft cover)
    1. English language—Rhetoric.   2. English language—
Grammar—1950–   I. Title.
PE1408.G559   1981   90-42433
808.'042—dc20   CIP

Copyright © 1991, 1987, 1984, 1981 by Holt, Rinehart and Winston, Inc.

All rights reserved. No part of this publication may be reproduced or transmitted in any form or by any means, electronic or mechanical, including photocopy, recording or any information storage and retrieval system, without permission in writing from the publisher.

Requests for permission to make copies of any part of the work should be mailed to: Copyrights and Permissions Department, Holt, Rinehart and Winston, Inc., 6277 Sea Harbor Drive, Orlando, Florida 32887.

Address for editorial correspondence: Holt, Rinehart and Winston, Inc., 301 Commerce Street, Suite 3700, Forth Worth, Texas 76102

Address for orders: Holt, Rinehart and Winston, Inc., 6277 Sea Harbor Drive, Orlando, Florida 32887. 1-800-782-4479, or 1-800-433-0001 (in Florida)

Printed in the United States of America

1 2 3 4   090   9 8 7 6 5 4 3 2 1

Holt, Rinehart and Winston, Inc.
The Dryden Press
Saunders College Publishing

FREE COPY   FREE COPY   FREE COPY   FREE COPY   FREE COPY
FREE COPY

FREE COPY

FREE COPY

FREE COPY

FREE COPY

FREE COPY

FREE COPY

To the Instructor

This book is for students who need to review the rules of English composition and who may profit from a simplified approach. The main features of the book are these:

1. It is truly basic. Only the indisputable essentials of spelling, grammar, sentence structure, and punctuation are included because research has shown that putting too much emphasis on mechanics is not the way to help students learn to write.
2. Little linguistic terminology is used. A conjunction is a connecting word; gerunds and present participles are *ing* words; a parenthetical constituent is an interrupter. Students work with words they already know.
3. It has abundant practice sentences and paragraphs—enough so that students learn to use the rules automatically and thus *carry their new skills over into their writing.*
4. It includes groups of thematically related, informative sentences on such subjects as the history of forks, Wayne Gretzky's first world record, plants that eat insects, the world's largest collection of canoes, patterns of snowflakes, the reason leaves turn red and yellow, Woolworth's first store, prices in the Sears 1908 catalogue, whales' songs, the hole in the ozone layer, Einstein's hatred of schoolwork . . . thus making the task of doing the exercises interesting.
5. It provides answers at the back of the book so that students can correct their own work, thus teaching themselves as they go.
6. It stresses writing. A writing section, EIGHT STEPS TO BETTER WRITING (pp. 206–46), provides writing assignments to be used along with the exercises. The section has been kept brief because **students learn to write by *writing* rather than by reading pages and pages *about* writing.** Even though the section is only 41 pages (compared to 204 for the first part of the text), students will no doubt spend more time on it than on all the rest of the book. (Instructors who prefer to begin with the paragraph may use pages 220–23 first and then return to the beginning of the writing section on page 206.)
7. It stresses thinking. As students write logically organized papers, they learn that *writing* problems are really *thinking* problems.
8. It includes at the end of the Writing Section five essays to read and summarize. Students improve their reading by learning to spot main ideas and their writing by learning to write concise summaries.

FREE COPY   FREE COPY   FREE COPY   FREE COPY

9. It can be used as a self-tutoring text. The simple explanations, abundant exercises, and answers at the back of the book provide students with a writing lab in their own rooms.

Students who have previously been overwhelmed by the complexities of English should, through mastering simple rules and through writing and rewriting simple papers, gain enough competence to succeed in further composition courses.

A packet of ready-to-photocopy tests covering all parts of the text (four for each section) is available to instructors. Also available is a disk of tests that will allow the instructor to send a class to a computer lab for testing. These aids are free upon adoption of the text and may be obtained from the local Holt representative or from the English Editor, Holt, Rinehart and Winston, 301 Commerce Street, Suite 3700, Fort Worth, Texas 76102.

TFG

Acknowledgments

I am grateful to the users of this text who have written to point out improvements that should be made, and as always I am indebted to my careful proofreaders: Teresa Edwards, Christopher Glazier, Kenneth Glazier, and Liz Roth.

FREE COPY   FREE COPY   FREE COPY   FREE COPY

Contents

To the instructor   v

WHAT IS THE LEAST YOU SHOULD KNOW?

1. SPELLING

Your own list of misspelled words   6
Words often confused   7
More words often confused   16
  Proofreading exercise   24
Contractions   25
Possessives   31
  Review of contractions and possessives   38
  Proofreading exercise   39
Words that can be broken into parts   40
Rule for doubling a final consonant   41
  Progress test   43
A list of frequently misspelled words   44
Using your dictionary   46

2. SENTENCE STRUCTURE

Finding subjects and verbs   55
  Proofreading exercise   60
Subjects not in prepositional phrases   61
More about verbs and subjects   66
  Proofreading exercise   71
Correcting run-together sentences   72
Correcting fragments   80
More about fragments   88
  Review of run-together sentences and fragments   93
  Proofreading exercise   96
Using standard English verbs   97
Using helping verbs and irregular verbs   104
Avoiding dialect expressions   110
  Proofreading exercise   113
  Progress test   114
Making subjects, verbs, and pronouns agree   115

FREE COPY   FREE COPY   FREE COPY   FREE COPY

Choosing the right pronoun 121
Making the pronoun refer to the right word 124
Correcting misplaced or dangling modifiers 128
    Proofreading exercise 132
Using parallel construction 133
Correcting shift in time 141
Correcting shift in person 145
Correcting wordiness 151
Avoiding clichés 155
    Review of sentence structure 157
    Proofreading exercise 159

3. PUNCTUATION AND CAPITAL LETTERS

Period, question mark, exclamation mark, semicolon, colon, dash 161
    Proofreading exercise 168
Commas (Rules 1, 2, and 3) 169
Commas (Rules 4, 5, and 6) 176
    Review of the comma 183
Quotation marks 185
Capital letters 193
    Review of punctuation and capital letters 197
    Proofreading exercises 200
    Comprehensive test on entire text 203

4. WRITING

EIGHT STEPS TO BETTER WRITING 206

I.   Do some free writing 206
II.   Limit your topic 207
    ASSIGNMENT 1 A Satisfying Moment 209
    ASSIGNMENT 2 A Place Important to Me 210
III. Write a thesis statement 212
IV. Support your thesis with reasons or points 215
    ASSIGNMENT 3 Two Thesis Statements with Points 216
V.   Organize your paper from your thesis 218
VI. Organize each paragraph 220
    ASSIGNMENT 4 Writing a Paragraph 223
    ASSIGNMENT 5 A Decision I Have Made 224
VII. Write and rewrite 225
    ASSIGNMENT 6 A Hobby 225
VIII. Proofread ALOUD 228
    ASSIGNMENT 7 My Best Class 228
    ASSIGNMENT 8 A Process Paper 228
    ASSIGNMENT 9 Most Important to Me 228
    ASSIGNMENT 10 Someone I Admire 228

ASSIGNMENT 11   Something I've Learned   229
ASSIGNMENT 12   A Thousand Dollars to Spend   229
ASSIGNMENT 13   An Achievement I'm Proud Of   229
ASSIGNMENT 14   A Quotation for Me   229
ASSIGNMENT 15   Advice That Changed My Life   229
ASSIGNMENT 16   My Opinion on a Current Problem   230
Writing a summary   231
ASSIGNMENT 17   A 100-Word Summary   231
   Juvenile Juries
ASSIGNMENT 18   A 100-Word Summary   234
   Darkness at Noon
ASSIGNMENT 19   A 100-Word Summary   237
   Turning Rails into Trails
ASSIGNMENT 20   A 100-Word Summary   239
   How to Keep Air Clean
ASSIGNMENT 21   A 100-Word Summary   241
   0 (Backward) Canada
Writing an Application   243
ASSIGNMENT 22   A Letter of Application   243
Writing an Evaluation
ASSIGNMENT 23   An Evaluation of My Performance   246

ANSWERS   248

INDEX   299

What Is the Least You Should Know?

What <u>Is</u> the Least You Should Know?

Most English textbooks try to teach you as much as they can. This one will teach you the least it can—and still help you learn to write acceptably. You won't have to bother with predicate nouns and subordinating conjunctions and participial phrases and demonstrative pronouns and all those terms you've been hearing about for years. You can get along without them if you'll learn thoroughly a few basic rules. You *do* have to know how to spell common words; you *do* have to recognize subjects and verbs to avoid writing fragments and run-together sentences; you *do* have to know a few rules of punctuation—but rules will be kept to a minimum.

Unless you know these few rules, though, you'll have difficulty communicating in writing. Take this sentence for example:

Let's eat mom before we start the housecleaning.

We assume the writer isn't a cannibal but merely failed to capitalize and put commas around the name of a person spoken to. If the sentence had read

Let's eat, Mom, before we start the housecleaning.

then no one would misunderstand. Or take this sentence:

The coach dropped Jeffrey and Curt and Don got to play.

Did Curt get to play? There's no way of knowing unless the writer puts a comma either after *Jeffrey* or after *Curt*. If the sentence reads

The coach dropped Jeffrey and Curt, and Don got to play.

2

we know that Curt was dropped, but if the sentence reads

The coach dropped Jeffrey, and Curt and Don got to play.

then we know Curt got to play. Punctuation makes all the difference. What you'll learn from this book is simply to make your writing so clear that no one will misunderstand it.

The English you'll learn to write is called standard English, and it may differ slightly from the English spoken in your community. All over the country, various dialects of English are spoken. In northern New England, for example, people leave the *r* off certain words and put an *r* on others. President Kennedy said *dollah* for *dollar*, *idear* for *idea*, and *Cubar* for *Cuba*. In black communities many people leave the *s* off some verbs and put an *s* on others, saying *he walk* and *they walks* instead of *he walks* and *they walk*.

But no matter what English dialect people *speak*, they all must *write* the same dialect—standard English. You can say, "Whacha doin? Cmon," and everybody will understand, but you can't *write* that way. If you want your readers to understand what you write, you'll have to write the way English-speaking people all over the world write—in standard English. Being able to write standard English is essential in college, and it probably will be an asset in your career.

It's important to master every rule as you come to it because many rules depend on the ones before. For example, unless you learn to pick out subjects and verbs, you'll have trouble with run-together sentences, with fragments, with subject-verb agreement, and with punctuation. The rules are brief and clear, and it won't be difficult to master all of them . . . *if you want to*. But you do have to want to!

Here's the way to master the least you should know:

1. Study the explanation of each rule carefully.
2. Do the first exercise (10 sentences). Correct your answers by those in the Answer Section at the back of the book. If you miss even one answer, study the explanation again to find out why.
3. Do the second exercise and correct it. If you miss a single answer, go back once more and study the explanation. You must have missed something. Be tough on yourself. Don't just think, "Maybe I'll hit it right next time." Go back and master the rules, and *then* try the next exercise. It's important to correct each group of 10 sentences before going on so that you'll discover your mistakes while you still have sentences to practice on.
4. You may be tempted to quit when you get several exercises perfect. Don't! Make yourself finish every exercise. It's not enough to

understand a rule. You have to *practice* it. Just as understanding the strokes in swimming won't help unless you actually get into the pool and swim, so understanding a rule about writing isn't going to help unless you practice using it.

If you're positive, however, after doing five exercises, that you've mastered the rules, take Exercise 6 as a test. If you miss even one answer, you must do all the rest of the exercises. But if you get Exercise 6 perfect, then spend your time helping one of your friends. Teaching is one of the best ways of learning.

5. But rules and exercises are not the most important part of this book. **The most important part begins on page 206–when you begin to write.** The Writing Assignments, grouped together in the back of the book for convenience, are to be used along with the exercises. At the end of most chapters in the front part of the book, you'll be referred to the Writing Assignments in the back. Also you'll sometimes be asked to do another kind of writing—Journal Writing, which calls for just a few sentences in your daily journal using the rules you've learned that day.

Mastering these essentials will take time. Generally, college students are expected to spend two hours outside of class for each hour in class. You may need more. Undoubtedly, the more time you spend, the more your writing will improve.

Spelling

1

1 Spelling

Anyone can learn to spell. You can get rid of most of your spelling errors by the time you finish this book if you want to. It's just a matter of deciding you're going to do it. If you really intend to learn to spell, master the first seven parts of this section. They are

YOUR OWN LIST OF MISSPELLED WORDS
WORDS OFTEN CONFUSED
CONTRACTIONS
POSSESSIVES
WORDS THAT CAN BE BROKEN INTO PARTS
RULE FOR DOUBLING A FINAL CONSONANT
A LIST OF FREQUENTLY MISSPELLED WORDS

Master these seven parts, and you'll be a good speller.

YOUR OWN LIST OF MISSPELLED WORDS

On the inside back cover of this book, write correctly all the misspelled words in the papers handed back to you. Review them until you're sure of them. That will take care of most of your errors.

WORDS OFTEN CONFUSED

By mastering the spelling of these often-confused words, you'll take care of many of your spelling problems. Study the words carefully, with their examples, before trying the exercises.

a, an

Use *an* before a word that begins with a vowel *sound* (*a*, *e*, *i*, and *o*, plus *u* when it sounds like *uh*). Note that it's not the letter but the *sound* of the letter that matters.

 an adult, an engine, an idea, an orange
 an hour, an honor (silent *h*)
 an uproar, an umpire (the *u*'s sound like *uh*)

Use *a* before a word that begins with a consonant sound (all the sounds except the vowels, plus *u* or *eu* when they sound like *you*).

 a daisy, a headline, a hammer
 a union, a uniform, a unit (the *u*'s sound like *you*)
 a eulogy, a European trip (*eu* sounds like *you*)

accept, except

Accept is a verb and means "to receive willingly."
 I *accept* your suggestion. (receive it willingly)
Except means "excluding" or "but."
 All were there *except* you. (but you)

advise, advice

Advise is a verb (pronounce the *s* like *z*).
 I *advise* you to keep trying.
Use *advice* when it's not a verb.
 She gave me good *advice*.

affect, effect

Affect is a verb and means "to influence."
 The weather does *affect* my moods.
Effect means "result." If *a*, *an*, or *the* is in front of the word, then you'll know it isn't a verb and will use *effect*.
 That letter had an *effect* on her plans.
 His warning had no *effect* on the players.

all ready, already

If you can leave out the *all* and the sentence still makes sense, then *all ready* is the form to use. (In that form, *all* is a separate word and could be left out.)

I'm *all ready* to go. (*I'm ready to go* makes sense.)

Lunch is *all ready*. (*Lunch is ready* makes sense.)

But if you can't leave out the *all* and still have the sentence make sense, then use *already* (the form in which the *al* has to stay in the word).

I'm *already* late. (*I'm ready late* doesn't make sense.)

are, or, our

Are is a verb.

We *are* going to the museum.

Or is used between two possibilities, as "tea *or* coffee."

Keep it *or* send it back.

Our shows we possess something.

Our house is painted blue.

brake, break

Brake means "to slow or stop motion." It's also the name of the device that slows or stops motion.

You *brake* to avoid an accident.

You slam on your *brakes*.

Break means "to shatter" or "to split." It's also the name of an interruption, as "a coffee break."

You *break* a dish or an engagement or a record.

You enjoy your Easter *break*.

choose, chose

I will *choose* fish rather than steak right now.

I *chose* fish yesterday.

clothes, cloths

Her *clothes* are always in style.

We used soft *cloths* to polish the silverware.

coarse, course

Coarse describes texture, as *coarse* cloth.

Her suit was made of *coarse* material.

Course is used for all other meanings.

Of *course* I enjoyed the poetry *course*.

complement, compliment

The one spelled with an *e* completes something or brings it to perfection.

A 30° angle is the *complement* of a 60° angle.

Her blue jewelry *complements* her gray dress.

The one spelled with an *i* has to do with praise. Remember "*I* like compliments," and you'll remember to use the *i* spelling when you mean praise.

She was waiting for a *compliment*.

He *complimented* her on her excellent talk.

conscious, conscience	*Conscious* means "aware."
	    I wasn't *conscious* that the taxi was waiting.
	 The extra *n* in *conscience* should remind you of NO, which is what your conscience often says to you.
	    My *conscience* told me to observe the speed limit.

dessert, desert	*Dessert* is the sweet one, the one you like two helpings of. So give it two helpings of *s*.
	    I ordered a sundae for *dessert*.
	 The other one, *desert*, is used for all other meanings.
	    Don't *desert* me.
	    The camel moved slowly across the *desert*.

do, due	You *do* something.
	    I *do* what I want to *do*.
	 But a payment or an assignment is *due;* it is scheduled for a certain time.
	    My bank loan is *due* next week.

does, dose	*Does* is a verb.
	    He *does* his work well. She *doesn't* care about cars.
	 A *dose* is an amount of medicine.
	    That was a bitter *dose* to swallow.

feel, fill	*Feel* describes your feelings.
	    I *feel* tired.
	 Fill is what you do to a cup.
	    Will you *fill* my cup again?

fourth, forth	The number *fourth* has *four* in it. (But note that *forty* does not. Remember the word *forty-fourth*.)
	    This is our *fourth* game.
	    That was our *forty-fourth* point.
	 If you don't mean a number, use *forth*.
	    She walked back and *forth*.

have, of	*Have* is a verb. When you say *could have*, the *have* may sound like *of*, but it must not be written that way. Always write *could have, would have, should have, might have*.
	    I should *have* finished my work sooner.
	    Then I could *have* gone home.
	 Use *of* only in a prepositional phrase (see p. 61).
	    I often think *of* him.

hear, here

The last three letters of *hear* spell "ear." You *hear* with your ear.

I can *hear* the phone ringing.

The other spelling *here* tells "where." Note that the three words indicating a place or pointing out something all have *here* in them: *here, there, where*.

Where are you? I'm right here.

it's, its

It's is a contraction and means "it is" or "it has."

It's time to go. (It is time to go.)

It's been a good game. (It has been a good game.)

Its is a possessive. (Possessives such as *its, yours, hers, ours, theirs, whose* are already possessive and never take an apostrophe. See p. 32.)

The team reached *its* goal.

knew, new

Knew has to do with knowledge (both start with *k*).

New means "not old."

He *knew* she wanted a *new* car.

know, no

Know has to do with knowledge (both start with *k*).

I *know* the answer.

No means "not any" or the opposite of "yes."

I have *no* time. *No*, I can't go.

EXERCISES

Underline the correct word. Don't guess! If you aren't sure, turn back to the explanatory pages. When you've finished 10 sentences, compare your answers with those at the back of the book. Correct each group of 10 sentences before continuing so you'll catch your mistakes while you still have sentences to practice on.

☐EXERCISE 1

1. We've rented a (knew, new) house, and (it's its) (all ready already) to move into.
2. (It's Its) location is (a an) asset because (it's its) near a park.
3. The park has (a an) outdoor swimming pool.
4. (It's Its) close enough that we can easily walk back and (forth fourth).
5. Of (coarse course) we (know no) the exercise will have a good (affect effect) on (are our) health.
6. I (hear here) the bus service in the area is excellent too.
7. That's (a an) important factor for (are our) family.

8. We like to (choose chose) between taking a bus (are or) driving (are our) car.

9. (Are Our) new location is also not far from a shopping mall.

10. I (do due) think we're making (a an) excellent move. We should (have of) made it sooner.

☐EXERCISE 2

1. Last summer we drove (are our) (knew new) car to Arizona.

2. We (choose chose) (a an) itinerary that took us along a scenic route.

3. We decided to (accept except) the (advice advise) of friends who'd been there.

4. They said (it's its) wise to (do due) the (desert dessert) driving at night.

5. We had had (know no) experience with such driving before.

6. We were (conscience conscious) that it would be different from the driving we (are our) used to (hear here).

7. The trip was a good (brake break) from (are our) busy lives.

8. Of (coarse course) I wish we could (have of) stayed longer.

9. I (know no) the (affect effect) of that scenery won't soon wear off.

10. Now we're (all ready already) dreaming of another trip.

☐EXERCISE 3

1. Last week (are our) son took part in a triathlon.

2. (It's Its) been called the fastest growing sport in (are our) country.

3. I wasn't (conscience conscious) that there are over 2,000 triathlons held each year.

4. A triathlon consists of (a an) ocean swim followed by a bike race followed by a marathon run.

5. I (hear here) that it all began when some people in Hawaii were arguing about which was the toughest sport—biking, running, (are or) swimming.

6. In a triathlon in Chicago I (know no) the contestants swam nine-tenths of a mile in Lake Michigan, biked 24 miles, and ran 6 miles.

7. More than 2,400 athletes came (forth fourth) for that event.

8. (All ready Already) there is talk of getting the triathlon on the Olympic agenda for 1992.

9. As for me, I (choose chose) to (do due) one sport at a time.

10. Of (coarse course) I (all ready already) (know no) which sport that will be.

☐EXERCISE 4

1. Before long there may be (know no) more giant pandas.

2. Fewer than 1,000 (are our) left in all of China.

3. And those few are (all ready already) dying off.

4. Naturalists (know no) that the principal food of pandas is bamboo.

5. In fact (it's its) almost the only food they'll (accept except).
6. Periodically, though, the bamboo forests put (forth fourth) their flowers and then die.
7. Since the pandas don't like anything (accept except) bamboo, they're left with nothing to eat.
8. They can't move to (knew new) forests because those too have died.
9. Of (coarse course) other factors are also hastening the extinction of the pandas: internal parasites and (a an) unusually low reproduction rate.
10. Scientists are trying to find some alternative food for the pandas before they become (a an) extinct species.

☐EXERCISE 5

1. I'm reading (a an) interesting (knew new) book on word origins.
2. I never (knew new) there were so many fascinating word stories.
3. The names of many of (are our) months, for example, come from the names of people—either real or mythological.
4. Of (coarse course) I (all ready already) (knew new) that July is named for Julius Caesar and August for Augustus Caesar.
5. I wasn't (conscience conscious), though, that January is named for the Roman god Janus, who had two faces looking in opposite directions (January looks toward both the past year and the new year).
6. And I didn't (know no) May is named after a Roman goddess Maia.
7. I should (have of) guessed that March is named for Mars, the Roman god of war, and that June is the month of the Roman goddess Juno.
8. I may (choose chose) a vocabulary (coarse course) next semester.
9. I (hear here) that (it's its) excellent and that it (does dose) have a good (affect effect) on one's vocabulary.
10. I (do due) want to learn more word stories.

☐EXERCISE 6

1. I'm now taking a field (coarse course) in botany.
2. Until now, I never (knew new) whether a plant was smartweed (are or) foxtail grass.
3. Now I (know no) (a an) amazing number of plants.
4. I should (have of) taken this (coarse course) earlier, for a knowledge of plants (does dose) add to the pleasure of hiking.
5. (It's Its) relaxing to put on old (clothes cloths) and spend a morning in the woods.
6. Of (coarse course) I'm (conscience conscious) there's more to learn.
7. But I (do due) (know no) now the difference between ragweed and Queen Anne's lace.
8. I'm going to the (desert dessert) next fall to learn about more plants.
9. I might even (choose chose) botany as my major.
10. I (hear here) there (are our) good jobs for field naturalists in (are our) national parks.

☐EXERCISE 7

1. I've just read (a an) article about some (knew new) plans for Yosemite.
2. Although Yosemite isn't as large as Yellowstone or as deep as the Grand Canyon, (it's its) one of (are our) most beautiful parks.
3. Someone has called Yosemite Valley (a an) enormous unroofed cathedral with Half Dome as (it's its) altar.
4. I wasn't (conscience conscious) of Yosemite's history, but now I (know no) a little about it.
5. In the midst of the Civil War, Lincoln (choose chose) to sign a bill to protect Yosemite, and in 1890 Congress made it a national park.
6. (It's Its) visited every year by 2.6 million people, and of (coarse course) the problem is how to allow the people to come without turning it into a Disneyland.
7. The (knew new) plans designate 89 percent of Yosemite as protected wilderness.
8. It (does dose) seem desirable to keep some parts undeveloped.
9. The managers are (all ready already) planning to relocate many park services outside the park.
10. One of the concession managers (accepts excepts) the plans, saying, "If we ruin Yosemite, the (affect effect) will be to cut (are our) own throats."

☐EXERCISE 8

1. My sister and I visited Chicago during (are our) spring (brake break).
2. We should (have of) planned (a an) itinerary.
3. As it was, we had time to do little (accept except) buy our tickets and pack our (clothes cloths).
4. I (know no) we should have got (advice advise) about what new things to see.
5. Of (coarse course) we (knew new) the main places.
6. We both (choose chose) to spend (are our) first day at the Art Institute.
7. (Know No) matter how much time I spend there, (it's its) never enough.
8. It was my (forth fourth) visit, but its (affect effect) is always the same.
9. The second day we decided to (accept except) the (advice advise) of a friend and go to the Museum of Science and Industry.
10. I had (all ready already) visited it several times, but there's always something (knew new) there.

☐EXERCISE 9

1. I wish I could (have of) spent several hours (are or) even days there.
2. Of course we had to (accept except) the fact that we couldn't see everything.
3. The next day we (choose chose) to visit the University of Chicago and (it's its) famous Oriental Institute.

4. We saw many (knew new) exhibits from Egypt.
5. The (desert dessert) climate of Egypt has helped preserve artifacts that would (have of) disintegrated elsewhere.
6. (It's Its) interesting that climate can (affect effect) (are our) knowledge of history.
7. After (are our) morning there, we took a tour of the campus although we (knew new) it fairly well.
8. Next we stopped at the chapel to (hear here) a carillon recital, which is something I'd (advice advise) any campus visitor not to miss.
9. By evening we were (conscience conscious) of our tired feet and were (all ready already) for some sit-down entertainment.
10. We went to Mandel Hall for the (forth fourth) play of the season and found it (a an) enjoyable experience.

☐EXERCISE 10

1. I must now (choose chose) my classes for the (knew new) semester.
2. I wasn't (conscience conscious) that (are our) college offers so many choices.
3. I need some (advice advise) because I don't (know no) which (coarses courses) will count toward my major.
4. (It's Its) my (forth fourth) year, and I've only now decided on my major.
5. Of (coarse course) I should (have of) chosen my major earlier.
6. Then I'd (all ready already) have some of my credits.
7. I (feel fill) that fashion design will be (a an) interesting field.
8. I like to design (clothes cloths) and to (choose chose) accessories that (complement compliment) an outfit.
9. I've had lots of (complements compliments) on my designing, and they've had an (affect effect) on my decision to major in design.
10. It (does dose) seem like a good field to enter.

JOURNAL WRITING

The surest way to learn these Words Often Confused is to use them immediately in your own writing. Therefore begin to keep a journal, writing each day at least three sentences making use of some words or rules you've learned that day. If you write about things that interest you, then you'll be inclined to reread your journal occasionally and thus review what you've learned.

WRITING ASSIGNMENT

The writing assignments, grouped together for convenience at the back of the book, are to be used along with the exercises. Turn to page 206 for your first writing assignment, or follow your instructor's directions concerning the assignments.

BEWARE

Don't assume that the Writing Section isn't important just because it's at the back of the book and has only 41 pages. IT'S THE MOST IMPORTANT PART OF THE BOOK, and you should spend more time on it than on all the rest of the book. It has been kept brief because **you learn to write by writing,** not by reading pages and pages *about* writing.

MORE WORDS OFTEN CONFUSED

Study these words carefully, with their examples, before attempting the exercises. When you've mastered all 40 word groups in these two sections, you'll have taken care of many of your spelling problems.

led, lead	The past form of the verb is *led*.
	She *led* her class in math last year.
	If you don't mean past time, use *lead*, which rhymes with *bead*. (Don't confuse it with the metal *lead*, which rhymes with *dead*.)
	She will *lead* her class again this year.
loose, lose	
	Loose means "not tight." Note how *l o o s e* that word is. It has plenty of room for two *o*'s.
	My shoestring is *loose*.
	The other one, *lose*, has room for only one *o*.
	We're going to *lose* the game.
moral, morale	
	Pronounce these two words correctly, and you won't confuse them—*móral, moróle*.
	Moral has to do with right and wrong.
	She has high *moral* standards.
	Morale means "the spirit of a group or an individual."
	The *morale* in that company is excellent.
passed, past	
	Passed is a verb.
	He *passed* the house.
	Use *past* when it's not a verb.
	He walked *past* the house. (It's the same as *He walked by the house*, so you know it isn't a verb.)
	He's coasting on his *past* reputation.
	In the *past* he had always *passed* his exams.
personal, personnel	
	Pronounce these two correctly, and you won't confuse them—*pérsonal, personnél*.
	He had a *personal* interest in the election.
	Personnel means "a group of employees."
	She was in charge of *personnel* at the factory.
piece, peace	
	Remember "piece of pie." The one meaning "a *piece* of something" always begins with *pie*.
	I gave him a *piece* of my mind.
	The other one, *peace*, is the opposite of war.
	They signed the *peace* treaty.

principal,
principle

Principal means "main." Both words have *a* in them:
principa*l*
m*a*in
The *principal* of the school spoke. (main teacher)
The *principal* problem is financial. (main problem)
He lost both *principal* and interest. (main amount of money)
A *principle* is a "rule." Both words end in *le*:
princip*le*
ru*le*
He had high moral principles. (rules)
I object to the *principle* of the thing. (rule)

quiet, quite

Pronounce these two correctly, and you won't confuse them. *Quiet* rhymes with *diet*.
Be *quiet*.
Quite rhymes with *bite*.
It's *quite* cold in here.

right, write

Right means "correct" or "proper."
I got ten answers *right*.
Write is what you do with a pen.
I'll *write* my paper tonight.

than, then

Than compares two things.
I enjoy ice skating more *than* skiing.
Then tells when (*then* and *when* rhyme, and both have *e* in them).
We finished studying; *then* we played chess.

their, there,
they're

Their is a possessive (see p. 32).
Their house is for sale.
There points out something. (Remember the three words indicating a place or pointing out something all have *here* in them: *here, there, where*.)
I left it over *there*.
There were clouds in the sky.
They're is a contraction and means "they are."
They're happy now. (They are happy now.)

threw, through

Threw means "to throw something" in past time.
He *threw* the ball. I *threw* away my chance.
If you don't mean "to throw something," use *through*.
I walked *through* the door.
She's *through* with her work.

two, too, to

Two is a number.
I have *two* brothers.
Too means "more than enough" or "also."
The lesson was *too* difficult and *too* long. (more than enough)
I found it boring *too*. (also)
Use *to* for all other meanings.
He likes *to* snorkel. He's going *to* the beach.

weather, whether

Weather refers to atmospheric conditions.
This *weather* is too hot for me.
Whether means "if."
I don't know *whether* I'll go.
Whether I'll go depends on the *weather*.

were, where

Were is a verb.
We *were* miles from home.
Where refers to a place. (Remember the three words indicating a place or pointing out something all have *here* in them: *here, there, where*.)
Where is he? There he is.
Where are you? Here I am.

who's, whose

Who's is a contraction and means "who is" or "who has."
Who's there? (Who is there?)
Who's been eating my pizza? (Who has been . . . ?)
Whose is a possessive. (Possessives such as *whose, its, yours, hers, ours, theirs* are already possessive and never take an apostrophe. See p. 32).
Whose book is this?

woman, women

Remember that the word is just *man* or *men* with *wo* in front of it.
wo man . . . *woman* . . . one woman
wo men . . . *women* . . . two women
That *woman* is my aunt.
Those *women* are helping with the canvass.

you're, your

You're is a contraction and means "you are."
You're very welcome. (You are very welcome.)
Your is a possessive.
Your toast is ready.

EXERCISES

Underline the correct word. When you've finished 10 sentences, compare your answers with those at the back of the book. WATCH OUT! Don't do more than 10 sentences at a time, or you won't be teaching yourself while you still have sentences to practice on.

☐EXERCISE 1

1. I just read (a an) article about the ozone layer.
2. I never (knew new) before what ozone is.
3. Now I (know no) that (it's its) a chemical that pollutes the environment but that it becomes valuable when it rises to the stratosphere from 6 to 20 miles above the earth.
4. (Their There) this ozone layer protects the earth by absorbing the ultraviolet rays of the sun.
5. If it didn't absorb them, they of (coarse, course) would penetrate the earth's atmosphere, and skin cancers would increase, animals and plants would be harmed, and life itself might not be possible.
6. During the (passed past) few years scientists have been worried about the hole in the ozone layer above Antarctica.
7. The hole is caused by chemicals used (hear here) on earth.
8. These chemicals (are our) chlorofluorocarbons or CFCs—some of the most widely used chemicals in the world.
9. They are used in aerosol sprays, in the making of foam for bedding, furniture, egg cartons, and coffee cups, and in many other manufacturing processes.
10. CFCs have (know no) harmful (affect effect) (hear here) on earth, but when they drift up to the stratosphere, they destroy the ozone layer.

☐EXERCISE 2

1. The level of the ozone layer has (all ready already) dropped, and researchers predict that CFCs could destroy the entire ozone layer in a hundred years.
2. That would of (coarse course) be a global catastrophe.
3. In 1989 in Helsinki 80 nations decided to (accept except) the (advice advise) of the scientists and phase out the production and consumption of CFCs entirely by the year 2,000.
4. Thus for the first time in history nations (are our) acting to prevent a catastrophe before it happens.
5. Du Pont is already phasing out (it's its) production of CFCs, and manufacturers (are our) searching for other chemicals to use instead of CFCs.
6. Firms are also doing (their there) part.

7. In the Congressional cafeterias in Washington, for example, (know no) foam plates or cups manufactured with CFCs are used.

8. Even McDonald's has announced that (it's its) going to stop serving food in foam containers made with CFCs, and other fast-food chains are following (it's its) lead.

9. These steps, however, may be (to too) little and (to too) late because most CFCs stay in the atmosphere for 75 or 100 years.

10. Even if all CFCs were banned tomorrow, it would take 100 years to replenish the ozone (all ready already) lost.

☐EXERCISE 3

1. When I was 12, I (knew new) (their there) must be (a an) easier way to make money (than then) delivering papers.

2. I decided to (right write) a lot of little cards offering to mow lawns for a dollar (a an) hour.

3. I walked (passed past) all the houses in the neighborhood and (threw through) a card on each porch.

4. But (know no) one called. (Than Then) finally a (woman women) called and asked me to come Saturday morning.

5. I was (quiet quite) pleased, and away I went with my old push mower.

6. When I got (were where) I was supposed to go, I was stunned.

7. The grass was a foot high, and (there they're) were (loose lose) leaves all over the place.

8. I didn't (know no) (weather whether) to begin (are or) not, but I felt I had a (moral morale) obligation.

9. My (conscience conscious) told me I had agreed to (do due) the job, and I'd better see it (threw through).

10. When I finished, I was (to too) exhausted to (do due) more (than then) drag myself home, but I did have (too two) dollars in my pocket.

☐EXERCISE 4

1. During (are our) spring (brake break), we visited Muir Woods.

2. Since (it's its) not far from San Francisco, we were (all ready already) (quiet quite) near.

3. We (choose chose) Muir Woods because we (knew new) it has one of the best stands of coastal redwoods in the United States.

4. (Their There) are some redwoods more than 73 meters tall.

5. Beneath the redwoods the ground is covered with ferns. The (principal principle) kinds are the evergreen fern and the lady fern.

6. (It's Its) the fog from the Pacific that produces the damp (weather whether) the redwoods need.

7. As we walked (through threw) the woods, we were (conscience conscious) of the unusual (peace piece) and (quiet quite).

8. The (affect effect) is like that in a great cathedral.

9. The only mammal found (their there) is the black-tailed deer. I (do due) wish we could (have of) seen one.

10. The day (passed past) all (to too) quickly. (Are Our) trip was definitely (a an) enjoyable one.

☐EXERCISE 5

1. We should (have of) known it might rain before we got back to (are our) car.

2. We had been fishing and (were where) a mile from (were where) we had parked.

3. Claps of thunder shattered the (quiet quite); (than then) big drops of rain began to fall.

4. We could see no shelter (accept except) a farmhouse not (to too) far away.

5. We pounded on the door, and a (woman women) opened it and said, "(You're Your) welcome to wait (here hear)."

6. The family were (all ready already) eating (their there) supper and were having pie for (desert dessert).

7. The (woman women) offered us each a (peace piece), which we didn't hesitate to (accept except).

8. Of (coarse course) we gave her (complements compliments) on her baking.

9. We (passed past) the time by talking with the family about the (affect effect) of the (knew new) tax laws.

10. When the (weather whether) cleared, we walked back (threw through) the fields to (are our) car.

☐EXERCISE 6

1. (Are Our) biology class saw (a an) interesting insect yesterday.

2. We were on the campus (were where) (there they're) are a lot of trees.

3. Suddenly someone pointed (to too) a strange insect on a leaf. It was about (too two) inches long.

4. (Are Our) instructor said, "(It's Its) a praying mantis. It (does dose) a lot of good because it eats other insects."

5. It sits with the front part of (it's its) body erect and (it's its) long forelegs held up and folded as if in prayer.

6. That's of (coarse course) how it got (it's its) name.

7. (It's Its) green coloring blends with the surroundings as it sits in wait for unwary insects.

8. When (a an) insect goes (passed past), the mantis grabs it.

9. Gardeners sometimes "plant" mantis eggs in (their there) gardens because mantises (are or) (quiet quite) effective in getting rid of garden pests.

10. I never (knew new) before that (their there) was such an insect.

☐EXERCISE 7

1. The captain (lead led) the team to (it's its) (forth fourth) victory.
2. By (than then) the (moral morale) of the team was high.
3. They should (have of) known that (their there) luck might not hold.
4. Of (coarse course) they were surprised to (loose lose) their next game.
5. They couldn't (quiet quite) (accept except) losing.
6. It had a bad (affect effect) on their (moral morale).
7. They wondered (who's whose) fault it had been, but (than then) they decided to forget the (passed past) and get on with their practicing.
8. The coach kept saying the (principal principle) thing was not winning but playing (a an) excellent game.
9. (Threw Through) hard work and by using some (knew new) tactics, they began to win again.
10. Now (their they're) looking forward (to too) next season.

☐EXERCISE 8

1. If (you're your) planning to participate in sports, I'd (advice advise) you to make sure (you're your) grades are at least average.
2. Spending (to too) much time on sports can have (a an) adverse (affect effect) on your grades.
3. You don't want to (loose lose) academic credit because your (principal principle) reason for being in college is academic.
4. If (you're your) (all ready already) finding your (coarses courses) difficult, (than then) leave sports until later.
5. My (advice advise) is based on (personal personnel) experience.
6. Last spring I was (to too) involved with sports to (right write) a good term paper and barely (passed past) economics.
7. (It's Its) not smart to try to (do due) (to too) much.
8. Now I (know no) enough to (choose chose) just the (right write) amount of extracurricular activity.
9. (Weather Whether) you go out for sports is of (coarse course) your own decision.
10. I (feel fill) that (you're your) the one to decide.

☐EXERCISE 9

1. I've applied for a (knew new) job as a bank teller, and if I get it, I (know no) I'll like it.
2. I hope I (hear here) soon (weather whether) I get it.
3. First I had to (right write) a letter of application; (than then) I (passed past) a test; finally I went for (a an) interview.
4. My (principal principle) reason for wanting that job is a (personal personnel) one; I want to work (were where) my girlfriend does.
5. Another reason is that I (all ready already) have been in my old job (to too) long, and (there they're) is no future in it.

6. Also the (moral morale) of the (personal personnel) there is poor.
7. Therefore I took the (advice advise) of my friends and applied at (quiet quite) a few places.
8. Of (coarse course) I'd rather have the bank job (than then) any other.
9. I hope the (woman women) in charge will soon call me.
10. It won't take me long to (accept except) because (it's its) the job I want.

☐EXERCISE 10

1. Yesterday I saw (a an) interesting movie about the human body.
2. Did you (know no) that your body has 60,000 miles of blood vessels (through threw) which the blood journeys endlessly?
3. Yet a tour of blood from the heart and back takes less (than then) a minute.
4. (Your You're) heart beats about 70 times a minute and pumps 2,000 gallons of blood a day.
5. I never (knew new) before that the stomach produces hydrochloric acid strong enough to burn a hole in a rug.
6. Did you know (there they're) are 2,000 pores per square inch in your fingertips?
7. Of the body's 206 bones, more than half (are our) in the hands and feet.
8. (Your You're) hand is a unique engineering feat with the ability to perform 58 distinct motions.
9. (Its It's) the servant of the brain and is the most versatile instrument on earth.
10. I wish I knew as much about my body as I now (do due) about these words often confused.

JOURNAL WRITING

In your journal write several sentences using any words you may formerly have had trouble with.

Journal writing is a good idea not only because it will help you remember these words often confused but also because it will be a storehouse for ideas you can later use in writing papers. Here are some ideas you might consider writing your sentences about:

— your goals
— your thoughts about a class discussion
— a new idea you've gained from a course
— your reaction to a movie or play
— an experience that has made you think
— what you've learned from a friendship
— how you're working through a problem
— how your values are changing

WRITING ASSIGNMENT

From now on, along with doing the exercises, you will be expected to follow your instructor's directions concerning the writing assignments which begin on page 206.

Proofreading Exercise

Can you find the four errors in this student paper before checking with the answers at the back of the book?

TIDEPOOL

It was a beautiful day to walk along the rocky shoreline. With careful footsteps I made my way along the jagged rocks. Than I noticed something bright in a little tidepool ahead of me. It was a group of small snail shells among the plants growing in the tidepool. As I looked closer, I saw a snail shell move, and then another. I remained still and watched as more and more of the shells began to jerk around and then crawl along. Tiny little feet came out from each shell to move it.

These little animals weren't the original inhabitants of the shells. I new these were hermit crabs, crabs that use old empty shells to live in. Some of the hermit crabs could barely fit into there shells and would probably be looking for bigger ones soon. It was fascinating to watch them move around in the little pool that was their whole world.

Animals that carry there homes with them are certainly strange, I thought, as I walked back to the camper van that I'd been traveling in all summer.

CONTRACTIONS

Two words condensed into one are called a contraction.

is not   isn't   you have   you've

The letter or letters that are left out are replaced with an apostrophe. For example, if the two words *do not* are condensed into one, an apostrophe is put where the *o* is left out.

do not   don't

Note how the apostrophe goes in the exact place where the letter or letters are left out in these contractions:

I am	I'm
I have	I've
I shall, I will	I'll
I would	I'd
you are	you're
you have	you've
you will	you'll
she is, she has	she's
he is, he has	he's
it is, it has	it's
we are	we're
we have	we've
we will, we shall	we'll
they are	they're
they have	they've
are not	aren't
cannot	can't
do not	don't
does not	doesn't
have not	haven't
let us	let's
who is, who has	who's
where is	where's

One contraction does not follow this rule: *will not* becomes *won't*.

In all other contractions that you're likely to use, the apostrophe goes exactly where the letter or letters are left out. Note especially *it's, they're, who's,* and *you're.* Use them when you mean two words. (See p. 32 for the possessive forms—*its, their, whose,* and *your*—which don't take an apostrophe.)

EXERCISES

Put an apostrophe in each contraction. Then compare your answers with those at the back of the book. Be sure to correct each group of 10 sentences before going on so you'll catch your errors while you still have sentences to practice on.

☐EXERCISE 1

1. Havent you wondered whether theres intelligent life out in space?
2. Doesnt the search for other planets sound exciting?
3. Its only in the last few years that weve begun to hunt for planets.
4. It wasnt until the mid-sixteenth century that anyone thought the earth wasnt the center of the Universe.
5. Then Copernicus showed that its not the sun going around the earth but the earth going around the sun.
6. In the nineteenth century astronomers discovered that the stars arent just little points of light; theyre suns.
7. Now were looking for planets around those suns.
8. "Its a way of finding out whether our sun is unique," says Carl Sagan, "or whether planetary systems are a dime a dozen. If its the latter, as I strongly suspect . . . there may be a large number of inhabited worlds."
9. Of course if theres even one more inhabited world, its possible that theres life and intelligence out there.
10. Its NASA's plan to conduct an all-sky search for planets with dozens of sweeps across the sky over a six-year period—as soon as Congress gives the go-ahead with funds.

Source: *Discover*, October 1987

☐EXERCISE 2

1. Arent you pleased that youve passed the Words Often Confused test?
2. Yes, its the first time Ive been sure of all those words.
3. What Im hoping is that Ill remember them all when Im writing papers.
4. You wont forget them if youve done all the exercises.
5. Oh, I dont skip any exercises. I know its practice thats important.
6. Ive always had trouble with *accept* and *except,* and now theyre easy.
7. I hadnt bothered to learn all those words before, and I didnt know any memory devices.
8. Its easy to remember *dessert* and *desert* now that weve learned a memory device for them, isnt it?
9. Yes, theyre easy, but now Ive got to think up ways to remember half a hundred more words I cant spell.
10. Our instructor says its just a matter of deciding youre going to do it.

☐EXERCISE 3

1. Wheres Charley? I cant imagine why he isnt here.
2. Oh, hes always late. Hes never on time for anything.
3. Doesnt he know hes keeping the whole group waiting?
4. Sure, but he doesnt care.
5. Ive heard that people who are always late are self-centered.
6. Hows that?
7. Well, theyre so wrapped up in themselves that they dont realize the whole world isnt glad to wait for them.
8. Thats a good description of Charley all right.
9. Lets go without him. Hes already 15 minutes late. Theres no reason to wait longer.
10. Im with you. Maybe hell get wise to what hes doing if he misses the trip to the lake. Hes been really looking forward to it.

☐EXERCISE 4

1. Id never seen any old manuscripts until I visited the Huntington Museum in San Marino, California.
2. Its famous for its collection of manuscripts.
3. First I saw a manuscript of Chaucer's Canterbury Tales. Its the most elaborately decorated Chaucer manuscript in existence.
4. It dates from about 1410, but its still in good condition.
5. Then theres the first book that was printed in Europe with movable type.
6. Its the Gutenberg Bible, which was printed about 1455 on vellum, which is the inner skin of a calf or sheep.
7. Its text is in black letters, but its chapter headings and capital letters are large red or blue painted initials.
8. Then I saw the Shakespeare "First Folio," which contains 36 plays.
9. Many of Shakespeare's plays wouldnt have survived if two of his theatrical associates hadnt put this Folio together after his death.
10. Finally I went out into the Museum's 130 acre Botanical Gardens, but thats another story.

☐EXERCISE 5

1. If you dont like roadside litter, think of the junk thats floating around in space.
2. Its a fact that about 3,400 pieces of trackable debris are orbiting the earth.
3. Theres everything from spent rocket boosters to broken solar panels.
4. Its not surprising that about 550 pieces of junk fall to the earth each year.

5. Space junk isnt much of a problem yet because most of it burns up on reentry into the Earth's atmosphere.
6. Its going to be more of a problem though as we send more things up.
7. The United Nations says that the nation thats launched the litter is responsible for any damage it causes.
8. When Skylab came down in 1978, the U.S. government wasnt surprised to get 42 claims for damages.
9. One was for $2.47 from someone who had had a nightmare about Skylab and had broken a lampshade, and one was from someone claiming mental anguish for $10 million.
10. They didnt get compensation.

Source: *National Wildlife,* April–May 1983

☐EXERCISE 6

1. Ive just learned why leaves turn red and yellow in autumn.
2. Its not the frost thats responsible because colors often appear before theres any frost.
3. Ive learned that leaves contain green and yellow and red pigments.
4. Its the green pigment, or chlorophyll, thats dominant in the summer.
5. Toward the end of summer its no longer produced, and then the yellow pigment becomes apparent.
6. Or if theres an abundance of red pigment, the leaf becomes red.
7. Its the sugar content in the leaf that produces red pigment, and the sugar content is dependent on sunlight.
8. So a leaf thats in the bright sunlight will have more sugar content than one thats in the shade and thus will turn red.
9. Thats why some leaves on the same tree may be yellow and others red.
10. Its simply that the red ones have received more sunlight.

☐EXERCISE 7

1. Ive learned, too, that different species have different chemical components.
2. A maple leaf is red because of its sugar content, but an oak leaf turns red because of its accumulation of tannic acid.
3. Theres lots to learn about the complex structure of plant life.
4. Then, too, Ive always wondered why theres more brilliant color in the woods some years than others.
5. Its temperature that causes the difference, with warm sunny days and cold nights producing the most sugar and hence the most red color.
6. Ive also learned why leaves fall from the trees.
7. When a leaf has lost its green chlorophyll, it cant make food for the tree any longer.

8. Since its no longer needed, it falls to the ground with its mission accomplished.
9. In the past when I walked in the woods, I didnt know all these facts.
10. Now whenever I see the fall colors, Im aware of whats happening.

☐EXERCISE 8

1. In our psychology class weve been learning about sleep.
2. I didnt know that a person doesnt sleep the same way all night long.
3. Ive learned that 90-minute periods of deep sleep alternate with 90-minute periods of light sleep.
4. Toward morning theres less deep sleep and more light sleep.
5. Also I didnt know that everybody dreams; some people simply cant remember their dreams.
6. A person who wakes slowly doesnt remember dreams as well as one who wakes quickly.
7. Dreaming occurs in REM (rapid eye movement) periods of sleep, and its usual to have five periods a night.
8. Dreams arent all the same length; theyre usually from five to thirty minutes.
9. Four out of five dreams, its been found, are in color.
10. Its important to dream because it lets one wake up refreshed and rested.

☐EXERCISE 9

1. Ive always wanted to go to Egypt, where theres so much of historical interest to be seen.
2. Its not likely, though, that Ill ever get there.
3. But Im hoping to go to New York City, where theres a 2,000-year-old temple thats been brought over from Egypt.
4. Its the Temple of Dendur from 400 miles up the Nile in Nubia.
5. The reason its in the United States is that its a gift from the Egyptian government.
6. As a result of Egypt's decision in 1953 to build a high dam across the Nile at Aswan, many monuments would have been covered with water if UNESCO hadnt started a fund to save them.
7. The Temple of Dendur wouldnt be in existence today if that fund, to which the United States gave $16 million, hadnt enabled an Egyptian team to dismantle the temple and number and store all its stone blocks.
8. It wasnt until 1965 that the Egyptian government offered the temple to the United States in appreciation.
9. Soon 640 tons of stones arrived in Manhattan, but it wasnt until 1974 that the stones were painstakingly reassembled into the temple.
10. Now its in a glass pavilion at the north end of the Metropolitan Museum overlooking Central Park.

☐EXERCISE 10

1. If you liked the King Tut exhibit, then youd probably enjoy the Temple of Dendur.
2. If youre interested in art, youd appreciate the wall reliefs.
3. If youre interested in history, youd learn something about daily life in Egypt at that time.
4. Temples in those days werent for people to worship in but for the gods to live in.
5. The reconstructed temple stands on a wide platform skirted by a moat of lapping water thats supposed to remind us of its original site on the Nile.
6. Ive heard that the ancient stones of the temple glow orange against the night sky as spotlights illumine them.
7. Our family is planning a trip to New York next summer, and were excited about it.
8. Im eager to see the Temple of Dendur, but thats only one of the things were going to see.
9. Everybodys been telling us about places we shouldnt miss.
10. Weve already made a list of what were going to do, and its certain well not waste a minute.

JOURNAL WRITING

Doing exercises helps you learn a rule, but even more helpful is using the rule in writing. In your journal write some sentences using contractions. You might write about your reaction to the week's news. Or choose your own subject.

WRITING ASSIGNMENT

Turn to the writing section at the back of the book for your writing assignment.

POSSESSIVES

The trick in writing possessives is to ask yourself the question, "Who (or what) does it belong to?" (Modern usage has made *who* acceptable when it comes first in a sentence, but some people still say, "*Whom* does it belong to?" or even "*To whom* does it belong?") If the answer to your question ends in *s*, simply add an apostrophe. If it doesn't end in *s*; then add an apostrophe and *s*.

one boys bike	Who does it belong to?	boy	Add *'s*	boy's bike
two boys bikes	Who do they belong to?	boys	Add *'*	boys' bikes
the mans hat	Who does it belong to?	man	Add *'s*	man's hat
the mens hat	Who do they belong to?	men	Add *'s*	men's hats
childrens game	Who does it belong to?	children	Add *'s*	children's game
a days work	What does it belong to?	day	Add *'s*	day's work

This trick will always work, but you must ask the question every time. Remember that the key word is *belong*. Who (or what) does it belong to? If you ask the question another way, you may get an answer that won't help you. Also, if you just look at a word without asking the question, you may think the name of the owner ends in *s* when it really doesn't.

TO MAKE A POSSESSIVE

Ask "Who (or what) does it belong to?"
If the answer ends in *s*, just add an apostrophe.
If it doesn't end in *s*, add an apostrophe and *s*.

Cover the right-hand column and see if you can write the following possessives correctly. Ask the question each time.

the womans dress _____ woman's
the womens ideas _____ women's
Stephens apartment _____ Stephen's
James apartment _____ James'
the Hardys house _____ the Hardys'
Mr. Hardys house _____ Mr. Hardy's

(Sometimes you may see a variation of this rule. *James' book* may be written *James's book*. That is correct too, but the best way is to stick to the simple rule. You can't be wrong if you follow it.)

A word of warning! Don't assume that because a word ends in *s* it is necessarily a possessive. Make sure the word actually possesses something before you add an apostrophe.

A few words are already possessive and don't need an apostrophe added to them. Memorize this list:

my, mine	its
your, yours	our, ours
his	their, theirs
her, hers	whose

Note particularly *its, their, whose,* and *your.* They are already possessive and don't take an apostrophe. (They sound just like the contractions *it's, they're, who's,* and *you're,* which stand for two words and of course have to have an apostrophe.)

As a practice exercise, cover the right-hand column below with a sheet of paper, and on it write the correct form (contraction or possessive). If you miss any, go back and review the explanations.

(It) cold today. _____	It's
(You) coat is beautiful. _____	Your
(Who) going with me? _____	Who's
(They) intending to go. _____	They're
The robin left (it) nest. _____	its
(Who) planning the dinner? _____	Who's
The hurricane lost (it) force. _____	its
(You) score was excellent. _____	Your
(They) garden is drying up. _____	Their
(It) all right. _____	It's
(You) correct. _____	You're
(They) house is up for sale. _____	Their
(They) planning a party. _____	They're
(Who) book is this? _____	Whose
(You) bound to win. _____	You're

Here's one more practice exercise. Cover the right-hand column with a sheet of paper, and on it write the possessives.

1. My cousins love their grandfathers house.

grandfather's (You didn't add an apostrophe to *cousins,* did you? The cousins don't possess anything.)

2. Students grades depend on their tests.

Students' (Who do the grades belong to?)

3. Charles stopped at my parents house.

parents' (Charles doesn't possess anything in this sentence.)

4. One of my friends went to Charles recital.

Charles' (The friends don't possess anything in this sentence.)

5. Anns job pays more than yours.

Ann's (*Yours* is already possessive and doesn't take an apostrophe.)

6. Last nights game was a tie.

night's (The game belonged to last night.)

7. The Browns cottage is spacious.

Browns' (Who does the cottage belong to?)

8. The Browns painted their cottage.

(No apostrophe in this sentence. *Their* is already possessive. The sentence merely tells what the Browns did.)

9. The womens team played the girls team.

women's, girls' (Did you ask who each team belongs to?)

10. The girls boast about their team.

(No apostrophe. *Their* is already possessive, and the girls don't possess anything in this sentence.)

11. The jurors verdict was fair.

jurors' (Who did the verdict belong to?)

12. The jurors gave a fair verdict.

(No apostrophe. The sentence merely tells what the jurors did.)

13. He's driving someone elses car.

someone else's. (Who did the car belong to?)

14. The sign by the gate said "The Smiths."

Smiths (meaning that the Smiths live there) or Smiths' (meaning that it's the Smiths' house).

EXERCISES

Put the apostrophe in each possessive. WATCH OUT! **First,** make sure the word really possesses something; not every word ending in *s* is a possessive. **Second,** remember that certain words are already possessive and don't take an apostrophe. **Third,** remember that even though a word seems to end in *s,* you can't tell where the apostrophe goes until you ask the question, "Who (or what) does it belong to?" In the first sentence, for example, "Who does the cottage belong to?" "Parents." Therefore you'll write *parents'*.

☐EXERCISE 1

1. Carla has invited our class out to her parents cottage for our reunion.
2. The Wilsons cottage is on Clear Lake and will be an ideal place.
3. Carlas mother has said we may have a barbecue.
4. Carlas dad will let us use his motorboat.
5. Mr. Wilsons motorboat is his hobby.
6. The Wilsons are very hospitable people.
7. We'll all go to Fridays game and then to the Wilsons cottage afterward.
8. The Wilsons boathouse down by the lake has shower rooms.
9. It has a mens shower room and a womens shower room.
10. That keeps all the wet bathing suits out of the Wilsons cottage.

☐EXERCISE 2

1. Miles is our reunion organizer, and he's planning our activities.
2. Besides swimming, there'll be mens volleyball and womens volleyball.
3. Miles plan is for everyone to bring something for the potluck.
4. Carla has offered to supply the steaks for the barbecue.
5. After supper we're sure to hear from Julies rock group and maybe from Kevins choral group.
6. We may have a problem getting to the cottage because we have only Michaels van and a few cars, but Miles dad may drive a carload out.
7. I spent a day with the Wilsons last fall at Mrs. Wilsons invitation.
8. I was impressed with Carlas diving and her moms swimming.
9. Then we had an exciting ride in her dads motorboat.
10. Finally supper on the beach ended the days activities.

☐EXERCISE 3

1. I'm going to take advantage of Saturdays sale to buy some gifts.
2. I'm looking for mens ties for my dad and boys T-shirts for my brother.
3. My mother-in-laws gift will be harder to decide upon.
4. Maybe I should look at books for her.
5. Then I need to look at childrens toys for my small nephew.
6. I'm sure of my husbands taste in compact disks, so that will be easy.

7. I've no ideas for my two grandfathers presents.
8. Maybe I'll look at mens shirts or sweaters.
9. I hope I can find an inexpensive childs watch for my niece.
10. By going to the sale I hope to get my moneys worth.

☐EXERCISE 4

1. Philips main interest was in cabinetmaking.
2. He was taking an advanced course in wood finishing, and each days instruction gave him satisfaction.
3. His work was better than any of the other students work.
4. He won a prize for some bookends he made for his fathers office.
5. Then he made a small desk for his mothers living room.
6. Making the drawers was the hardest part.
7. With his instructors help, however, he made them fit beautifully.
8. Finally he was satisfied with his semesters work.
9. Eventually he was rewarded by his mothers surprise and pleasure.
10. Woodworking will probably always be Philips favorite hobby.

☐EXERCISE 5

1. Three students papers were read and discussed in class.
2. The instructors comments were helpful, but the students comments were even more helpful.
3. Sues paper was about how to construct a childs play grocery store.
4. One students criticism was that the thesis statement wasn't clear.
5. Terrys comment was that the paper had interesting specific details.
6. Ashleys paper was about voter apathy in the last election.
7. All the students comments about that paper were favorable.
8. Jasons paper was read next; it was about the pollution of our rivers.
9. The students comments indicated that he should narrow his subject.
10. Angelas suggestion was that he should write about a local creek.

☐EXERCISE 6

1. Mikes car won't run, and he has to get a new one.
2. Three of his friends are trying to sell him their cars.
3. Teds Toyota gets good mileage, but its tires are old.
4. Tonys Camaro is classy but expensive.
5. Rudys Mustang needs a new paint job.
6. Mike can't decide which of his three friends cars he'll buy.
7. What he'd really like is to drive his fathers car.
8. But his dads work schedule makes that impractical.
9. Mike's going to accept his dads offer to help with the financing though.
10. Since Mikes bank account is low, his fathers help will be welcome.

☐EXERCISE 7

1. For coping with winters chill, animals and birds have some interesting mechanisms.
2. The red foxs method of keeping warm while sleeping is to wrap its tail around its head as a muff.
3. Similarly the gray squirrels method when it goes out in search of food is to flatten its tail against its back and neck as an insulating windbreaker.
4. The cardinals feathers are fluffed out to reduce heat loss.
5. One of the few woodland creatures able to thrive during winters worst weather is the chickadee.
6. At night the chickadee fluffs its outer feathers over the layer of soft down next to its skin.
7. A snowshoe hares protection against winter chill is the fur snowshoes that it grows on the bottom of its feet each fall.
8. The hares snowshoes are more than an inch thick and provide warm and skid-proof overshoes.
9. A white-tailed deers gray-brown winter coat is made of thousands of brittle hollow hairs filled with air.
10. And a soft undercoat of fine hair serves as the deers thermal underwear.

Source: *National Wildlife,* February–March 1988

☐EXERCISE 8

1. The worlds largest collection of canoes is in the Kanawa Museum near Dorset, Ontario, Canada.
2. The collection includes about 600 canoes, kayaks, and other paddle-powered craft.
3. Kirk Wipper, a University of Toronto professor, created Kanawa to house one of Canadas most interesting historical collections.
4. The log buildings set in a dense pine forest are a fitting background for Wippers collection.
5. Wippers love of the canoe extends back to his childhood when he paddled his fathers canoe in Manitoba.
6. Wipper hunts from New York to California for canoes for his museum and brings back many of Canadas early canoes.
7. Restoring the canoes to their original state is Rick Nashs job. He uses only Indian tools and materials.
8. The new popularity of canoeing has added to peoples interest in the history of the canoe.
9. In spite of its out-of-the-way location, many visitors are discovering the museum.
10. Kanawas collection of aboriginal and historical watercraft is unmatched in the world.

☐EXERCISE 9

1. The Mens Club and the Womens Club in our town are more than social clubs.
2. The Mens Club sponsors a Boys Club and the Womens Club sponsors a Girls Club.
3. Also the members of both clubs participate in educational programs.
4. The Womens Club devotes one evening a month to poetry.
5. The evenings program includes the work of a poet such as Wordsworth or Keats.
6. My mother took part one evening in the reading of John Keats poems.
7. Another evening the Clubs program was on Shakespeare sonnets.
8. The Mens Club programs usually include out-of-town speakers who talk on current topics.
9. The Mens Club sponors a grade school boys track meet.
10. They also present a scholarship to one of the Colleges needy students.

☐EXERCISE 10

1. Cologne Cathedral is one of the worlds most magnificent buildings and one of Germanys best known architectural landmarks.
2. Since the laying of the cornerstone in 1248, wars have ravaged the exterior and interior of the cathedral.
3. Yet none of that damage equals the damage caused by todays devastating environmental pollution.
4. The master architects report blames sulfur dioxide emissions from cars, industrial plants, and house chimneys.
5. The atmospheric pollutants have eroded the stone walls of the cathedral, turning them into plaster of Paris and causing them to crumble.
6. The master architects job is to try to prevent the erosion and to keep Europes largest church from falling down.
7. Routing traffic away from the church has helped to slow the corrosion, and the stones are being sprayed with silicone to repel the pollutants.
8. The architects report also says the priceless stained glass windows are deteriorating, and about 380,000 separate pieces of glass must be removed and treated.
9. The craftsmens job is going to be a race against time.
10. If corrosive emissions continue at the present rate, the prevention and restoration measures won't be swift enough to save Germanys most impressive cathedral.

JOURNAL WRITING

In your journal write some sentences using the possessive forms of the names of the members of your family or the names of your friends.

Review of Contractions and Possessives

Add the necessary apostrophes. Try to get these exercises perfect. Don't excuse an error by saying, "Oh, that was just a careless mistake." A mistake is a mistake. Be tough on yourself!

☐EXERCISE 1

1. What can one person do? Its amazing.

2. When Will Toor enrolled as a graduate student in Physics at the University of Chicago, he was surprised to discover that the University didnt do any recycling.

3. It wasnt long before he organized an environmental group, and he didnt rest until the group planned a paper recycling project called UCRecycle.

4. The University cooperated, and UCRecycle began in 1988 by collecting paper from the offices in seven buildings.

5. Then offices in other buildings asked to be included, and soon UCRecycles program included 40 buildings.

6. At the years end, the total collection amounted to 135 tons of paper— the equivalent of 2,300 trees.

7. UCRecycles next step was to include other recyclable materials—aluminum, glass, newspapers, cardboard, and cans.

8. By the end of the second year, over 30 tons of recyclable material were being collected each month.

9. Now UCRecycles goal is to collect 50 tons each month.

10. Isnt it amazing what one person can do?

☐EXERCISE 2

1. Ive been helping on Saturdays at the Thrift Store, which is run by the Salvation Army.

2. People donate some excellent clothes: womens dresses, mens suits, and boys and girls clothes.

3. They bring in all sizes of mens, womens, and childrens shoes too.

4. Someones discarded clothing often becomes someone elses prized possession.

5. Weve also been given such articles as a babys crib, a toddlers swing, and a childs bed.

6. Occasionally somebody brings in an article thats valuable.

7. Last week a woman brought in her uncles antique clock.

8. Its possible that it will bring a good price, but then again it may not.

9. Ive found that something old is called a "collectors item" when Im trying to buy it.

10. When Im trying to sell it, its called "obsolete."

Proofreading Exercise

Can you find the 12 errors in this student paper? Challenge your instructor to find all 12 on the first try! No answers are provided at the back of the book for this exercise.

"HI, DAD"

Do you know what its like never being able to talk to your father? Well, I do. Ever since I can remember, Ive always been afraid of Dad. The only time we ever communicated was when he was yelling at me.

Dad used to go away on business trips a lot, and Mom would threaten us that if we didnt behave, Dad would take care of us. It made Dad sound like the villain, but it helped Mom control us. Im sure this had a great affect on how we thought of him. As I became older, I grew very far from Dad. We never talked about anything.

About the third week of college, I decided to call home. My dad answered, and instead of immediately handing the phone to Mom, he said, "Hi, how's college?" I couldnt believe it. Those were the first "nice" words hed really ever spoken. After talking to Mom, I hung up and started crying. I was crying because I was so happy.

Than one night I called home and talked to my Mom. Dad wasnt around, but Mom said shed have him call me. I didn't think he would, but two hours later the phone rang, and it was Dad. I was so excited. We started talking like we had known each other for years.

My being here at college has given my dad and me a chance to no each other. I dont think it would have happened any other way.

WORDS THAT CAN BE BROKEN INTO PARTS

Breaking words into their parts will often help you spell them correctly. Each of the following words is made up of two shorter words. Note that the word then contains all the letters of the two shorter words.

book keeper . . .	bookkeeper	room mate . . .	roommate
over run	. . . overrun	tail light	. . . taillight
over rate	. . . overrate	with hold	. . . withhold

Becoming aware of prefixes such as *dis, inter, mis,* and *un* is also helpful. Then when you add a prefix to a word, the spelling will be correct.

dis appear	disappear	mis informed	misinformed
dis appoint	disappoint	mis spell	misspell
dis approve	disapprove	mis step	misstep
dis satisfied	dissatisfied	un aware	unaware
dis service	disservice	un natural	unnatural
inter act	interact	un necessary	unnecessary
inter racial	interracial	un nerve	unnerve
inter related	interrelated	un noticed	unnoticed

Note that no letters are dropped, either from the prefix or from the word.

Have someone dictate the above list for you to write and then mark any words you miss. Memorize the correct spellings by noting how each word is made up of a prefix and a word.

RULE FOR DOUBLING A FINAL CONSONANT

Most spelling rules have so many exceptions that they aren't much help. But here's one that has almost no exceptions and is worth learning.

Double a final consonant when adding an ending that begins with a vowel (such as *ing, ed, er*) if all three of the following are true:

1. **the word ends in a single consonant,**
2. **which is preceded by a single vowel (the vowels are *a, e, i, o, u*),**
3. **and the accent is on the last syllable (or the word has only one syllable).**

We'll try the rule on a few words to which we'll add *ing, ed,* or *er.*

begin   1. It ends in a single consonant—*n,*
           2. preceded by a single vowel—*i,*
           3. and the accent is on the last syllable—*be gin'.*
           Therefore we double the final consonant and write *beginning, beginner.*

stop   1. It ends in a single consonant—*p,,*
           2. preceded by a single vowel—*o,*
           3. and the accent is on the last syllable (there is only one).
           Therefore we double the final consonant and write *stopping, stopped, stopper.*

motor   1. It ends in a single consonant—*r,*
           2. preceded by a single vowel—*o,*
           3. But the accent isn't on the last syllable. It's on the first—*mo'tor.*
           Therefore we don't double the final consonant. We write *motoring, motored.*

sleep   1. It ends in a single consonant—*p,*
           2. but it isn't preceded by a single vowel. There are two *e*'s.
           Therefore we don't double the final consonant. We write *sleeping, sleeper.*

Note that *qu* is treated as a consonant because *q* is almost never written without *u.* Think of it as *kw.* In words like *equip* and *quit,* the *qu* acts as a consonant. Therefore *quit* does end in a single consonant preceded by a single vowel, and the final consonant is doubled—*quitting.*

Also note that *bus* may be written either *bussing* or *busing.* The latter, contrary to our rule, is more common.

EXERCISES

Add *ing* to these words. Correct each group of 10 before continuing so you'll catch any errors while you still have words to practice on.

☐EXERCISE 1

1. put
2. control
3. admit
4. mop
5. plan
6. hop
7. jump
8. knit
9. mark
10. creep

☐EXERCISE 2

1. return
2. swim
3. sing
4. benefit
5. loaf
6. nail
7. omit
8. occur
9. shop
10. interrupt

☐EXERCISE 3

1. begin
2. spell
3. prefer
4. interpret
5. hunt
6. excel
7. wrap
8. stop
9. wed
10. scream

☐EXERCISE 4

1. feel
2. murmur
3. turn
4. weed
5. subtract
6. stream
7. expel
8. miss
9. get
10. stab

☐EXERCISE 5

1. forget
2. misspell
3. fit
4. plant
5. pin
6. trust
7. sip
8. flop
9. reap
10. fight

Progress Test

This test covers everything you've studied so far. One sentence in each pair is correct. The other is incorrect. Read both sentences carefully before you decide. Then write the letter of the correct sentence in the blank.

_____ 1. A. The Benson's apartment is too far from the city.
         B. My mother's principal interest is cooking.

_____ 2. A. His plans won't have any effect on my decision.
         B. It dosen't matter whether he goes with me or not.

_____ 3. A. I'm hoping to spend next year's vacation in Maine.
         B. She past me a piece of pie, and I took it.

_____ 4. A. I know its a good idea to cut down on desserts.
         B. The Fosters have invited us over for the evening.

_____ 5. A. He admitted that he didn't know the answer.
         B. It occurred to me that they weren't cooperating.

_____ 6. A. Is this bracelet hers or yours?
         B. He's quiet sure that he's right in protesting that rule.

_____ 7. A. Of coarse I know that you're planning to come.
         B. He omitted the fourth problem in the test.

_____ 8. A. I've all ready made quite a large deposit in my account.
         B. I'd like an honest opinion on the matter.

_____ 9. A. He should of given her more moral support.
         B. She wasn't conscious that they were critical of her.

_____ 10. A. It's quite an honor to know such an important person.
         B. The mens' athletic club needs a new building.

_____ 11. A. I already knew what she was planning to do.
         B. Our parakeet got out of it's cage and ruined our upholstery.

_____ 12. A. Your going to be quite busy with those two projects.
         B. I'm not sure whether it's too early to begin.

_____ 13. A. Who's motorcycle is that in the Jefferson's driveway?
         B. Won't he be through with his new assignment soon?

_____ 14. A. If I lose my notes, I'm sunk.
         B. Rebeccas' advice is good.

_____ 15. A. He knew little about history, but he lead his class in math.
         B. My counselor's advice was too difficult for me to follow.

A LIST OF FREQUENTLY MISSPELLED WORDS

Have someone dictate this list of commonly misspelled words to you and mark the ones you miss. Then memorize the correct spellings.

Pronounce these words correctly, and you won't misspell them: *athlete, athletics, nuclear*. And be sure to pronounce every syllable in these words: *environment, government, mathematics, probably, studying*. Also try to think up memory devices to help you remember correct spellings. For example, you *labor* in a *laboratory*; the two *l*'s in *parallel* are parallel; and the *r* separates the two *a*'s in separate.

1. absence	33. disastrous	65. humorous
2. across	34. discipline	66. immediately
3. actually	35. discussed	67. independent
4. a lot	36. disease	68. intelligence
5. amateur	37. divide	69. interest
6. among	38. dying	70. interfere
7. analyze	39. eighth	71. involved
8. appearance	40. eligible	72. knowledge
9. appreciate	41. eliminate	73. laboratory
10. argument	42. embarrassed	74. leisure
11. athlete	43. environment	75. length
12. athletics	44. especially	76. library
13. awkward	45. etc.	77. likely
14. becoming	46. exaggerate	78. lying
15. beginning	47. excellent	79. marriage
16. belief	48. exercise	80. mathematics
17. benefit	49. existence	81. meant
18. buried	50. experience	82. medicine
19. business	51. explanation	83. neither
20. certain	52. extremely	84. ninety
21. college	53. familiar	85. ninth
22. coming	54. February	86. nuclear
23. committee	55. finally	87. occasionally
24. competition	56. foreign	88. opinion
25. complete	57. government	89. opportunity
26. consider	58. grammar	90. parallel
27. criticism	59. grateful	91. particular
28. definitely	60. guarantee	92. persuade
29. dependent	61. guard	93. physically
30. develop	62. guidance	94. planned
31. development	63. height	95. pleasant
32. difference	64. hoping	96. possible

97. practical	115. sacrifice	133. success
98. preferred	116. safety	134. suggest
99. prejudice	117. scene	135. surprise
100. privilege	118. schedule	136. thoroughly
101. probably	119. secretary	137. though
102. professor	120. senior	138. tragedy
103. prove	121. sense	139. tried
104. psychology	122. separate	140. tries
105. pursue	123. severely	141. truly
106. receipt	124. shining	142. unfortunately
107. receive	125. significant	143. unnecessary
108. recommend	126. similar	144. until
109. reference	127. sincerely	145. unusual
110. relieve	128. sophomore	146. using
111. religious	129. speech	147. usually
112. repetition	130. straight	148. Wednesday
113. rhythm	131. studying	149. writing
114. ridiculous	132. succeed	150. written

USING YOUR DICTIONARY

By working through the following 13 exercises, you'll become familiar with what you can find in an up-to-date desk dictionary.

1. PRONUNCIATION

Look up the word *automaton* and copy the pronunciation in this space.

Now under each letter with a pronunciation mark over it, write the key word having the same mark. You'll find the key words at the bottom of one of the two dictionary pages open before you. Note especially that the upside-down *e* (ə) always has the sound of *uh* like the *a* in *ago* or *about*. Remember that sound because it's found in many words.

Next, pronounce the key words you have written, and then slowly pronounce *automaton,* giving each syllable the same sound as its key word.

Finally note which syllable has the heavy accent mark. (In most dictionaries the accent mark points to the stressed syllable, but in one dictionary it is in front of the stressed syllable.) The stressed syllable is *tom.* Now say the word, letting the full force of your voice fall on that syllable.

When more than one pronunciation is given, the first is more common. If the complete pronunciation of a word isn't given, look at the word above it to find the pronunciation.

Look up the pronunciation of these words, using the key words at the bottom of the dictionary page to help you pronounce each syllable. Then note which syllable has the heavy accent mark, and say the word aloud.

anonymity   nuclear   esoteric   ingenuous

2. DEFINITIONS

The dictionary may give more than one meaning for a word. Read all the meanings for each italicized word and then write a definition appropriate to the sentence.

1. She accepted the job offer with *alacrity*. _____

_____

2. The child felt *ambivalent* toward the new baby in the family. _____

_____

3. She was a *meticulous* housekeeper. _____

_____

4. His job was a *sinecure* because his dad owned the company. _____

_____

5. She *vacillates* between love and hate for her brother. _____

_____

3. SPELLING

By making yourself look up each word you aren't sure how to spell, you'll soon become a better speller. When two spellings are given in the dictionary, the first one (or the one with the definition) is the more common.

Underline the more common spelling of each of these words.

enclose, inclose   judgement, judgment

jeweler, jeweller   monolog, monologue

4. COMPOUND WORDS

If you want to find out whether two words are written separately, written with a hyphen between them, or written as one word, consult your dictionary. For example:

half sister	is written as two words
brother-in-law	is hyphenated
stepson	is written as one word

Write each of the following correctly:

blue jay _____   school room _____

ginger ale _____   self propelled _____

living room _____   short tempered _____

5. CAPITALIZATION

If a word is capitalized in the dictionary, that means it should always be capitalized. If it is not capitalized in the dictionary, then it may or may not be capitalized, depending on how it is used (see p. 193). For example:

Chinese is always capitalized

college is capitalized or not, according to how it is used
She's attending college.
She's attending Tacoma Community College.

Write these words as they are given in the dictionary (with or without a capital) to show whether they must always be capitalized or not.

Arctic _____   Heaven _____

Buddhism _____   Mexican _____

Congress _____   Woodpecker _____

6. USAGE

Just because a word is in the dictionary does not mean that it's in standard use. The following labels indicate whether a word is used today and, if so, where and by whom.

obsolete	no longer used
archaic	not now used in ordinary language but still found in some biblical, literary, and legal expressions
colloquial informal	used in informal conversation but not in formal writing
dialectal regional	used in some localities but not everywhere
slang	popular but nonstandard expression
nonstandard substandard	not used by educated people

Look up each italicized word and write the label indicating its usage. Dictionaries differ. One may list a word as slang whereas another will call it colloquial. Still another may give no label, thus indicating that that particular dictionary considers the word in standard use.

1. The poor *critter* came in last in the race. _____

2. *Quoth* the raven, "Nevermore." _____

3. Her *sweet tooth* keeps her from losing weight. _____

4. His new car is really *cool*. _____

5. When he decided to stop smoking, he quit *cold turkey*. _____

6. Cooking isn't exactly my *bag*. _____

7. I thought *you-all* were helping with the bloodmobile. _____

8. We couldn't find the book *nowheres*. _____

7. DERIVATIONS

The derivations or stories behind words will often help you remember the current meanings. For example, *symbiosis* is a word you'll often encounter in biology texts. When you look up its derivation, you'll find that SYM means "together" and BIO means "life." Therefore *symbiosis* is the "living together" of two dissimilar organisms. The hermit crab, for example, lives among the petal-like tentacles of the sea anemone and is protected from enemies by the stinging power of those tentacles. The anemone, on the other hand, is carried in the claws or on the back of the hermit crab to new feeding grounds. Thus the *symbiosis* or "living together" is beneficial to both.

Look up the derivation of each of these words. You'll find it in square brackets either just before or just after the definition.

derrick _____

hamburger _____

holiday _____

marathon _____

curfew _____

8. SYNONYMS

At the end of a definition, a group of synonyms is sometimes given. For example, at the end of the definition of *beautiful*, you'll find several synonyms. And if you look up *handsome* or *pretty*, you'll be referred to the synonyms under *beautiful*.

List the synonyms for the following italicized words.

1. She didn't *answer* my question. _____

_____

2. Everyone agreed that the decision of the jury was *fair*. _____

_____

3. Having lived in a communist country, she appreciated American *freedom*.

_____

9. ABBREVIATIONS

Find the meaning of the following abbreviations.

kg _____   mpg _____

a.k.a. _____   UNICEF _____

10. NAMES OF PEOPLE

The names of famous people will be found either in the main part of your dictionary or in a separate Biographical Names section at the back.

Identify the following.

Lewis Carroll _____

Georgia O'Keeffe _____

Johannes Gutenberg _____

Jonas Salk _____

11. NAMES OF PLACES

The names of places will be found either in the main part of your dictionary or in a separate Geographical Names section at the back.

Identify the following.

Juneau _____

Death Valley _____

Stonehenge _____

Oahu _____

12. FOREIGN WORDS AND PHRASES

Give the language and the meaning of the italicized expressions.

1. His usual *joie de vivre* helped him forget his disappointment. _____

   _____

2. Although the school was supposed to be integrated, there was *de facto*

   segregation. _____

3. Unaware of the social conventions, he made one *faux pas* after another.

   _____

4. At the archeological dig, we saw several ancient burials *in situ.* _____

   _____

13. MISCELLANEOUS INFORMATION

Find these miscellaneous bits of information in your dictionary.

1. What is the meaning of the British term *bobby*? _____

2. What is the plural of *handful*? _____

3. How many liquid quarts are in a liter? _____

4. What is the capital of Saskatchewan? _____

5. What is the population of Albuquerque? _____

6. In what novel is the land of Shangri-la found? _____

7. Where is Big Ben? _____

8. From what country do we get the word *boomerang*? _____

9. When did Albert Schweitzer live? _____

10. In what country and by whom was the saxophone invented? _____

    _____

11. What is the mythological character Romulus noted for? _____

    _____

Sentence Structure

2

2 Sentence Structure

The most common errors in freshman writing are fragments and run-together sentences. Here are some fragments:

Having worked hard to make the team
The game that I really hoped to play in
Although everyone was expecting to win

They don't make complete statements. They leave the reader wanting something more.

Here are some run-together sentences:

The lightning flashed the thunder roared.
It was a great trip I enjoyed every minute of it.
They invited Maria she couldn't come.

Unlike fragments, they make complete statements, but the trouble is they make *two* complete statements, which shouldn't be run together into one sentence without correct punctuation. The reader has to go back to see where there should have been a pause.

Both fragments and run-together sentences bother the reader. Not until you get rid of them will your writing be clear and easy to read. Unfortunately there is no quick, easy way to learn to avoid them. You have to learn a little about sentence structure—mainly how to find the subject and the verb in a sentence so that you can tell whether it really is a sentence.

FINDING SUBJECTS AND VERBS

When you write a sentence, you write about *something* or *someone*. That's the subject. Then you write what the subject *does* or *is*. That's the verb.

Birds <u>fly</u>.

The word *Birds* is the something you are writing about. It's the subject, and we'll underline it once. *Fly* tells what the subject does. It shows the action in the sentence. It's the verb, and we'll underline it twice. Because the verb often shows action, it's easier to spot than the subject. Therefore always look for it first. For example, in the sentence

Pat drives in the stock car races.

which word shows the action? <u>Drives</u>. It's the verb. Underline it twice. Now ask yourself who or what drives. <u>Pat</u>. It's the subject. Underline it once.

Study the following sentences until you understand how to pick out subjects and verbs.

Last night the rain flooded our basement. (Which word shows the action? Flooded. It's the verb. Underline it twice. Who or what flooded? Rain. It's the subject. Underline it once.)

My brother ran in the two-mile relay. (Which word shows the action? Ran. Who or what ran? Brother.)

This year my sister plays the clarinet in the college orchestra. (Which word shows the action? Plays. Who or what plays? Sister.)

Often the verb doesn't show action but merely tells what the subject *is* or *was*. Learn to spot such verbs—*is, are, was, were, seems, appears* . . .

Brian is smart. (First spot the verb <u>is</u>. Who or what is? <u>Brian</u> <u>is</u>.)

That guy on first base is a pro. (First spot the verb <u>is</u>. Who or what is? <u>Guy</u> <u>is</u>.)

Natalie seems happy these days. (First spot the verb <u>seems</u>. Who or what seems? <u>Natalie</u> <u>seems</u>.)

The goalie appears nervous. (First spot the verb <u>appears</u>. Who or what appears? <u>Goalie</u> <u>appears</u>.)

Sometimes the subject comes after the verb.

On her desk were her unopened books. (Who or what were? <u>Books</u>
<u>were</u>.)
<u>Where</u> is the coach? (Who or what is? <u>Coach</u> <u>is</u>.)
There was a big crowd at the recital. (Who or what was? <u>Crowd</u>
<u>was</u>.)
There were storm clouds in the west. (Who or what were? <u>Clouds</u>
<u>were</u>.)
Here is my car key. (Who or what is? <u>Key</u> <u>is</u>.)

Note that *there* and *here* (as in the last three sentences) are never subjects. They simply point out something.

In commands, the subject often is not expressed. It is *you* (understood).

Open the door! (<u>You</u> <u>open</u> the door.)
Hold that line! (<u>You</u> <u>hold</u> that line.)

As you pick out subjects in the following exercises, you may wonder
whether you should say the subject is, for example, *trees* or *redwood
trees*. It makes no difference so long as you get the main subject, *trees*,
right. In the answers at the back of the book, usually—but not always—
the single word is used. Don't waste your time worrying whether to
include an extra word with the subject. Just make sure you get the
main subject right.

EXERCISES

Underline the subject once and the verb twice. Find the verb first, and then
ask **Who** or **What**. When you've finished 10 sentences, compare your answers carefully with those at the back of the book.

☐EXERCISE 1

1. At one time 30 to 60 million bison roamed this country.
2. Bison is another name for buffalo.
3. Great herds roamed from Mexico to Canada in the early days.
4. Herds often extended from six to ten miles.

5. Often they blocked the way of trains.
6. Sometimes they even derailed the trains.
7. The bison's massive head is its most characteristic feature.
8. The adult bison is about eight feet high at the shoulders.
9. It weighs from 1,000 to 3,000 pounds.
10. It travels swiftly in spite of its size and bulk.

☐EXERCISE 2

1. The bison's hide furnished material for Indian tepees and robes.
2. Its meat furnished food for the Indians.
3. Early pioneers shot the bison by the thousands.
4. By 1900 the bison was nearly extinct.
5. Then the government established a refuge in Montana.
6. Soon 325–400 bison roamed on the Montana Bison Range.
7. With few fences the bison roamed almost free.
8. Before long, state parks developed herds.
9. Today there are about 75,000 bison in the United States.
10. They also roam in every province in Canada.

☐EXERCISE 3

1. I took a walk through a groove of 2,000-year-old redwood trees.
2. Redwood trees grow in families.
3. The parent tree is in the center with the offspring in a circle around it.
4. Each young tree grows from a burl, or root, of the parent tree.
5. The roots extend 25 feet horizontally but only about six feet deep.
6. Redwood bark is fire-resistant.
7. The wood also resists fungus growths.
8. Therefore redwood trees live a long time.
9. They are the largest living things in the world today.
10. The largest redwood tree is the General Sherman in Sequoia National Park in California with a circumference of 101.5 feet.

☐EXERCISE 4

1. The Great Wall of China is one of the modern wonders of the world.
2. It is 2,000 years old.
3. The wall is as high as a two-story house.
4. It runs over mountains, rivers, and deserts for 1,500 miles.
5. That is as far as from New York to Dallas.
6. Along the top of the wall runs a road about 10 feet wide.
7. There are watchtowers about every 100 yards along the top.
8. Once there were 15,000 towers.
9. Sentries in those towers kept a lookout for the enemy.
10. The wall was a defense against the tribesmen from the north.

☐EXERCISE 5

1. The highest waterfall in the world is Angel Falls in Venezuela.
2. It drops down the face of a 3,200-foot cliff.
3. An almost impenetrable jungle surrounds the falls.
4. For many years no one saw it close up.
5. Only airplane pilots spotted it from the air.
6. Then finally some explorers reached it.
7. Victoria Falls in Africa is another impressive falls.
8. It is more than a mile wide.
9. Niagara Falls is almost as wide as Victoria Falls.
10. Visit Niagara Falls someday.

☐EXERCISE 6

1. Some people fear spiders.
2. But spiders are friends of people.
3. Except for black widows and tarantulas, spiders are harmless.
4. They destroy fleas, mosquitoes, grasshoppers, and other insects.
5. Spiders are excellent civil engineers in making their webs.
6. They calculate the strain on each part of the web precisely.
7. The grass spider's web is usually in the shape of a broad funnel.
8. The spider lies in wait at the end of the funnel for its prey.
9. The open end is an escape hatch for the spider.
10. Dew upon the web makes the web visible.

☐EXERCISE 7

1. The whooping crane is a majestic white bird with black wing tips.
2. Once there were 1,300 to 1,500 whooping cranes in this country.
3. Then the flocks dwindled to a single flock of only 18 birds.
4. The two causes of the decrease were excessive hunting and the destruction of the prairie wetlands.
5. Development projects also disturbed the roosting sites of the birds along their migratory route.
6. The 18 remaining whooping cranes nested in northern Canada.
7. They wintered on the Texas coast.
8. Finally the U.S. Fish and Wildlife Service protected the stopover sites along the migration path of this endangered species.
9. The Canadian National Railway even changed the route of a branch line to avoid the nesting site of the cranes.
10. By 1990 the whooping cranes numbered about 200.

☐EXERCISE 8

1. In 1877 Edison invented the phonograph almost by accident.
2. He spoke "Mary Had a Little Lamb" into the invention.

3. Astonishingly, the device worked the first time.
4. People marveled at the reproduction of the human voice.
5. The phonograph was an immediate success in show business.
6. It gave an evening's entertainment to audiences throughout the country.
7. Skeptics tested it for themselves.
8. People listened with astonishment to their own voices.
9. Then they applauded with gusto.
10. The machine recorded the voices of Florence Nightingale, Woodrow Wilson, Queen Victoria, Mark Twain, and many other famous people.

☐EXERCISE 9

1. The phonograph also played John Philip Sousa marches and Stephen Foster melodies.
2. But Edison disapproved of the use of the phonograph for entertainment.
3. He intended it for office dictation.
4. Eventually Edison considered the phonograph his most original invention.
5. His first phonograph is now in the Edison Museum in West Orange, New Jersey.
6. My grandparents once had an old phonograph with a crank to wind it.
7. They had lots of records for it too.
8. But then they wanted a new electric record player.
9. So they discarded the old machine.
10. An old machine like that is valuable today.

☐EXERCISE 10

1. There are only three ways to make music.
2. One is by the vibration of a string, as in a violin.
3. Another is by the vibration of an air column inside a hollow tube, as in a clarinet.
4. The third way is by the vibration of a solid substance, such as a bell or gong or cymbals.
5. Thus there are three main families of musical instruments.
6. One is the string family with such instruments as the violin, viola, cello, double bass, harp, piano, guitar, and banjo.
7. The second family is the wind family with such instruments as the flute, piccolo, oboe, English horn, clarinet, bassoon, saxophone, trumpet, trombone, and tuba.
8. The wind family includes both woodwinds and brasses.
9. The third family is the percussion with such instruments as the drums, bells, cymbals, and gongs.

10. The modern orchestra is still much the same as the orchestra of Beethoven's time.

WRITING ASSIGNMENT

As you get back your writing assignments, are you keeping a list of your misspelled words on the inside back cover of this book?

Proofreading Exercise

Can you correct the five errors in this paragaph? No answers are provided at the back of the book.

The first muscle-powered flight across the English Channel took place in the summer of 1979. In his strange contraption of a bicycle with wings, Bryan Allen made the crossing in less than three hours. His pedal-powered craft, the *Albatross,* looked like a giant dragonfly. It's width was 96 feet. That's 2½ feet more then the width of a DC 9. The weight of the machine was only 75 pounds, and yet it was strong enough to withstand the sudden gusts in the Channel. Allen said, "If you start sinking, youve got to pedal faster." At one point Allens legs almost gave out, and the craft dipped to within six inches of the water. But Allen pedaled on in spite of leg cramps. Spectators cheers greeted Allen as he touched down in France after his long pedaling trip.

SUBJECTS NOT IN PREPOSITIONAL PHRASES

A prepositional phrase is simply a preposition and the name of someone or something. (See the examples in the columns below.) We don't use many grammatical terms in this book, and the only reason we're mentioning prepositional phrases is to get them out of the way. They're a bother in analyzing sentences. For example, you might have difficulty finding the subject and verb in a long sentence like this:

> During the summer one of my friends drove to her parents' home near Akron in southern Ohio.

But if you cross out all the prepositional phrases like this:

> ~~During the summer~~ one ~~of my friends~~ drove ~~to her parents' home near Akron in southern Ohio~~.

then you have only two words left—the subject and the verb. Even in short sentences like the following, you might pick the wrong word as the subject if you didn't cross out the prepositional phrases first.

> One ~~of my friends~~ lives ~~in St. Petersburg~~.
> Most ~~of the team~~ went ~~on the trip~~.

The subject is never in a prepositional phrase. Read this list several times to learn to recognize prepositional phrases.

about the desk	**beyond** the desk	**on** the desk
above the desk	**by** the desk	**outside** the desk
across the desk	**down** the street	**over** the desk
after vacation	**during** vacation	**past** the desk
against the desk	**except** the desk	**since** vacation
along the street	**for** the desk	**through** the desk
among the desks	**from** the desk	**to** the desk
around the desk	**in** the desk	**toward** the desk
at the desk	**inside** the desk	**under** the desk
before vacation	**into** the desk	**until** vacation
behind the desk	**like** the desk	**up** the street
below the desk	**near** the desk	**upon** the desk
beneath the desk	**of** the desk	**with** the desk
beside the desk	**off** the desk	**within** the desk

NOTE: Don't mistake *to* and a verb for a prepositional phrase. For example, to *run* is not a prepositional phrase because *run* is not the name of something. It's a verb.

EXERCISES

Cross out the prepositional phrases. Then underline the subject once and the verb twice. Correct each group of 10 sentences before going on.

☐EXERCISE 1

1. Most of my friends are in this English course.
2. All of us realize our need for a refresher course.
3. In high school most of us did little writing.
4. Every one of us needs practice in writing.
5. A few of us need help with punctuation.
6. Many of us need a review of sentence structure too.
7. Practically all of us need some work on spelling.
8. The goal of the course is not beautiful writing.
9. The goal of the course is simply clear writing.
10. With a lot of practice we hope to write better.

☐EXERCISE 2

1. In the country, springtime is frog time.
2. From ponds and puddles and ditches come the calls of the frogs.
3. Only the males sing.
4. On warm evenings they sing to attract their mates.
5. A frog closes his mouth in calling.
6. He pushes air from his lungs into his mouth and through special openings to vocal sacs or resonance chambers.
7. The resonance chambers give volume to the call.
8. Each species of frog has its own distinctive note.
9. The spring peeper, for example, emits a high piping note.
10. Dozens of them produce a noise like the sound of sleigh bells.

☐EXERCISE 3

1. The largest animals in the world are the whales.
2. Beside them a 10-ton elephant is small.
3. None of the ancient dinosaurs were as large as whales.
4. The dimensions of the blue whale, for example, are enormous.
5. Many of the blue whales are 100 feet long.
6. Some of them weigh 150 tons.
7. Whales are mammals.
8. Therefore all of them come to the surface of the water for air.

9. The sperm whale stays under water for half an hour at a time.

10. Most whales, however, come to the surface more frequently.

☐EXERCISE 4

1. In the Antarctic Ocean, whales are numerous.

2. There they feed on the abundant plankton of the Antarctic waters.

3. Most of the time they swim near the surface of the water.

4. But sometimes they dive half a mile in search of food.

5. The stomach of a whale is enormous.

6. The stomach of one small orca whale contained 24 seals.

7. Sometimes whales leap from the water just for fun.

8. In fish the tail fin is vertical.

9. In whales the tail is horizontal.

10. Most whales make sounds under water.

☐EXERCISE 5

1. Seventy percent of the total surface of the earth is water.

2. The Pacific is the largest ocean on earth.

3. It represents 45 percent of the world's ocean surface.

4. The deepest part of the oceans is in the Marianas Trench in the Pacific.

5. There the water is 35,760 feet deep in some places.

6. The average depth of the Pacific is 14,000 feet.

7. Under the ocean there are also mountains.

8. The highest of the Pacific underwater mountains is between Samoa and New Zealand.

9. It rises 28,500 feet from the seabed.

10. That underwater mountain comes within 500 feet of the height of Mount Everest.

Underline the subject once and the verb twice. If you aren't sure, cross out the prepositional phrases first.

☐EXERCISE 6

1. In his earliest years Einstein showed no sign of genius.

2. He did not talk until age three.

3. In high school he hated the drill-sergeant manner of his teachers.
4. He annoyed them with his rebellious attitude.
5. After his father's business failure, the family moved to northern Italy.
6. Einstein spent a year in the mountains and in museums.
7. Then he decided to enroll in the famed Swiss Federal Institute of Technology in Zurich.
8. However, with deficiencies in botany, zoology, and languages, he failed the entrance exam.
9. Only after a year of study at a Swiss high school, was he finally admitted.
10. Yet his rebelliousness continued. He cut lectures. He tinkered in school labs. He incurred the wrath of his teachers.

Source: *Time,* February 19, 1979

□EXERCISE 7

1. Not only scientists pioneer in scientific fields.
2. At the turn of the century a Vermont farmer became an authority on snow crystals and snowflakes.
3. With a simple microscope and a camera, Wilson A. Bentley developed a technique of microphotography.
4. In a shed on a hillside he collected snow crystals on a small black-velvet-covered tray.
5. He photographed from 50 to 75 crystals in each good snowstorm.
6. From his photographs he learned the anatomy of snow crystals.
7. In all of his study, he never found two exactly alike.
8. Most of them, however, are six-pointed.
9. Each of them develops from a droplet of cloud moisture.
10. Several of the crystals then combine into a snowflake.

□EXERCISE 8

1. The six delicate spokes of the snow crystal make a flowerlike pattern.
2. Each of the crystals contains ridges, grooves, and cavities in its hexagonal pattern.
3. In his lifetime Bentley photographed over 6,000 snow crystals.
4. The U.S. Weather Bureau bought large quantities of his prints.
5. Manufacturers copied his prints of the lovely snow crystals for jewelry, china, glass, and fabrics.
6. Every work on meteorology used his pictures for illustrations of snow crystals.
7. People called him Snowflake Bentley.

8. With the appearance of his most important book, *Snow Crystals,* he became an authority in the scientific world.
9. He wrote it with a professor of meteorology at the U.S. Weather Bureau.
10. Eventually the scientists in the American Association for the Advancement of Science made Bentley a member.

☐EXERCISE 9

1. In the Dickson Mounds Museum near Lewistown in central Illinois is one of the greatest study collections of prehistoric human skeletal remains in the world.
2. Here are the exposed remains of 237 Indians of the Mississippian period.
3. The burials date from A.D. 1150 to A.D. 1350.
4. Some of the burials are individual.
5. Many are group burials with from two to twelve individuals in one grave.
6. Many of the burials contain dishes.
7. The reason for the inclusion of dishes is unknown.
8. Mr. Dickson excavated from 1927 to 1931.
9. In 1972 the state of Illinois built a museum above the excavation at a cost of $2.5 million.
10. Now thousands of visitors come to the Dickson Mounds Museum each year.

☐EXERCISE 10

1. Visitors look through a glass partition at the 237 partially excavated graves.
2. Each of the bodies is in its original burial position.
3. A loudspeaker describes the different parts of the excavation.
4. Visitors see the places being discussed.
5. Archeologists determine the age of the individual from the development of the skull.
6. The life expectancy of these Indians was about 23½ years.
7. The high mortality of infants and of women in childbirth lowered the general life expectancy.
8. From the skeletons archeologists determine the diseases of these people.
9. They had pyorrhea, arthritis, and many other modern diseases.
10. Other exhibits in the museum span 12,000 years of prehistory.

MORE ABOUT VERBS AND SUBJECTS

Sometimes the verb is more than one word. Here are a few of the many forms of the verb *drive*:

I drive	I will be driving	I may drive
I am driving	I will have been driving	I could drive
I have driven	I will have driven	I might drive
I have been driving	I am driven	I should drive
I drove	I was driven	I would drive
I was driving	I have been driven	I must drive
I had driven	I had been driven	I could have driven
I had been driving	I will be driven	I might have driven
I will drive	I can drive	I should have driven

Note that words like the following are never part of the verb even though they may be in the middle of the verb:

already	even	never	only
also	ever	not	really
always	finally	now	sometimes
before	just	often	usually

Stephanie is not going far. She has finally decided on her route.

Two verb forms—*driving* and *to drive*—look like verbs, but neither can ever be the verb of a sentence. No *ing* word by itself can ever be the verb of a sentence; it must have a helping verb in front of it.

Derek driving home. (not a sentence because there is no proper verb)
Derek was driving home. (a sentence)

And no verb with *to* in front of it can ever be the verb of a sentence.

To drive north along the coast. (not a sentence because there is no proper verb and no subject)
I like to drive north along the coast. (a sentence with *like* as the verb)

These two forms, *driving* and *to drive,* may be used as subjects, or they may have other uses in the sentence.

Driving costs a lot.   To drive costs a lot.

But neither of them can ever be the verb of a sentence.

Not only may a verb be composed of more than one word, but also there may be more than one verb in a sentence:

Dan trimmed the bushes and planted some flowers.

Also there may be more than one subject.

Dan and Allison trimmed the bushes and planted some flowers.

EXERCISES

Underline the subject once and the verb twice. Be sure to include all parts of the verb. Also watch for more than one subject and more than one verb. It's a good idea to cross out the prepositional phrases first.

☐EXERCISE 1

1. Frank W. Woolworth's first store in Utica, New York, was a failure.
2. Woolworth pondered the cause of his failure.
3. He had had a good idea and had worked hard.
4. Perhaps the location was wrong.
5. He heard of good business opportunities in Lancaster, Pennsylvania.
6. The inhabitants of Lancaster were thrifty Pennsylvania Dutch farmers.
7. Woolworth took $30 and explored Lancaster.
8. In a few months he closed his Utica store and opened one in Lancaster.
9. The store was the world's first successful five-and-ten-cent store.
10. That store was the beginning of Woolworth's empire.

☐EXERCISE 2

1. Bunky Knudson was the son of General Motors onetime president William S. Knudson.
2. On his 14th birthday, Bunky was given a new Chevrolet by his father.
3. Bunky was ecstatic.
4. His father told him to go to the plant to get the car.
5. Bunky hurried to the plant in great excitement.
6. There the car was waiting for him—in several thousand pieces.

7. Bunky took a couple of months to assemble the car.
8. But eventually it was ready to run.
9. Bunky knew a lot about cars at the finish.
10. It had been a really good birthday present.

□EXERCISE 3

1. A woman in a Boston hotel phoned the manager.
2. She complained to him about the noise down the hall.
3. A piano had been banging away all day long.
4. It was impossible to rest with all that racket.
5. The manager was sympathetic but did nothing.
6. He merely told her the name of the pianist.
7. Paderewski would be giving a concert the next day and was practicing for it.
8. From that moment the woman sat in her room in rapt attention and listened to every note.
9. She considered it the opportunity of a lifetime.
10. Yet nothing had changed except her attitude.

□EXERCISE 4

1. Almost anything can be reproduced in a model except the universe.
2. It would be impossible to make such a model.
3. Here is the reason.
4. Imagine the earth as a ball one inch in diameter.
5. Then the nearest star in the model would be nearly 50,000 miles away.
6. The vastness of the universe is beyond comprehension.
7. For example, in the night sky we can see the Milky Way.
8. But we don't think of its composition.
9. To the early Greeks the Milky Way was a band of mythical milk across the heavens.
10. We know more about the Milky Way today but still know very little.

□EXERCISE 5

1. Galileo was the first to study the Milky Way.
2. He turned his newly invented telescope upon it and realized its makeup.
3. It is composed of at least 200 billion stars.
4. Our sun is one of those stars and is only an insignificant speck in the entire galaxy.
5. I have learned some of the constellations in the Milky Way.
6. On a dark night I can always find Orion and the Pleiades.
7. The Milky Way is only one of the billions of galaxies in the universe.
8. One hundred million galaxies can be counted in the bowl of the Big Dipper alone.

9. There are at least as many stars as grains of sand upon all the sea-shores of the earth.
10. Yet they are strewn very thinly throughout space.

□EXERCISE 6

1. Sir James Jeans, an eminent astronomer, made this observation about the vastness of space.
2. Imagine only three wasps in the airspace above Europe.
3. Space in the universe is even less crowded with stars than that.
4. Time in the universe also is beyond comprehension.
5. Our sun was born five billion years ago.
6. The light from one galaxy started to come to us 100 million years ago.
7. That was at the time of the dinosaurs.
8. That light is only now reaching us.
9. All this time it has been traveling 186,000 miles per second.
10. Try to comprehend the distance of that galaxy from the earth.

□EXERCISE 7

1. The great Edison industries in New Jersey were practically destroyed by fire in 1914.
2. In one night Thomas A. Edison lost two million dollars' worth of equipment.
3. And the record of much of his life's work was consumed by the flames.
4. Edison stood and watched the fire.
5. The next morning he walked among the charred embers of his work and then made a statement.
6. "There is great value in disaster. All of our mistakes are destroyed. We can start anew."
7. And at the age of 67 he did start again.
8. A less brilliant man might have surrendered to despair.
9. But Edison could see into the future further than most.
10. Adversity became a spur to still greater achievement.

□EXERCISE 8

1. Some of my friends and I took a trip last summer and visited a number of interesting places.
2. One of the most interesting was Heritage Park in Calgary, Alberta.
3. It's an authentic portrayal of a western village prior to 1917.
4. A few of the buildings were in the Calgary area originally.
5. Many have been moved from other parts of the Canadian West.
6. Among the business buildings is a grand old two-story hotel.
7. All of the rooms are furnished with iron bedsteads, handmade quilts, and china washbasins.

8. One of the business buildings is the general store.
9. There one can buy licorice sticks, horehound candy, and candy corn.
10. In the drugstore are old bottles of patent medicines.

☐EXERCISE 9

1. Many of the homes are old mansions with elegant furniture.
2. But some are primitive houses with crude homemade furnishings.
3. In the kitchens we saw wooden washing machines and churns.
4. At noon we had a hearty lunch in the hotel dining room.
5. Then we took a ride on an old steam train with plush seats.
6. It took us to the merry-go-round with its authentic horses and calliope music.
7. Riding on that merry-go-round was fun.
8. Then we returned to the business part of the village and bought some homemade bread at the old bakery.
9. A melodrama at the theater ended our tour.
10. Visit Heritage Park someday and learn about turn-of-the-century living.

☐EXERCISE 10

1. The Mojave Desert covers 25,000 square miles in southeastern California and is a place of contrasts.
2. It includes Mount Whitney, the second tallest mountain in the United States, and also Death Valley, the lowest elevation in the western hemisphere.
3. Death Valley, 282 feet below sea level, was named by pioneers in 1849.
4. Palm trees, cactuses, mountains, sandy plains, and even a lake can all be seen in the Mojave.
5. The Mojave is small in comparison with big deserts like the Sahara but attracts 15,000 visitors a month even in the hot weather.
6. The Mojave alternately bakes and freezes and therefore is sparsely populated even by animals.
7. The kangaroo rat can live its entire life without ever drinking any water and therefore is a natural resident.
8. The pronghorn, the jackrabbit, and the pack rat also live there.
9. The cactus wren and the roadrunner are desert residents too.
10. The Mojave has been called the Devil's Playground because of its wild and varied landscape.

Proofreading Exercise

Can you correct the five errors in these paragraphs? No answers are provided at the back of the book.

THE THREAT TO AFRICAN WILDLIFE

Heavily armed gangs of poachers were invading Africas animal preserves, evading the park rangers, and killing elephants and rhinos for there tusks and horns. Kenya's elephant population has declined 85 percent in the passed 15 years, and the African population of black rhinos has dwindled to a few thousand. Experts at the World Wildlife Fund estimate that at least 100 elephants were being killed illegally every week. Their ivory tusks were selling for about $125 a pound; and rhino horns, prized as dagger handles in the Mideast, were bringing $24,000 each. It was a frightening situation for world wildlife.

Than in October 1989 at a meeting in Lausanne, Switzerland, 76 nations supported a decision to place elephants on the roll of animals close to extinction. This decision triggered a worldwide ban on the ivory trade. Although four African nations say they may defy the ban, yet if the major consumer nations block imports, their will be little market for ivory. Thus the elephants and rhinos may still be saved.

CORRECTING RUN-TOGETHER SENTENCES

Any group of words having a subject and verb is a clause. The clause may be independent (able to stand alone) or dependent (unable to stand alone). Every sentence you have worked with so far has been an independent clause because it has been able to stand alone. It has made a complete statement.

If two independent clauses are written together with no punctuation or with merely a comma, they are called a run-together sentence. (Some textbooks call them a run-on sentence, a comma splice, or a comma fault.) Here are some examples.

> The girls made the fire the boys cooked the steaks.
> The girls made the fire, the boys cooked the steaks.
> The book was interesting therefore I read it rapidly.
> The book was interesting, therefore I read it rapidly.

Run-together sentences can be corrected in one of three ways:

1. Make the two independent clauses into two sentences.

> The girls made the fire. The boys cooked the steaks.
> The book was interesting. Therefore I read it rapidly.

2. Connect the two independent clauses with a semicolon.

> The girls made the fire; the boys cooked the steaks.
> The book was interesting; therefore I read it rapidly.
> I turned my paper in; then I began to review.
> I worked hard; finally I was ready for the test.

When a connecting word such as

also	however	otherwise
consequently	likewise	then
finally	moreover	therefore
furthermore	nevertheless	thus

is used between two independent clauses, it always has a semicolon before it, and it may have a comma after it, especially if there seems to be a pause between the word and the rest of the sentence.

> The lecture was boring; nevertheless, I sat through it.
> I admire that candidate; furthermore, I intend to work for her.

> I like to help in elections; also, it's my civic duty.
> The speaker was late; however, he was worth waiting for.

The semicolon before the connecting word is required. The comma after it is a matter of choice.

3. Connect the two independent clauses with a comma and one of the following words: *and, but, for, or, nor, yet, so.*

> The book was interesting, and I read it rapidly.
> The girls made the fire, but the boys cooked the steaks.
> I couldn't go to the movie, for I had no money.
> I must hurry, or I'll never finish.
> I haven't seen that movie, nor do I want to.

But be sure there are two independent clauses. The first sentence below has two independent clauses. The second sentence is merely one independent clause with two verbs, and therefore no comma should be used.

> She washed her car, and then she wrote her paper.
> She washed her car and then wrote her paper.

The Three Ways to Punctuate Independent Clauses

I began to study. I had a test the next day.
I began to study; I had a test the next day.
I began to study, for I had a test the next day.

Learn these three ways, and you'll avoid run-together sentences. (On page 85 you'll learn a fourth way.)

You may wonder when to use a period and capital letter and when to use a semicolon between two independent clauses. In general, use a period and capital letter. Only if the clauses are closely related in meaning should you use a semicolon.

EXERCISES

In each independent clause underline the subject once and the verb twice. Then be ready to give a reason for the punctuation.

☐EXERCISE 1

1. The country is in motion. The nation is on its feet.

2. Joggers pound the streets in the morning, and dancers carry the movement into the night.

3. Runners cross the country. Hikers scale the peaks.

4. Skiers, skateboarders, rope jumpers, and roller skaters add to the movement. Exercise is "in."

5. We hiked to the mountains last week. The views were breathtaking.

6. We followed a good trail, but it was steep.

7. Finally we stopped. We could climb no farther.

8. We saw an empty cabin and went in.

9. The cabin was cold; furthermore there was no firewood.

10. Still we were grateful for shelter and spent a few hours there.

Most—but not all—of the following sentences are run-together. If the sentence has two independent clauses, separate them with the correct punctuation—comma, semicolon, or period with a capital letter. In general, use the period with a capital letter rather than the semicolon. But either way is correct. Thus your answers may differ from those at the back of the book.

☐EXERCISE 2

1. The World Health Organization sent pesticide to Borneo to kill mosquitoes it worked well.
2. But the pesticide had another effect roaches accumulated the pesticide in their bodies.
3. Lizards in the thatched huts then ate the roaches and the pesticide accumulated in the bodies of the lizards.
4. The pesticide slowed the lizards down thus the cats caught them.
5. The cats then accumulated the pesticide in their bodies and they died.
6. Without the cats, the rats moved in and they carried a threat of the plague.
7. Furthermore, the pesticide killed a parasite enemy of the caterpillars therefore the caterpillars multiplied in the huts.

8. The caterpillars fed on the roof thatching then the roofs started to cave in.

9. No one had foreseen such happenings the World Health Organization had merely wanted to kill mosquitoes.

10. It is difficult to predict the results of interfering with nature the results can be helpful, or they can be catastrophic.

□EXERCISE 3

1. I have been learning about lasers I never knew about them before.

2. The word *laser* is an acronym an acronym is made from the first letters of several words.

3. The acronym *laser* stands for *l*ight *a*mplification by *s*timulated *e*mission of *r*adiation.

4. Ordinary light spreads out in traveling but laser light doesn't.

5. Laser light can be focused and aimed it is the most powerful light on earth.

6. Laser beams are used in eye surgery and scientists use them to cut concrete and steel.

7. The laser is the second most versatile invention of the twentieth century only the computer is more versatile.

8. Many uses are being found for the laser someday laser light may replace electricity as a source of energy.

9. The laser is also being used in weaponry thus the laser can be put to both beneficial and destructive uses.

10. The laser field is in its early stages but it is developing fast.

□EXERCISE 4

1. Learning the stories behind words is a fascinating hobby it helps us remember words too.

2. There are many interesting stories behind common words our word *alphabet* is an example.

3. *Alpha* is the first letter in the list of Greek letters and *beta* is the second.

4. The Greeks used those first two letters to stand for their entire list of letters thus they called their entire list *alphabetos*.

5. We do the same in English we call our entire list our *ABCs*.

6. But we also have taken over those two Greek words to mean our entire list of letters and thus we speak of our *alphabet*.

7. *Bonfire* is another interesting word it goes back to the Middle Ages.

8. In times of plague, bodies were burned on funeral pyres the fires were called *bonefires* (fires of bones).

9. Later the word came to mean any open-air fire and the spelling changed to *bonfire*.

10. Today we enjoy bonfires and never think of their gruesome beginning.

☐EXERCISE 5

1. In ancient times, salt was not easily obtained and Roman soldiers were given a special allowance for the purchase of salt.
2. This allowance was called *salarium* or "salt money" and from that Latin word we get our word *salary*.
3. Thus a salary is literally "salt money" a salary today, however, buys more than salt.
4. Another interesting word is *trivial* it comes from two Latin words.
5. *Tri* means three and *via* means way or road.
6. In Roman times the *trivium* was the crossing of three roads farmers' wives on their way to market would gather at the crossing of the three roads and chat about unimportant matters.
7. Gradually that kind of unimportant talk came to be called *trivial* or "three roads" talk.
8. Today anything unimportant is called trivial but we seldom think of the origin of the word.
9. Learning word origins is fun their derivations are often surprising.
10. The origin of most words can be found in a dictionary it will be in square brackets either at the beginning or at the end of the definition.

☐EXERCISE 6

1. *Gymnasium* is an interesting word its origin would surprise most athletes.
2. Athletics was important in Greece and the athletes exercised nude.
3. *Gymnos* in Greek means nude and therefore the exercise place for the nude athletes was called the *gymnasion*.
4. From it we get our *gymnasium* we have retained the idea of an exercise place but not of nudity.
5. Many English words come from Latin and Greek but we also get a number from German and French and Spanish.
6. The American Indian too has given us many words *moccasin, toboggan, wigwam,* and *chipmunk* are examples.
7. The most commonly spoken language today is Mandarin it is spoken by 68 percent of the Chinese.
8. The next most common and the most widespread is English it is spoken by an estimated 360,000,000 people.
9. There are 5,000 languages and dialects in the world today about 845 are spoken in India.
10. The oldest written language is Egyptian some Egyptian inscriptions date back to 3100 B.C.

□EXERCISE 7

1. In its 10,000-year history agriculture was an individual undertaking but today it's a mass-production business.
2. A farmer used to cultivate 80 acres with a horse and plow but now one person can cultivate ten or a hundred times that much with modern machinery.
3. Throughout the world today one farmer can feed five people but in the United States one farmer grows enough to feed 59 people.
4. In the early part of this century, one out of every three people lived on a farm by 1977 only one out of 28 people in the U.S. lived on a farm.
5. The largest farms today are the collective farms of Russia some are 60,000 acres.
6. For farmers, money used to be scarce every penny had to go to maintain the farm and support the family.
7. Now farmers have more money they often have more than city workers.
8. Agriculture is this nation's most efficient and productive industry and it is an enormous force in holding down the trade deficit.
9. Food production has increased worldwide yet more than a third of the people in the world suffer from malnutrition.
10. Almost a third of the world's babies die of malnutrition before the age of five and 300 million more will not have the ability to learn because of inadequate diet.

□EXERCISE 8

1. The first snowmobiles were developed in the 1920s they were used by mail carriers in the northern states.
2. In the 1950s the recreational snowmobile was developed it moves over the snow with two skis in front and an engine-driven track to propel it.
3. Thus it floats over the top of the snow it can attain a speed of 112 km per hour.
4. My dad doesn't like snowmobiles nor will he allow them on his farm.
5. He has placed warning signs everywhere nevertheless snowmobiles do come in.
6. The farm is large therefore the snowmobilers enter on the far side.
7. My father doesn't see them but he finds their tracks.
8. The noise frightens the cattle and it is scaring the wildlife away.
9. One small gully used to be a favorite place for rabbits foxes could sometimes be seen there too.
10. Now we seldom see them also fewer birds are nesting in that area.

☐EXERCISE 9

1. An attempt is being made to save the animals of the Bible from extinction Israel's Nature Reserve Authority is trying to save 13 endangered species.
2. The age-old scarcity of water and foliage in the Bible lands has always limited the animal population but modern factors have made it even more difficult for the animals to survive.
3. Speeding automobiles, pollution of rivers, pesticides, and poachers have all reduced the population of animals of the Bible now efforts to save them are proving successful.
4. A roadside feast of horse meat, beef, and freshly killed chicken is left at the edge of a desert road and the animals come at night to eat.
5. First come the foxes and then come wolves, jackals, hyenas, and occasionally a leopard.
6. One after another they help themselves to the food and ignore the nearby human observers.
7. Such a feast is left in five locations on the Negev and Judean deserts every two weeks and already there's an increase in the animal population.
8. The project, however, can't save all the desert's endangered species only the bolder animals come to the feeding stations.
9. Also the officials have to be careful not to leave too much food otherwise the animals quit fending for themselves.
10. The program has been under way since 1970 and the authorities hope to repopulate the land with the animals of ancient times.

Punctuate this paragraph so that there will be no run-together sentences.

☐EXERCISE 10

The first state to honor working people was Oregon it set aside a day for them in 1887. In 1894 Labor Day became a national legal holiday it marks the end of summer. Of course summer really ends with the autumnal equinox about September 23 after that the nights become longer than the days. Soon leaves begin to fall and that gives another name to autumn. It's the only season with two names it's as often called fall as autumn. Autumn usually has pleasant weather but surprises may occur. It was −7° F in Yellowstone National Park on September 24, 1926 and Denver got 21.3 inches of snow on September 27, 1936. The weather can also go to the other extreme San Diego reached 111° F on September 26, 1963. Of course in the southern hemisphere the trend is the opposite and the first signs of spring are appearing.

Source: *Travel and Leisure,* Sept. 1984

JOURNAL WRITING

Write three sentences to illustrate the three ways of punctuating two independent clauses in a sentence. Master this section before you go on. It will take care of many of your punctuation errors.

WRITING ASSIGNMENT

Continue with your writing assignments. Have someone dictate to you your list of spelling words on the inside back cover. Can you spell them all correctly now?

CORRECTING FRAGMENTS

There are two kinds of clauses: independent (which we have just finished studying) and dependent. A dependent clause has a subject and a verb just like an independent clause, but it can't stand alone because it begins with a dependent word (or words) such as

after	since	whereas
although	so that	wherever
as	than	whether
as if	that	which
because	though	whichever
before	unless	while
even if	until	who
even though	what	whom
ever since	whatever	whose
how	when	why
if	whenever	
in order that	where	

Whenever a clause begins with one of the above dependent words (unless it's a question, which would never give you any trouble), it is dependent. If we take an independent clause such as

We finished the game.

and put one of the dependent words in front of it, it becomes dependent:

After we finished the game
Although we finished the game
As we finished the game
Before we finished the game
Since we finished the game
That we finished the game
While we finished the game

As you read the clause, you can hear that it doesn't make a complete statement. It leaves the reader expecting something more. Therefore it can no longer stand alone. It's a fragment and must not be punctuated as a sentence. To correct such a fragment, add an independent clause:

After we finished the game, we went to the clubhouse.
We went to the clubhouse after we finished the game.
We were happy that we finished the game early.
While we finished the game, the others waited.

In other words, **EVERY SENTENCE MUST HAVE AT LEAST ONE INDEPENDENT CLAUSE.**

Note in the examples that when a dependent clause comes at the beginning of a sentence, it is followed by a comma. Often the comma prevents misreading, as in the following sentence:

By the time I had finished, my lunch was cold.

Without a comma after *finished,* the reader would read *By the time I had finished my lunch* before realizing that that was not what the author meant. The comma prevents misreading. Sometimes if the dependent clause is short and there is no danger of misreading, the comma is omitted, but it is safer simply to follow the rule that a dependent clause at the beginning of a sentence is followed by a comma.

You'll learn more about the punctuation of dependent clauses on page 85, but right now just remember the above rule.

Note that sometimes the dependent word is the subject of the dependent clause:

I took the highway that was finished just last month.

Sometimes the dependent clause is in the middle of the independent clause:

The highway that was finished last month goes to Missoula.

And sometimes the dependent clause is the subject of the entire sentence:

What I was doing was not important.

Also note that sometimes the *that* of a dependent clause is omitted.

This is the house that Jack built.
This is the house Jack built.
I thought that you were coming with me.
I thought you were coming with me.

And finally the word *that* doesn't always introduce a dependent clause. It may be a pronoun (That is my book) or a describing word (I like that book).

EXERCISES

Underline the subject once and the verb twice in both the independent and the dependent clauses. Then put a broken line under each dependent clause.

☐EXERCISE 1

1. When I was 10, we moved to a farm.

2. Ever since I can remember, I dreamed of living on a farm.

3. I never thought that my dream would come true.

4. When we had finished unpacking, we put all the furniture in place.

5. We worked until we were exhausted, but we were happy.

6. Then we went out to the yard, which interested us most.

7. When we saw the old well, we immediately had to pump some water.

8. Then we ran out into the orchard that was behind the house.

9. There we picked almost a bushel of apples that had fallen to the ground.

10. When it began to get dark, we knew that our exploring would have to wait for another day.

Underline each dependent clause with a broken line.

☐EXERCISE 2

1. Since I had always wanted to see Alaska, I decided to go there last summer.
2. I drove along the Alaska Highway, which goes through the Yukon Territory in Canada.
3. The highway, which is 1,500 miles long, is the only land route to Alaska.
4. Most tourists go to Alaska by air although some go by ship.
5. Because Denali National Park is Alaska's main tourist attraction, I headed there.
6. I saw Mount McKinley, which is the tallest mountain in North America.

7. Much of Alaska is uninhabited, and glaciers cover hundreds of square miles.
8. I was surprised that the mainland of Alaska at its most western point is only 50 miles from the mainland of Russia.
9. Alaska's coastline, which is 6,640 miles in length, is the longest coastline in the United States.
10. I stayed a week in Anchorage, which is the largest city.

☐EXERCISE 3

1. Alaska has a chain of volcanic islands that go more than a thousand miles into the Bering Sea.
2. It is farther from Alaska's westernmost island to its easternmost point than it is from San Francisco to New York.
3. Alaska, which is more than twice the size of Texas, has the fewest people of any state.
4. But even isolated villages now have airstrips, where bush pilots can land small planes.
5. Along the Arctic Coast, Eskimos still hunt and fish as their ancestors did.
6. Salmon is one of the leading exports of Alaska although the number of salmon has been decreasing.
7. In 1867 the United States bought Alaska from Russia for $7,200,000, which was about two cents an acre.
8. Many thought that the land was a worthless waste of ice and snow.
9. But Alaska, which means "great land," proved to be rich in fish, minerals, oil, timber, and water power.
10. Alaska was a territory of the United States from 1912 until 1959, when it became the 49th state.

☐EXERCISE 4

1. Cross-country skiing, which has more than three million devotees, has become the fastest growing sport in the country today.
2. People who are summer backpackers or bicyclists or joggers find it a good way to keep fit in the winter.
3. In California, ski resorts that a few years ago had only 100 to 200 cross-country skiers now have thousands.
4. For downhill skiing one must go to the mountains and depend on lifts whereas cross-country skiing can be done anywhere.
5. Snow-covered golf courses or cow pastures or city parks are excellent places for those who enjoy cross-country skiing.
6. The equipment for cross-country skiing is simpler than you might think.
7. Of course some skiers use skis that require various kinds of waxes for different temperatures.

8. Most cross-country skiers, however, choose a waxless ski that is grooved with patterns to provide both grip and glide.
9. During the big snows in the East, some business people who had difficulty getting to their offices finally got there on their skis.
10. Cross-country, which used to be a poor cousin to downhill, has at last caught on.

If the clause is independent and therefore a sentence, put a period after it. If the clause is dependent and therefore a fragment, add an independent clause either before or after it to make it into a sentence. Remember that if the dependent clause comes first, it should have a comma after it.

□EXERCISE 5

1. He is a wonderfully kind and compassionate person

2. Whom everyone loves and admires

3. Whose leadership and experience are outstanding

4. I had been getting bored with studying

5. When I could have been doing something much more exciting

6. When I had done everything possible and felt discouraged

7. He suggested jogging a couple of miles

8. Which always puts me in a better mood

9. Whenever I want exercise

10. Which I really enjoy

On pages 72–73 you learned three ways of correcting run-together sentences. Now that you are aware of dependent clauses, you may use a fourth way. In the following run-together sentence

The forecast was for a blizzard we canceled our trip.

you can make one of the two independent clauses into a dependent clause by putting a dependent word in front of it, as in the following examples:

Because the forecast was for a blizzard, we canceled our trip.
Since the forecast was for a blizzard, we canceled our trip.
We canceled our trip when the forecast was for a blizzard.

This fourth way of correcting a run-together sentence is often the best because it puts the more important of the two ideas in the independent clause and thus makes it stand out.

Correct the following run-together sentences by making one of the clauses dependent. In some sentences you will want to put the dependent clause first; in others you may want to put it last or in the middle of the sentence. Since various words can be used to start a dependent clause, your answers may differ from those suggested at the back of the book.

□EXERCISE 6

1. I decided to go home for the weekend I hadn't been home for weeks.

2. I decided to walk it's only about two miles.

3. I don't get enough exercise walking is good for me.

4. I have an office job most of my time is spent sitting.

5. I was walking down the avenue there in front of me I saw a gray fluffy kitten.

6. I can never resist a cuddly kitten I stopped and picked it up.

7. I was in a hurry I finally put it down again.

8. Eventually I got to our house I was surprised at the new car in the driveway.

9. It was a new station wagon my mother had been wanting one for months.

10. Immediately I dashed into the house I wanted to hear her comments.

☐EXERCISE 7

1. We were driving through New Mexico last fall someone told us about Carlsbad Caverns.

2. I had never heard of them before I was immediately interested.

3. I've visited several national parks I'm always eager to see another.

4. We decided to see the park it meant driving several hundred miles out of our way.

5. The weather was good the drive was pleasant.

6. We finally got there we had to wait an hour for a tour to begin.

7. Then we hiked along a trail it was more than 700 feet underground.

8. One room is called The Big Room it is the largest subterranean chamber in the world.

9. Its ceiling is as high as a 22-story building its floor space would hold 14 football fields.

10. The amazingly beautiful formations have been formed by dripping groundwater they include stalactites, stalagmites, columns, and draperies.

☐EXERCISE 8

1. My courses are difficult I need to improve my study habits.

2. Part of my problem is lack of planning I'm going to make a list of things to do.

3. I'll study one subject at a time then I won't get hopelessly bogged down.

4. I'll turn off the stereo then I can concentrate better.

5. I want to concentrate I need complete quiet.

6. I have a paper to write for tomorrow I'll begin it first.

7. Then I'll put my first draft aside I'll study another subject.

8. I'll come back later to my first draft I'll see ways to improve it.

9. Then I'll again put it aside I'll work on something else.

10. My paper will go through several drafts then finally it will be finished.

JOURNAL WRITING

Now that you are aware of independent and dependent clauses, you can vary your sentences. Write three sentences, each containing two independent clauses connected by one of the following words. Be sure to use the correct punctuation—comma or semicolon.

and	for	or
but	however	then
consequently	nevertheless	

Now rewrite the three sentences using one independent and one dependent clause in each. Use some of the following dependent words. If you put the dependent clause first, put a comma after it.

after	if	until
although	since	while
because	unless	

MORE ABOUT FRAGMENTS

We've seen that a dependent clause alone is a fragment. Any group of words that doesn't have a subject and verb is also a fragment.

> Paid no attention to his parents (no subject)
> Rick thinking about all his problems (no adequate verb. Although *ing* words look like verbs, no *ing* word by itself can ever be the verb of a sentence. It must have a helping verb in front of it.)
> Speeding along the highway (no subject and no adequate verb)
> The announcement that we had expected (no verb for an independent clause)

To change these fragments into sentences, we must give each a subject and an adequate verb:

> He paid no attention to his parents. (We added a subject.)
> Rick was thinking about all his problems. (We put a helping verb in front of the *ing* word to make an adequate verb.)
> Speeding along the highway, he had an accident. (We added an independent clause.)
> The announcement that we had expected finally came. (We added a verb for the independent clause.)

Sometimes you can tack a fragment onto the sentence before or after it.

> Wondering why she had not come.   I finally phoned her.
> Wondering why she had not come, I finally phoned her.

Or you can change a word or two in the fragment and make it into a sentence.

> I wondered why she had not come.

Are fragments ever permissible? Increasingly, fragments are being used in advertising and in other kinds of writing. In Exercises 5 through 8, you'll find advertisements that make use of fragments effectively to give a dramatic pause between individual parts of a sentence. But such fragments are used by writers who know what they're doing. The fragments are used intentionally, never in error. Until you're an experienced writer, stick with complete sentences. Especially in college writing, fragments should not be used.

EXERCISES

Put a period after each sentence. Make each fragment into a sentence either by adding an independent clause before or after it or by changing some words in it. Sometimes changing just one word will change a fragment into a sentence.

□EXERCISE 1

1. My resolution to work four hours on my studies every night.

2. The important thing being to get every assignment in on time

3. Having written my thesis statement, I started my paper

4. Getting more and more ideas as I went along

5. After writing for three hours, I decided to go to bed

6. Hoping that my paper would sound better when I read it in the morning

7. To get an idea across and not distract the reader with sentence errors

8. Write simply

9. Make it brief

10. Searching the dictionary for the spelling of every word

□EXERCISE 2

1. She did the best that she could

2. Which is all that anybody can do

3. Since there was nothing more to say

4. Nothing that had not already been said

5. The notice on the bulletin board stating that there would be play practice that evening

6. Hoping all the time that she would call him again

7. A person who was always ready to help

8. Which I have always enjoyed

9. Haven't had so much fun in years

10. Realizing that our next move was important

Make each of the following into a smooth paragraph by getting rid of the fragments. Each of these particular fragments can be tacked on to the sentence before it. Simply cross out the period, and show that the capital letter should be a small letter by putting a diagonal line through it.

☐EXERCISE 3

I came across the little house by accident. As I hiked through the green rolling hills. It sat on one side of a clearing of waving brown grass. With the trees all around fencing in the little area like a yard. I looked inside the battered wooden planks. That framed the opening where a door had once been. The sun shone through the one window opening. And through the cracks in the walls onto the warped wooden floorboards. Which did not quite keep the grass from poking through. I wondered who had built the house. I guessed an old man. Might have lived there alone. I imagined him hoeing his garden. And wiping the sweat from his brow with an old red handkerchief. How long ago was that? And how many years had the house stood empty without him? It would stand for a few more years, but eventually the trees would retake the clearing, and the grass would grow through the old planks. Some night the boards would blow over to rejoin the earth. And new trees would grow. Where the old house had stood.

☐EXERCISE 4

No one knows who invented eyeglasses. Monks first used a magnifying glass. That was laid flat on a manuscript. At the end of the thirteenth century someone put two magnifying glasses in frames, riveted the frames together, and balanced them on the bridge of the nose. But people found that keeping the glasses on the nose was difficult. Then in the sixteenth century Spanish spectacle makers attached to the frames silk ribbons. That were looped over the ears. The Chinese added to the ends of the ribbons little weights. That dangled on the chest and helped to hold the glasses in place. In 1730 an optician in London invented rigid sidepieces. That finally kept the glasses firmly on the nose. Bifocals, which Benjamin Franklin invented in the 1780s, were the next step in the evolution of glasses. At first people were self-conscious about wearing glasses. Even in the first part of the twentieth century, Dorothy Parker wrote her famous line: "Men seldom make passes at girls who wear glasses." Only in the latter part of the twentieth century have glasses become an item of style. With frames that are fashioned by famous designers.

Source: *The Smithsonian,* March 1983

In the following excerpts from advertisements, the writers have chosen to use fragments. Although the fragments are effective in the ads, they wouldn't be acceptable in formal writing. On a separate sheet rewrite each ad, turning it into acceptable college writing.

☐EXERCISE 5

"Baked Necks."

We cook 'em for breakfast over an open fire in the outback. Then eat 'em with damper bread and billy tea.

What are they? Why bacon and eggs, of course! Just the right way to start off a day of exploring the Aboriginal rock paintings in the outback.

Australia—The Wonder Down Under

☐EXERCISE 6

The world is waiting.

Be an exchange student.

Step into an adventure filled with opportunities and challenges. For many Americans, that adventure remains the most incredible experience of their lives. An experience rich in lifelong friendships and memories.

As part of International Youth Exchange, a Presidential Initiative for peace, you travel to another country. Live abroad with your new host family. Learn new skills. Go to new schools. Make new friends. And return with knowledge and experience that could make a difference in your future. . . .

Youth Exchange
Pueblo, Colorado

□EXERCISE 7

Come talk to the animals.

Whisper to a walrus. Patter to a penguin. Sing to a sea lion.

Pet a smiling dolphin or hug that world-famous killer whale, Shamu. He's the biggest friend you'll ever make! Plan to visit a beautiful Sea World park this summer. Where else can you reach out to so many different marine animals? To talk. To touch. To laugh. To love. To understand each other. And where else can you and your family be so entertained by your new animal friends? With a whole day of fabulous shows, shows, shows! It can only happen at Sea World. Where you can talk to the animals. And they can talk to you.

Sea World
Orlando, San Diego, Cleveland

□EXERCISE 8

We'd like to uncover a hidden natural resource.

Did you know that empty plastic soft drink bottles you throw away every day can be transformed into carpet yarn or automotive parts or fiberfill for ski parkas?

That used glass bottles and aluminum cans can be transformed into new ones?

And that yesterday's newspaper can be transformed into tomorrow's?

It all happens because of recycling. . . .

Amoco Chemical

□EXERCISE 9

The eagle has landed. In Oklahoma and Mississippi. Georgia and Alabama. Where few bald eagle nests have produced young in the last 50 years. Using precious eggs and dedicated effort, the Sutton Avian Research Center is successfully raising eaglets from fuzzy to fierce. And releasing them into the habitats bald eagles used to call home. Phillips Petroleum supports this unique program to re-establish our endangered national symbol. . . .

Phillips Petroleum

Review of Run-together Sentences and Fragments

Six Sentences That Show How to Punctuate Clauses

I gave a party. Everybody came. I gave a party; everybody came.	(two independent clauses)
I gave a party; moreover, everybody came.	(two independent clauses connected by a word such as *also, consequently, finally, furthermore, however, likewise, moreover, nevertheless, otherwise, then, therefore, thus*)
I gave a party, and everybody came.	(two independent clauses connected by *and, but, for, or nor, yet, so*)
When I gave a party, everybody came.	(dependent clause at beginning of sentence)
Everybody came when I gave a party.	(dependent clause at end of sentence) The dependent words are *after, although, as, as if, because, before, even if, even though, ever since, how, if, in order that, since, so that, than, that, though, unless, until, what, whatever, when, whenever, where, whereas, wherever, whether, which, whichever, while, who, whom, whose, why*.

If you remember these six sentences and understand the rules for their punctuation, most of your punctuation problems will be taken care of. It is essential that you learn the italicized words in the above table. If your instructor reads some of the words, be ready to tell which ones come between independent clauses and which ones introduce dependent clauses.

Put periods and capital letters in these paragraphs so there will be no run-together sentences or fragments.

1. Our land is more valuable than your money it will last forever it will not perish as long as the sun shines and the water flows, and through all the years it will give life to men and beasts it was put there by the Great Spirit, and we cannot sell it because it does not belong to us.

   —Chief Crowfoot

2. Green is the clue to creating a garden the most beautiful gardens in the world show few flowers they depend for their beauty on tree and stone and water.

   —Osbert Sitwell

3. There is a school of psychiatrists who think that "blowing one's top" is a good way to work off something bad this view is held mostly by psychiatrists who cannot control their own tops there is nothing to it blowing one's top serves no good purpose one blowing sets the habit more firmly for the next blowing children blow their tops it is a childish adult who finds it necessary to do so.

   —John A. Schindler

4. Who says youth can't accomplish things? Newton was 24 when he formulated the law of gravitation Victor Hugo had taken three prizes at the French Academy before he was 20 Jefferson was 33 when he drafted the Declaration of Independence Charles Dickens was 25 when he wrote *Oliver Twist* McCormick was 23 when he invented the reaper.

5. But older people have done things too Verdi at 74 produced his masterpiece *Otello* and at 85 the famous *Ave Maria* Goethe at 80 completed *Faust* Tennyson at 85 wrote "Crossing the Bar" Benjamin Franklin at 81 took part in the Constitutional Convention Frank Lloyd Wright created the Guggenheim Museum in New York City when he was close to 90 Grandma Moses took up painting in her seventies and painted more than a thousand canvases before her death at 101.

6. Some long-distance phone calls are routed through satellites that are orbiting 23,000 miles above the earth if you make a call, for example, from the Midwest to California, your voice might travel over land lines to a satellite earth station in Illinois then it would travel up to a satellite next it would travel back down to an earth station near Los Angeles finally it would travel over land lines to the listening party all that would happen in about half a second.

7. Before the days of Shakespeare, there were no forks a servant would bring the meat to the table on the spit or rod on which it had been impaled for cooking the servant would hold the meat while the guest cut off chunks and laid them on a huge slab of thickly cut bread that served as a plate then the meat was eaten with the fingers toward the end of the seventeenth century forks were finally accepted into polite society, but using them was considered rather effeminate.

8. Many state names come from Indian words Wisconsin comes from a word meaning "meeting place of waters" Minnesota comes from a word meaning "sky-tinted water" Dakota comes from a word meaning "friends" or "allies" Mississippi comes from two words meaning "great river."

9. Coral reefs are the largest structures in the world made by living things they are composed of fire corals, lace corals, bead corals, bubble corals, organ-pipe corals, and many others the largest coral reef is the Great Barrier Reef in Australia, which stretches more than a thousand miles the chief enemy of such reefs is man anchors and mooring lines of yachts do considerable damage to corals.

Put periods and capital letters in this student paper so there will be no run-together sentences.

"HERE, BOY"

Early one morning I was sailing out of the harbor on my way to do some salmon fishing I was quietly enjoying the calm water and gray mist over the distant shoreline when to my surprise I saw that I was not alone just a few feet away I saw a dog in the water calmly staring at me with big black eyes.

"A dog out here? This far from land? Impossible!" I thought. But there he was with big eyes, whiskers on his nose, and a sort of friendly curiosity.

I didn't know what to do I slowed my boat and started thinking that I should try to help him to shore he just kept staring, effortlessly floating there with just his face showing above the calm water I looked at him, and he looked at me.

"Here, boy," I said, trying to coax him closer so I could save him he just kept watching, so I slowly swung my boat closer. But he slipped beneath the surface and didn't reappear.

"He's drowned," I thought as the minutes ticked by while I waited for him to surface.

"What was he doing out here in the early morning anyway?" I asked myself. Then I realized how silly I'd been I turned up my motor and with a smile headed off for fishing that was no dog with those big eyes and long whiskers I'd been trying to save a curious harbor seal.

Proofreading Exercise

In this paragraph you may find errors from all the material you have studied so far. Try to find all six errors. You're on your own now. No answers are provided at the back of the book for this paragraph.

It rains every hour on the hour in the new rain forests of "Tropic World" in the Brookfield Zoo near Chicago. "Tropic World" reproduces rain forests that are rapidly disappearing in three parts of the world: Africa, Asia, and South America. When its completed it will be the largest indoor animal exhibit in the world. It will be equal to six stories in height and one and a half football fields in length. Its glass-covered jungle includes 6,000 tropical plants, 50-foot trees, 50-foot waterfalls, rivers, and treetop walkways. Instead of keeping animals in separate cages, the zoo is putting gorillas, orangutans, gibbons, lizards, hippos, and birds all together just as they live in nature. Of coarse animals that have a predatory-prey relationship cant be placed together but many animals live together peacefully. People will see them in their natural setting and the zoo keepers hope that with more room to roam the animals will behave more naturally and produce offspring.

USING STANDARD ENGLISH VERBS

This chapter and the next are for those who need practice in using standard English verbs. Many of us grew up speaking a dialect other than standard English, whether it was in a farm community where people said *I ain't* and *he don't* and *they was* or in a black community where people said *I be* and *it do* and *they has*. Such dialects are effective in their place, but in college and in the business and professional world, the use of standard English is essential. Frequently, though, after students have learned to speak and write standard English, they go back to their home communities and are able to slip back into their community dialects while they are there. Thus they have really become bilingual, able to use two languages—or at least two dialects.

The following tables compare four verbs in one of the community dialects with the same four verbs in standard English. Memorize the standard English forms of these important verbs. Most verbs have endings like the first verb *walk*. The other three verbs are irregular and are important because they are used not only as main verbs but also as helping verbs. We'll be using them as helping verbs in the next chapter.

Don't go on to the exercises until you have memorized the forms of these standard English verbs.

REGULAR VERB: WALK

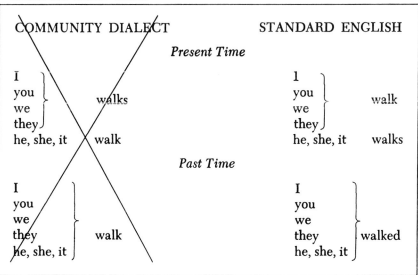

IRREGULAR VERB: HAVE

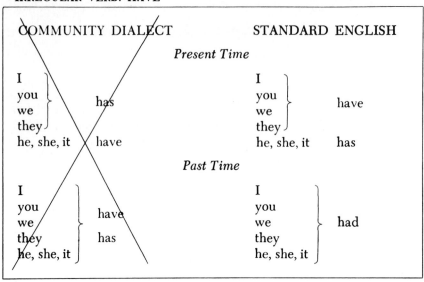

IRREGULAR VERB: BE

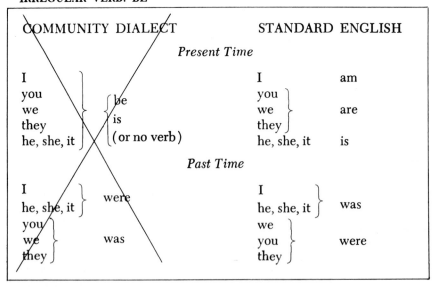

IRREGULAR VERB: DO

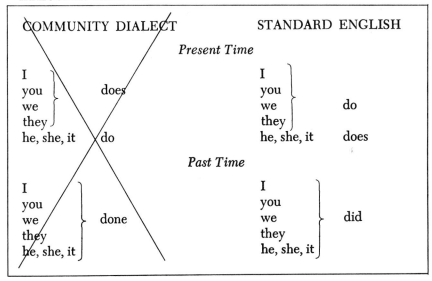

Sometimes students have difficulty with the correct endings of verbs because they don't hear the words correctly. As you listen to your instructor or to TV, note carefully the *s* sound and the *ed* sound at the end of words. Occasionally the *ed* is not clearly pronounced, as in *He asked me to go*, but most of the time you can hear it if you listen.

Try reading the following sentences aloud, making sure that you say every sound.

1. He seems to enjoy his two new friends.
2. He likes his job and hopes to stay with it.
3. It costs a dollar to go by bus, so she walks.
4. He rests for ten minutes before he starts again.
5. I supposed everyone had left.
6. He composed a piece for the piano.
7. She's prejudiced against pop singers.
8. I decided to jog a mile before I started to work.

Now read some other sentences aloud from this text, making sure you sound all the *s*'s and *ed*'s. Listening to others and reading aloud will help you use the correct verb endings automatically.

A good way to learn to speak standard English is to make a pact with a friend that you will both speak only standard English when you are together. By helping each other, you'll soon find yourselves speaking more easily.

EXERCISES

In these pairs of sentences, use the present form of the verb in the first sentence and the past form in the second. All the verbs follow the pattern of the regular verb *walk* except the three irregular verbs *have, be,* and *do.* Keep referring to the tables if you're not sure which form to use. Correct your answers for each exercise before going to the next.

☐EXERCISE 1

1. (learn) I _____ quickly when I try. I _____ all that last week.

2. (like) I _____ this weather. I _____ last week's weather too.

3. (need) He_____ you now. He _____ you then.

4. (open) She _____ the door now. She _____ the door then.

5. (start) He _____ home early these days. He _____ home two hours ago.

6. (suppose) I _____ that I'll go. He _____ that I had gone.

7. (want) He _____ dinner right now. He _____ dinner last night.

8. (have) He _____ a job now. He _____ a job last year.

9. (be) She _____ happy now. She _____ happy then.

10. (do) They _____ their best now. They _____ their best last term.

Underline the standard English verb form. All of the verbs follow the pattern of the regular verb *walk* except the three irregular verbs *have, be,* and *do.*

☐EXERCISE 2

1. About a month ago I (decide decided) to come to evening college.
2. I (work works) during the day, but last week I (sign signed) up for this evening course.
3. When I (arrive arrived) this evening, I (be was) the first one here.

4. Soon, though, a few more students (arrive arrived), and then before long all of the students (was were) here.
5. I (need needs) the kind of drill this class (offer offers).
6. I (intend intends) to work hard, I (hope hopes) to learn a lot.
7. My friend Derek (enroll enrolled) for the class too. We both (want wants) to improve our English.
8. We (work works) at the same company and (live lives) not far from each other.
9. Our children (play plays) together and (attend attends) the same school.
10. Derek and I both (hope hopes) to get college degrees. We (want wants) to advance in our jobs.

☐EXERCISE 3

1. I (do does) everything that the instructor (assign assigns).
2. I (discover discovers) that the assignments (are is) interesting.
3. I (use uses) standard English now, and I (doesn't don't) have much difficulty.
4. When I (watch watches) TV, I (listen listens) to the sounds of the words.
5. Listening carefully (benefit benefits) me, and I (imitate imitates) the speech of the newscasters.
6. When I (talk talks) with my friends, we (use uses) standard English.
7. That (be is) the only way to learn. It (help helps) me a lot.
8. Standard English (be is) the language of the business world. I (intend intends) to master it.
9. I (decide decided) yesterday to speak only standard English for six weeks. I (expect expects) that to help.
10. Last night I (ask asked) Derek to follow my plan. He (agree agreed).

☐EXERCISE 4

1. Some of us (intend intends) to take a trip to Springfield during spring vacation. We (plan plans) to see the Old State Capitol.
2. We (want wants) to spend some time in the Illinois State Museum. I (want wants) to see the habitat groups.
3. Then we (expect expects) to see the home of Abraham Lincoln. It (be is) furnished with period pieces, many associated with the Lincoln family.
4. The Lincoln Memorial Garden features the plants and animals that (was were) familiar to Lincoln.
5. I also want to see the Lincoln Law Offices, where Lincoln (practice practiced) law.
6. Finally I (intend intends) to visit the State Capitol Building. It (be is) majestic.

7. We (has have) New Salem next in our plans. It (be is) 20 miles northwest of Springfield.
8. New Salem (be is) where Lincoln (live lived) for six years before he (move moved) to Springfield.
9. New Salem is a reconstructed pioneer town. It (has have) timber houses, stores, and a school—all furnished as they (was were) in 1830.
10. We (look looks) forward to our trip. That's all we (talk talks) about these days.

In these sentences cross out the community dialect expressions and write the standard English ones above.

□EXERCISE 5

1. We was at the play last night.

2. You was there too, wasn't you?

3. I listen to every word last night.

4. All the actors be well cast.

5. At intermission I talk with some friends. We discuss the play.

6. We also talk about the music camp we all attend last summer.

7. I play the drums then, but now I plays the xylophone.

8. My brother attend the camp too, and he play the flute in the orchestra.

9. He have a solo in one of the performances at the camp.

10. He practice six hours a day now and plan to make a career of music.

□EXERCISE 6

1. Last summer I work with a lawn crew and like it.

2. I mow lawns and trim hedges all last summer.

3. I learn how to edge a lawn.

4. Learning to prune trees require time.

5. My boss be patient and help me learn.

6. He show me how to prune a branch close to the trunk.

7. Then he help me seal the cut.

8. I also learn to prune flowering shrubs.

9. The whole crew work together and have a good time that summer.

10. I hopes to work with that same crew again.

☐EXERCISE 7

1. Yesterday Darrell receive a low grade on a math test, and he decide to do something about it.

2. He realize yesterday that he need a study schedule.

3. He never have one until now.

4. He intend to study two hours outside of class for every hour in class.

5. That be a lot more than he study before.

6. Also he plan to go to the library to study every evening.

7. In the library there be no interruptions.

8. No friends asks him to go out for a snack.

9. Nobody drop by for a chat.

10. On his next math test he be hoping to make a better grade.

JOURNAL WRITING

In your journal write about something that interests you at the moment using verbs you may formerly have had trouble with.

WRITING ASSIGNMENT

Continue with your writing assignments. Have someone dictate to you your list of spelling words on the inside back cover. Can you spell them all correctly now?

USING HELPING VERBS AND IRREGULAR VERBS

In the last chapter you studied the present and past forms of the regular verb *walk*. Other forms of regular verbs may be used with helping verbs. Here is a table showing all the forms of some regular verbs and the various helping verbs they are used with.

REGULAR VERBS

BASE FORM (Use after *can, may, shall, will, could, might, should, would, must, do, does, did.*)	PRESENT	PAST	PAST PARTICIPLE (Use after *have, has, had*. Or use after some form of *be* to describe the subject.)	*ING* FORM (Use after some form of *be*.)
ask	ask (*s*)	asked	asked	asking
dance	dance (*s*)	danced	danced	dancing
decide	decide (*s*)	decided	decided	deciding
enjoy	enjoy (*s*)	enjoyed	enjoyed	enjoying
finish	finish (*es*)	finished	finished	finishing
happen	happen (*s*)	happened	happened	happening
learn	learn (*s*)	learned	learned	learning
like	like (*s*)	liked	liked	liking
need	need (*s*)	needed	needed	needing
open	open (*s*)	opened	opened	opening
start	start (*s*)	started	started	starting
suppose	suppose (*s*)	supposed	supposed	supposing
walk	walk (*s*)	walked	walked	walking
want	want (*s*)	wanted	wanted	wanting

Sometimes a past participle is used after some form of the verb *be* (or verbs that take the place of *be* like *appear, seem, look, feel, get, act, become*) to describe the subject.

He is satisfied.
He was confused.
He has been disappointed.
He appeared pleased. (He was pleased.)
He seems interested. (He is interested.)
He looked surprised. (He was surprised.)

He feels frightened. (He is frightened.)
He gets bored easily. (He is bored easily.)
He acts concerned. (He is concerned.)

Usually these past participles are called describing words that describe the subject rather than being called part of the verb of the sentence. What you call them doesn't matter. The only important thing is to be sure you use the correct form of the past participle (*ed* for regular verbs).

When do you write *ask, finish, suppose, use*? And when do you write *asked, finished, supposed, used*? Here's a rule that will help you decide.

Write *asked, finished, supposed, used*

1. when it's past time:

She *asked* him to dinner last night.
She *finished* her paper yesterday.
When I saw you, I *supposed* you had had lunch.
I *used* to play in the band last year.

2. when some form of *be* or *have* comes before the word:

He has *asked* her to go with him.
She is *finished* with her paper now.
I was *supposed* to give you this note.
I am *used* to late hours.

IRREGULAR VERBS

All the verbs in the table on page 104 are regular. That is, they're all formed in the same way—with an *ed* ending on the past form and on the past participle. But many verbs are irregular. Their past and past participle forms change spelling instead of just adding an *ed*. Here's a table of some irregular verbs. (The present and the *ing* forms aren't usually given in a list of principal parts because they're formed easily from the base form and cause no trouble.) Refer to this list when you aren't sure which verb form to use. Memorize all the forms you don't know.

BASE FORM	PAST	PAST PARTICIPLE
be	was, were	been
become	became	become
begin	began	begun
break	broke	broken
bring	brought	brought
buy	bought	bought
build	built	built
catch	caught	caught
choose	chose	chosen
come	came	come
cost	cost	cost
do	did	done
draw	drew	drawn
drink	drank	drunk
drive	drove	driven
eat	ate	eaten
fall	fell	fallen
feel	felt	felt
fight	fought	fought
find	found	found
fit	fitted *or* fit	fitted *or* fit
forget	forgot	forgotten *or* forgot
forgive	forgave	forgiven
freeze	froze	frozen
get	got	got *or* gotten
give	gave	given
go	went	gone
grow	grew	grown
have	had	had
hear	heard	heard
hold	held	held

BASE FORM	PAST	PAST PARTICIPLE
hurt	hurt	hurt
keep	kept	kept
know	knew	known
lay (to place)	laid	laid
lead (rhymes with "bead")	led	led
leave	left	left
lie (to rest)	lay	lain
lose	lost	lost
make	made	made
meet	met	met
pay	paid	paid
read (pronounced "reed")	read (pronounced "red")	read (pronounced "red")
ride	rode	ridden
ring	rang	rung
rise	rose	risen
run	ran	run
say	said	said
see	saw	seen
sell	sold	sold
shake	shook	shaken
shine (to give light)	shone	shone
shine (to polish)	shined	shined
sing	sang	sung
sleep	slept	slept
speak	spoke	spoken
spend	spent	spent
stand	stood	stood
steal	stole	stolen
strike	struck	struck
swim	swam	swum
swing	swung	swung
take	took	taken
teach	taught	taught
tear	tore	torn
tell	told	told
think	thought	thought
throw	threw	thrown
try	tried	tried
wear	wore	worn
win	won	won
write	wrote	written

EXERCISES

Write the correct form of each verb. Refer to the tables and explanations on the preceding pages if you aren't sure which form to use after a certain helping verb. Do no more than 10 sentences at a time before checking your answers.

□EXERCISE 1

1. (try, need) I am _____ to do more walking because I _____ the exercise.

2. (walk) I have _____ to campus every day this week, and I'll _____ more this weekend.

3. (intend, do) I _____ to walk four miles a day now, and I usually _____ it.

4. (walk) I am not only _____ more these days, but I'm also _____ faster.

5. (walk) I have _____ farther than anyone else in the family this week, and I _____ farther than anyone last week too.

6. (walk) My sister _____ downtown twice a day now, and she usually also _____ home.

7. (walk, do) My dad _____ to work each morning for a month, but now he _____ not walk very often.

8. (start) Have you _____ a walking program?

9. (walk) We could _____ through the park, and then we might _____ along the lake.

10. (know, be) I _____ walking _____ good for my health.

□EXERCISE 2

1. (surprise, eat) I was _____ to learn that some plants _____ insects.

2. (know, eat) I always had _____ that many insects _____ plants.

3. (realize, work) I had never before _____ that it _____ the other way too.

4. (live, eat) Plants that _____ in bogs can't get enough nitrogen from their surroundings and therefore _____ insects to get it.

5. (use, be) I _____ to think pitcher plants _____ just pretty plants.

6. (learn, use) Now I have _____ that they _____ their pitcher-shaped leaves to capture insects.

7. (fill, lure) The leaves are _____ with a sweetish liquid that _____ insects to their doom.

8. (prevent) The insects are _____ from escaping by stiff, downward-pointing hairs.

9. (be, escape) The Venus flytrap _____ another plant that insects can't _____ from.

10. (touch, clamp) When an insect _____ the hairs on a leaf of the Venus flytrap, the leaf will _____ shut, crushing the victim.

☐EXERCISE 3

1. (use) I never _____ to read a weekly newsmagazine.

2. (read) Now I am _____ one every week.

3. (find, help) I have _____ that it _____ my writing.

4. (begin) I have _____ to notice the *ed* on verbs.

5. (pay) I had never _____ any attention to verb endings before.

6. (help) Thus reading has _____ me with my writing.

7. (note) Also I have _____ carefully the use of apostrophes.

8. (see, use) I've _____ how they are _____ in possessives and contractions.

9. (notice, use) Now that I've _____ how they are _____, I'll use them correctly.

10. (do) I _____ well on my exam last week.

Avoiding Dialect Expressions

Although verbs cause the most trouble for those who have grown up speaking a dialect other than standard English, certain other expressions, more common in speech than in writing, should be avoided.

DIALECT	STANDARD ENGLISH
anywheres, nowheres, somewheres	anywhere, nowhere, somewhere
anyways	anyway
hisself, theirselves	himself, themselves
this here book, that there book, those there books	this book, that book, those books
them books	those books
he did good, she sang good	he did well, she sang well
my brother he plays ball	my brother plays ball
haven't none, haven't got none haven't no, haven't got no haven't never haven't nothing wasn't no wasn't never (These are called double negatives.)	have none, haven't any have no, haven't any have never, haven't ever have nothing, haven't anything was no, wasn't any was never, wasn't ever
ain't	am not, isn't, aren't, hasn't, haven't
ain't got no	have no, haven't any
we was, you was, they was she don't, he don't, it don't	we were, you were, they were she doesn't, he doesn't, it doesn't

EXERCISES

Cross out the dialect expressions and write the standard English ones above.

___

☐EXERCISE 1

1. I can't find that book nowheres.

2. There ain't no use looking no more.

3. Maybe I didn't never bring it home.

4. Now how can I study for my test if I ain't got no book?

5. I wanted to do good on that test tomorrow.

6. Now I probably ain't going to.

7. I ain't never been good in English, but I done o.k. on my last test.

8. My instructor say anyone who don't do good just ain't working.

9. Anyways I hear the test don't count as much as daily work.

10. Now if I could just find that there book, I wouldn't have no problem.

☐EXERCISE 2

1. We was talking about taking a trip this summer.

2. Then my dad he say that instead of going somewheres else we should see more of our own city.

3. So we be doing just that, and we ain't finished yet.

4. We went to the zoo and seen animals we ain't never seen before.

5. There was this here New Zealand kiwi; the zoo ain't never had one before.

6. And we be having picnic suppers in parks.

7. Downtown there's a art gallery where my sisters enjoyed theirselves.

8. One night we all went to a theater and seen a Shakespeare play.

9. And we ain't seen nothing yet; there's still places to go.

10. This here city have plenty to keep us busy all summer.

□EXERCISE 3

1. Loretta hadn't never seen a Little League game.

2. So me and her went to the stadium last night because I want to see my son Leroy play.

3. I seen him in only one game this season.

4. Loretta don't know nothing about baseball.

5. And I never tried to explain a game to nobody before.

6. But I try to tell her what Leroy be doing.

7. I must of done good because she watch him all the time.

8. And afterward she say she enjoy the game.

9. Well, Leroy didn't make no hits or nothing.

10. Still Loretta and me eat popcorn and have a good time.

□EXERCISE 4

1. My parents wasn't never much interested in county fairs.

2. In fact I don't think they have ever went to a fair before.

3. But yesterday they decide to go because my sister has enter the flower arranging contest.

4. She work hard on her arrangement, and we all thought she done real good.

5. Then we discover there was 20 entries, and my sister feel sure she ain't got no chance to win.

6. We went around and seen a lot of other exhibits.

7. Finally we come back to the flower booth.

8. The judges had just finish, and ribbons was attach to three arrangements.

9. My sister give a little shout because attach to her arrangement was the blue ribbon.

10. My parents say they sure is glad they went to the county fair yesterday.

JOURNAL WRITING

Write some sentences using words you have used incorrectly in the exercises or in your papers.

Proofreading Exercise

See if you can find all nine errors in this student paper before you check with the answer sheet.

IT'S THE KID IN ME

Its hard to buy presents for friends. I hate trying to think of something clever. Of course I can always get after-shave for men and perfume for women if I can't think of anything else but those are such usual gifts.

Now my little nephew is another matter he's five and I go wild getting toys for him. I walk into a toy store and get all excited about toy rockets and building kits and battery-powered trucks last Christmas I got him a combination-lock coin bank and a water pistol and a yo-yo and a rubber-band-powered airplane. Of coarse I had to try them all out for hours just to make sure that he'd like them. I suppose it's the kid in me that makes me still enjoy playing with such things but I hope I never grow to old to get a kick out of toys.

Actually I still play. Its just that I have a real car now and build real things when I play.

Progress Test

This test covers everything you've studied so far. One sentence in each pair is correct. The other is incorrect. Read both sentences carefully before you decide. Then write the letter of the correct sentence in the blank.

_____ 1. A. Whether our team wins or loses is not our main concern.
B. You're new car is sharper than those you've had in the past.

_____ 2. A. I've joined a cross-country ski group it's good exercise.
B. My principal interest is in conservation.

_____ 3. A. Doing the best he could and finally passing the course.
B. Doesn't she do quite a bit of homework every night?

_____ 4. A. I've went over all the exercises, and now I know all the rules.
B. Their trip across the desert was too tiring.

_____ 5. A. She doesn't lose her cool easily.
B. When my tutor came in, he ask me to do the fourth exercise.

_____ 6. A. I was suppose to call her, but I forgot.
B. I'm glad I chose this course, for I know it's helping me.

_____ 7. A. If you can't write well, you're at a disadvantage.
B. I worked until midnight, then I went to bed.

_____ 8. A. He did good on the exam, and now he's sure of passing.
B. I painted my kitchen; then I bought new curtains.

_____ 9. A. I chose a green color scheme for my clothes last fall.
B. We was planning a trip, but we had to give it up.

_____ 10. A. Not having enough money to do the things I wanted to do.
B. My golden retriever puppy broke its chain and ran away.

_____ 11. A. If you miss an answer, make sure you know why.
B. I finish all my exercises last night; then I started my paper.

_____ 12. A. When I start my paper early, I have time to revise it.
B. Because revising a paper is really important for success.

_____ 13. A. I made a new kind of salad and set the table in the living room.
B. I enjoyed entertaining the group however I was tired afterward.

_____ 14. A. It don't matter whether many go on the hike or not.
B. I'm not sure who's going.

_____ 15. A. They was trying out a microwave oven.
B. Finally they sent it back and ordered a different one.

MAKING SUBJECTS, VERBS, AND PRONOUNS AGREE

All parts of a sentence should agree. In general if the subject is singular, the verb should be singular; if the subject is plural, the verb should be plural.

Each of the boys has his own car.

Both have their own cars.

He and I were at the movie.

Many of the class were absent.

There were vacant seats in the front row.

The following words are singular and take a singular verb:

(*one* words)	(*body* words)	
one	anybody	each
anyone	everybody	either
everyone	nobody	neither
no one	somebody	
someone		

One of my friends is a senior.

Everybody in the class expects to vote.

Either of the candidates is a good choice.

The following "group" words take a singular verb if you're thinking of the group as a whole, but they take a plural verb if you're thinking of the individuals in the group:

audience	family	kind
band	flock	lot
class	group	number
committee	heap	none
crowd	herd	public
dozen	jury	team

My family *is* behind me. . . . . .My family *are* all scattered.
The number present *was* small. . . . .A number *are* going to the rally.
A dozen rolls *is* enough. . . . . .A dozen *are* going.
The jury *is* ready. . . . . .The jury *are* still arguing.

Here are some subject-verb pairs you can *always* be sure of. No exceptions!

you were	(*never* you was)
we were	(*never* we was)
they were	(*never* they was)
he doesn't	(*never* he don't)
she doesn't	(*never* she don't)
it doesn't	(*never* it don't)

Not only should subject and verb agree, but a pronoun also should agree with the word it refers to. If the word referred to is singular, the pronoun should be singular; if that word is plural, the pronoun should be plural.

Each of the boys has *his* own room.

The pronoun *his* refers to the singular subject *Each* and therefore is singular.

Both of the boys have *their* own rooms.

The pronoun *their* refers to the plural subject *Both* and therefore is plural.

Today many people try to avoid sex bias by writing sentences like the following:

If anyone wants a ride, he or she can go in my car.
If anybody calls, tell him or her that I've left.
Somebody has left his or her textbook here.

But those sentences are wordy and awkward. Therefore some people, especially in conversation, turn them into sentences that are not grammatically correct.

> If anyone wants a ride, they can go in my car.
> If anybody calls, tell them that I've left.
> Somebody has left their textbook here.

Such ungrammatical sentences, however, are not necessary. It just takes a little thought to revise each sentence so that it avoids sex bias and is also grammatically correct.

> Anyone who wants a ride can go in my car.
> Tell anybody who calls that I've left.
> Somebody has left a textbook here.

Another good way to avoid the awkward *he or she* and *him or her* is to make the words plural. Instead of writing, "Each of the students was in his or her place," write, "All the students were in their places," thus avoiding sex bias and still having a grammatically correct sentence.

EXERCISES

Underline the correct word. Check your answers 10 at a time.

☐EXERCISE 1

1. Most of my friends (has have) interesting hobbies.
2. One of them (has have) been learning Japanese brush painting.
3. There (are is) about 10 people in the class.
4. Each of the paintings (are is) done with jet black ink on rice paper.
5. Several of the paintings that my friend has made (are is) worth framing.
6. Another of my friends (has have) taken up pottery making.
7. There (are is) plenty of opportunities to work at the local pottery.
8. Each of the vases that she has designed (has have) been a work of art.
9. One of my brothers (play plays) the drums, and both of my sisters (play plays) the piano and (hope hopes) to make music (her their) career.
10. All of us at one time or another (sing sings), and everyone in the family (enjoy enjoys) music.

☐EXERCISE 2

1. This summer all our family (are is) going to drive to Sequoia National Park.
2. None of us (has have) ever been there.

3. Each of us (has have) a different reason for wanting to go.
4. Of course all of us (look looks) forward to seeing the giant sequoias.
5. My parents (has have) always wanted to see the General Sherman tree, which is the world's largest living thing.
6. The General Sherman stands 272.4 feet high and (measure measures) 101.5 feet around the base.
7. Based on the studies of growth rings of similar trees, scientists (estimate estimates) its age at 3,500 years.
8. My sister (want wants) to see the Crystal Cave and take one of the guided tours through it.
9. My brother (think thinks) he'd like to take some of the tours that (are is) conducted by a ranger naturalist.
10. Of course all of us (want wants) just to stand in the sequoia groves and marvel at their enormity and beauty.

☐EXERCISE 3

1. One of the best courses I've taken in college (are is) psychoiogy.
2. The texts in that course (explain explains) how our minds work.
3. One of the ideas I found interesting (are is) psychological maturity.
4. Plenty of people mature physically but (doesn't don't) mature psychologically.
5. The most dangerous members of our society (are is) grownups with childish motives.
6. Human misbehaviors (are is) simply immature ways of solving problems.
7. One of the challenges of twentieth-century psychology (are is) to help people mature psychologically.
8. One of the characteristics of a mature person (are is) a sense of responsibility.
9. Another characteristic (are is) being able to tell the important from the unimportant.
10. Some of these ideas (help helps) me to understand myself better.

☐EXERCISE 4

1. Everyone in our history class (are is) going to Colonial Williamsburg this weekend.
2. All of us (has have) been studying eighteenth-century history and (are is) eager to see the reconstructed town.
3. Each of us (has have) different things we want to see.
4. Several in the class (are is) mainly interested in the architecture since half the major buildings (are is) original structures that have been restored.
5. Most of us (want wants) to watch the craftspeople in their shops.

6. The craftshops (include includes) silversmiths, bookbinders, black-smiths, coopers, cabinetmakers, and wigmakers.
7. I have read that the cabinetmakers (use uses) eighteenth-century tools to make handmade furniture.
8. I want to watch a shoemaker, for I understand it (take takes) 12 hours to make two pair of shoes.
9. All of us (intend intends) to see the Raleigh Tavern, which was a place for patriots' meetings.
10. And of course everyone (look looks) forward to having a lunch that would have been served in the eighteenth century.

☐EXERCISE 5

1. A number of articles (has have) appeared recently about the destruction of the tropical rain forests which (form forms) a green band around the earth at the equator.
2. More than half of the world's plant and animal species (live lives) in those forests.
3. Most of the Third World countries (are is) cutting down the forests for farmland or other development.
4. The farmers of course (think thinks) they can make more money from farmland than from trees.
5. None of the farmers (realize realizes) that cutting down the forests will cause global warming and threaten life on our planet.
6. Also, burning of the forests (put puts) carbon dioxide in the atmosphere and (contribute contributes) to the "greenhouse effect," which also may cause global warming.
7. The tropical forests, according to an article in the *Los Angeles Times,* (are is) being cut down at the rate of 54 acres every minute.
8. In desperation, some conservation organizations now (are is) offering a "Debt for Nature" swap to Third World countries.
9. The swap (cancel cancels) part of a country's debt in return for that country's preserving its rain forests.
10. Bolivia, Costa Rica, and Ecuador have agreed to the swap, and those concerned about conservation now (hope hopes) that more Third World countries will also agree.

Source: *Los Angeles Times* 1989

☐EXERCISE 6

1. All the things that my counselor did for me during my high school days (has have) made me realize how much I owe him.
2. One of my best memories of high school (are is) of my talks with him.
3. He convinced me that a person who (doesn't don't) read much will have difficulty in college.

4. I began reading more, and all the books that I read (has have) been of value.

5. Several of the books that I read (has have) been mentioned in my English class.

6. One of the books (was were) discussed in my psychology class.

7. Just having become a reader (has have) improved my study habits.

8. Now when I have to read a book for a course, it (doesn't don't) floor me.

9. Oh, there (has have) been some problems since I came to college.

10. But it usually (doesn't don't) take me long to solve them.

JOURNAL WRITING

Write about something that interests you using at least four words from your Spelling List on the inside back cover of this book.

CHOOSING THE RIGHT PRONOUN

Of the many kinds of pronouns, the following cause the most difficulty:

SUBJECT GROUP	NONSUBJECT GROUP
I	me
he	him
she	her
we	us
they	them

A pronoun in the Subject Group may be used in two ways:

1. as the subject of a verb:

> *He* is my brother. (*He* is the subject of the verb *is.*)
> We girls gave a party. (*We* is the subject of the verb *gave.*)
> Joe is taller than *I*. (The sentence is not written out in full. It means "Joe is taller than *I* am." *I* is the subject of the verb *am.*) Whenever you see *than* in a sentence, ask yourself whether a verb has been left off the end of the sentence. Add the verb, and then you'll automatically use the correct pronoun. In both speaking and writing, always add the verb. Instead of saying, "She's smarter than (I, me)," say, "She's smarter than I am." Then you can't fail to use the correct pronoun.

2. as a word that means the same as the subject:

> I was sure that it was he. (*He* means the same as the subject *it*. Therefore the pronoun from the Subject Group is used.)
> It was she who phoned. (*She* means the same as the subject *It*. Therefore the pronoun from the Subject Group is used.)

Modern usage allows some exceptions to this rule however. *It is me* and *it is us* (instead of the grammatically correct *it is I* and *it is we*) are now established usage; and *it is him, it is her,* and *it is them* are widely used, particularly in informal speech.

Pronouns in the Nonsubject Group are used for all other purposes.

In the following sentence, *me* is not the subject, nor does it mean the same as the subject. Therefore it comes from the Nonsubject Group.

He came with Lynn and *me.*

A good way to tell which pronoun to use is to leave out the extra name. By leaving out *Lynn*, you will say, *He came with me*. You would never say, *He came with I*.

> We saw *him* and Kimberly last night. (We saw *him* last night.)
> He gave *us* boys a pony. (He gave *us* a pony.)
> The firm gave my wife and *me* a trip. (The firm gave *me* a trip.)

EXERCISES

Underline the correct pronoun. Remember the trick of leaving out the extra name to help you decide which pronoun to use. Use the correct grammatical form even though an alternate form may be acceptable in conversation.

☐EXERCISE 1

1. The orchestra director suggested that Jon and (I me) plan a party to be held after our final concert.
2. The director left all the details to Jon and (I me).
3. Since Heather likes that sort of thing, we asked (she her) and Brenda to take charge of the food.
4. That didn't leave much for Jon and (I me) to do.
5. Between you and (I me), it was a good party.
6. Jon and (I me) got a lot of praise for organizing it.
7. Because Heather did most of the work, we said the praise should go to (she her) and Brenda.
8. During spring break some of (we us) orchestra members are giving an extra concert.
9. It's good for all of (we us) beginners to get extra practice in performing.
10. (We Us) new members are eager to play as much as possible.

☐EXERCISE 2

1. Dad and (I me) made the breakfast this morning.
2. It wasn't a big job for either Dad or (I me).
3. My uncle has asked my brother and (I me) to visit his farm.
4. He wants to know whether my brother and (I me) would like to work for him during the summer.
5. Naturally my brother and (I me) are excited about the prospect.
6. It will be a new experience for both my brother and (I me).
7. Neither (he nor I, him nor me) have ever worked on a farm.
8. Both (he and I, him and me) have always had jobs in the city.
9. Now it's up to (we us) two to do our best on the farm.
10. (He and I, Him and me) are certainly going to try.

□EXERCISE 3

1. My girlfriend Debbie and (I me) went to McDonald's last night.
2. Debbie thought maybe Andrea would be there, and sure enough we saw (she her) and Scott.
3. Scott and (I me) used to hang around together.
4. They came over and asked Debbie and (I me) to join them.
5. Then they suggested that (Debbie and I, me and Debbie) go waterskiing with them the next day.
6. Waterskiing was new to both Debbie and (I me).
7. But both Debbie and (I me) were eager to try.
8. So the next day Debbie and (I me) picked up Andrea and Scott and went to the lake.
9. It turned out to be more fun for Andrea and Scott than for Debbie and (I me) however.
10. Debbie and (I me) spent most of our time in the water.

□EXERCISE 4

1. When we were little, Mom used to make waffles for (we us) kids.
2. The first one always had to be divided between my brother and (I me).
3. My sister and (I me) got the next one.
4. Then my brother would yell, and the third one would be divided between (he him) and Mom.
5. Finally my brother and (I me) would get to split the last one.
6. Today when Mom makes waffles, my brother and (I me) often remember those early days.
7. Sometimes we say, "Hey, that waffle is supposed to be split between (we us) two."
8. My brother and (I me) now get along famously.
9. We're in some of the same classes at college, and (he and I, him and me) often study together.
10. It works out well for both him and (I me).

□EXERCISE 5

1. The instructor is trying to get all of (we us) students ready for the final.
2. He gave a practice test to my friend and (I me).
3. My friend has always been a better student than (I me).
4. Now all of (we us) students feel ready for the final.
5. (My friend and I, Me and my friend) are hoping for A's.
6. Next semester my friend and (I me) plan to take another English course.
7. (He Him) and I like to take the same course and study together.
8. It helps both (he him) and (I me).
9. Some of the assignments are difficult for (he him) and (I me).
10. But when (he him) and (I me) work together, we do well.

MAKING THE PRONOUN REFER TO THE RIGHT WORD

When you write a sentence, *you* know what it means, but your reader may not. What does this sentence mean?

> She asked the candidate to come back when she had more time.

When who had more time? She or the candidate? The simplest way to correct such a faulty reference is to use a direct quotation:

> She said to the candidate, "Why don't you come back when I have more time?"

Here's another sentence with a faulty reference:

> I've always been interested in farming and finally have decided to be one.

Decided to be a farming? There's no word for *one* to refer to. We need to write

> I've always been interested in farming and finally have decided to become a farmer.

Another kind of faulty reference is a *which* clause that doesn't refer to any specific word, thus making it difficult to tell what part of the sentence it refers to.

> He finally quit college and took a job which his parents disapproved of.

Did the parents disapprove of the job or of the fact that he quit college and took a job? The sentence should read

> His parents disapproved of his quitting college and taking a job.

or

> His parents disapproved of the job he took after he quit college.

EXERCISES

Most—but not all—of these sentences aren't clear because we don't know what word the pronoun refers to. Revise such sentences, making the meaning clear. Remember that using a direct quotation is often the easiest way to clarify what a pronoun refers to. Since there are more ways than one to rewrite each sentence, yours may be as good as the one at the back of the book. Just ask yourself whether the meaning is clear.

☐EXERCISE 1

1. The manager said he might be transferred to another state.

2. The instructor told him that he hadn't proofread the paper carefully.

3. I'm going to save my summer wages for college which won't be easy.

4. I ordered the roast lamb, which I enjoyed.

5. Her mother suggested that she wear her new suede jacket to the game.

6. He told the foreman that he was too inexperienced for the job.

7. She told her girlfriend that she was being too pessimistic.

8. He complained to his dad about his shabby clothes.

9. When she talked to her daughter that noon, she was having problems.

10. When he talked to his lawyer, he didn't know how the case would turn out.

☐EXERCISE 2

1. The salesman told him he had made an error in addition.

2. As I put the canary's food in the dish, it began to sing.

3. He told his brother that his tape recorder wasn't working properly.

4. Diane told Becky that she had received a letter from her boyfriend.

5. He told his friend he was probably making a mistake in taking the job.

6. As soon as the mechanic changed the tire, I drove it home.

7. Whenever I approached the baby's high chair, it screamed.

8. My car swerved into a fence, but it wasn't damaged.

9. She told her sister she needed a new hairstyle.

10. We studied only two novels in that course that I really enjoyed.

☐EXERCISE 3

1. When her sister finally arrived, she was in tears.

2. I read about the famous basketball coaches and players and hope someday I'll be one.

3. The congressman asked him to give his bill some more thought.

4. He told the supervisor that his design didn't work.

5. The manager told the clerk she had made an error in the day's total.

6. I learned to play table tennis, which I really enjoy.

7. She told her sister she needed to take time to think about the problem.

8. I refused to listen to Dad's advice which turned out to be a good thing.

9. The coach told the captain that he had blamed the wrong player.

10. He is a whiz at math but poor in chemistry; this is why he got a scholarship.

☐EXERCISE 4

1. I made up my mind to major in business which wasn't easy.

2. Since her great ambition is to be a figure skater, she spends all her spare time practicing it.

3. His son told him he was getting poor mileage from his old car.

4. I've always wanted to do secretarial work and finally have decided to go to secretarial school.

5. The weather was cold on the trip which was disappointing.

6. When she went to visit her daughter, she was underweight.

7. They quit spanking the child which was just what the child needed.

8. I decided to take another job, which my parents disapproved of.

9. He told the filling station attendant he had lost the cap to the gas tank.

10. When he showed the smashed taillight to his father, he was upset.

☐EXERCISE 5

1. In Japan they have exquisite little gardens.

2. He told his dad he was a clever manager.

3. His instructor told him he was mistaken.

4. I finally found a job which made me happy.

5. As I came near the bittern's nest, it flapped its wings and flew away.

6. When the doctor talked with him, he was really worried.

7. She told her mother that her entire wardrobe needed updating.

8. I went to a committee meeting, which happened to be an important one.

9. Only a few attended the meeting, which annoyed the president.

10. Persons experiencing chest pains and shortness of breath should be encouraged to rest and should be watched until they have completely disappeared.

CORRECTING MISPLACED OR DANGLING MODIFIERS

A modifier gives information about some word in a sentence, and it should be as close to that word as possible. In the following sentence the modifier is too far away from the word it modifies to make sense:

> Leaping across the road we saw two deer.

Was it *we* who were leaping across the road? That's what the sentence says because the modifier *Leaping across the road* is next to *we*. Of course it should be next to *deer*.

> We saw two deer leaping across the road.

The next example has no word at all for the modifier to modify:

> At the age of 10 my dad was transferred to Louisiana.

Obviously the father was not 10. The modifier *At the age of 10* is dangling there with no word to attach itself to, no word for it to modify. We can get rid of the dangling modifier by turning it into a dependent clause.

> When I was 10, my dad was transferred to Louisiana.

Here the clause has its own subject—*I*—and there's no chance of misunderstanding the sentence.

Here's another dangling modifier:

> After running six blocks, the bus pulled away as I reached it.

Had the bus run six blocks? Who had? You can change the sentence in one of two ways. You can insert *I* to make clear who did the running:

> After running six blocks, I saw the bus pull away as I reached it.

Or you can turn the dangling modifier into a dependent clause:

> After I had run six blocks, the bus pulled away as I reached it.

Either way of getting rid of the dangling modifier makes the sentence clear.

EXERCISES

Most—but not all—of these sentences contain misplaced or dangling modifiers. Some you can correct simply by shifting the modifier so it will be next to the word it modifies. Others you'll need to rewrite. Since there is more than one way to correct each sentence, your way may be as good as the one at the back of the book.

☐EXERCISE 1

1. Studying really hard last fall, my grades improved.

2. Before leaving for vacation, my final paper had to be written.

3. While sitting at my desk doodling, my thesis statement became clear.

4. Completely exhausted, my books fell to the floor.

5. When I quit studying at 2 A.M., I found some leftover pickled herring in the refrigerator.

6. When pickled, I'll eat almost anything.

7. The next day, sleepy from too many late nights, the professor failed to get through to me.

8. Before I finished her test, the prof called time, and I ran for the bus.

9. Excited about my trip, the bus took off as soon as I boarded it.

10. After a two-year absence, the house looked just the same.

☐EXERCISE 2

1. Last summer my parents bought a cottage from a man with no inside plumbing.

2. Needing considerable repair, they were able to buy it for very little.

3. When I got home, I discovered Mom mopping the kitchen floor, and I decided to mop the floor with her.

4. While walking on the beach one day, I saw two spotted sandpipers.

5. Stepping gracefully on long thin legs, I watched them hunting for food.

6. Then darting suddenly into some bushes, I lost sight of them.

7. Chirping continuously, I watched some sparrows building their nest.

8. The cows, chewing their cud in the pasture, paid no attention to us.

9. Boldly taking food from our picnic table, I sat and watched a blue jay.

10. Then I put the food back into the picnic basket that we had not eaten.

☐EXERCISE 3

1. At the age of 12, Dad changed jobs, and we moved to San Jose.

2. We gave some of our old furniture to a charity that we had no use for.

3. On the plane we saw all the little farms flying over Kansas.

4. In our new house the dining room has a buzzer for summoning a maid under the table.

5. While we were eating lunch the first day, a telegram arrived.

6. Excited by the news, my plate of food was almost untouched.

7. After mowing the lawn that afternoon, my dog wanted to go for a walk.

8. In our neighborhood a dog must be accompanied by an adult on a leash.

9. Later that day a cement truck arrived for a walk through our backyard.

10. The next day my father bought a book that told him how to add an extra room to our house for $6.95.

☐EXERCISE 4

1. Our house is near the fairground, where I was born.

2. When six years old, my mother married again.

3. When I was seven, my mother made me start piano lessons.

4. After playing in the Little League, Mom entered me in a diving contest.

5. Swimming in the shallow water, my big toe was cut on a clamshell.

6. Hanging from a telephone wire, I saw my favorite kite.

7. When only a youngster in grade school, my father taught me to box.

8. Barking furiously, the man was obviously unnerved by the little mongrel.

9. While on a week's vacation, our neighbor's car was stolen.

10. We read that the thief had been caught in the morning paper.

☐EXERCISE 5

1. Dressed in a long evening gown, I thought my wife looked elegant.

2. I had a stain on my tie that could not be removed.

3. Standing at the top of the gorge, the way the earth had originally shifted became clear.

4. Peering through the dense fog, I saw a police officer following me.

5. Suddenly becoming confused, my car slid off the road.

6. Skidding on the icy pavement, a woman was almost hit by my car.

7. By clever steering, however, my car just missed her.

8. You'll appreciate the advice I'll give you years later.

9. Our office intends to hire a secretary who'll be more efficient after Christmas.

10. Being obviously a crook, the banker refused the man a loan.

JOURNAL WRITING

Make up a sentence with a misplaced or dangling modifier, and then write the correction.

Proofreading Exercise

Can you correct the seven errors in this paragraph? No answers are provided.

THE PYRAMID OF CHEOPS

I new the pyramids were big but I had no idea how big. I thought the base of the biggest one, the pyramid of Cheops at Gizeh near Cairo, was maybe half the size of a basketball court. Now Ive learned it would cover 13 acres. It was built of an estimated 2,300,000 blocks of stone weighing from 2 to 15 tons each. The blocks were cut at the quarry, set on sledges, and pulled by men over the land. One investigator reported that it must of taken 100,000 men 20 years to build the Great Pyramid. Even more amazing than it's size is the accuracy with which it was built. The exterior blocks were cut so perfectly that not even a postcard can be inserted between them and the sides of the Great Pyramid vary by not more then eight inches.

USING PARALLEL CONSTRUCTION

Your writing will be clearer if you use parallel construction. That is, when you make any kind of list, put the items in similar form. If you write

I enjoy swimming, skiing, and to hunt.

the sentence lacks parallel construction. The items don't all have the same form. But if you write

I enjoy swimming, skiing, and hunting.

then the items are parallel. They all have the same form. They are all *ing* words. Or you could write

I like to swim, to ski, and to hunt.

Again the sentence uses parallel construction because the items all have the same form. They all use *to* and a verb. Here are some more examples. Note how much easier it is to read the column with parallel construction.

LACKING PARALLEL CONSTRUCTION	HAVING PARALLEL CONSTRUCTION
He expected a woman to have a good job, to be beautiful, and who would pamper his whims.	He expected a woman to have a good job, to be beautiful, and to pamper his whims. (All three items start with *to* and a verb.)
His experience made him sullen, bitter, and a cynic.	His experience made him sullen, bitter, and cynical. (All three are words describing him.)
She asked me whether I could take shorthand and my experience.	She asked me whether I could take shorthand and what experience I had had. (Both items are dependent clauses.)
She wanted a house with seven rooms, a two-car garage, and it should be in a good location.	She wanted a house with seven rooms, a two-car garage, and a good location. (All three are words that can be read smoothly after the preposition *with*.)

The supporting points for a thesis statement (see p. 215) should always be parallel. For the following thesis statements, the supporting points in the left-hand column are not all constructed alike. Those in the right-hand column are; they are parallel.

NOT PARALLEL	PARALLEL
Working at a resort last summer was valuable.	Working at a resort last summer was valuable.
1. I earned money for college.	1. I earned money for college.
2. Job experience.	2. I gained job experience.
3. Recreation.	3. I had time for recreation.
College students should not live at home.	College students should not live at home.
1. Waste time commuting.	1. Commuting wastes time.
2. Independence needed.	2. Students need independence.
3. Friendships in a dorm.	3. Friendships are made in dorms.

Using parallel construction will make your writing more effective. Note the effective parallelism in these well-known quotations:

We cannot dedicate, we cannot consecrate, we cannot hallow this ground.

—Abraham Lincoln

Money may be the husk of many things, but not the kernel. It brings you food, but not appetite; medicine, but not health; acquaintance, but not friends; servants, but not loyalty; days of joy, but not peace or happiness.

—Henrik Ibsen

Ask not what your country can do for you; ask what you can do for your country.

—John F. Kennedy

With this faith we will be able to work together, to pray together, to struggle together, to go to jail together, to stand up for freedom together, knowing that we will be free one day.

—Martin Luther King, Jr.

EXERCISES

Most—but not all—of these sentences lack parallel construction. Cross out the part that is not parallel and write the correction above.

☐EXERCISE 1

1. The movie ended with the cowboy leaping on his horse, waving to his friends, and he rode away into the sunset.

2. He had worked in a pharmacy, the post office, and as a filling station attendant.

3. I went to Honolulu to enjoy the warm weather and for getting some practice in surfing.

4. We are looking for a house with a double garage, four bedrooms, and having a large garden.

5. Listening to his stereo and science fiction are my brother's chief pleasures.

6. No one can go through life just depending on others and never take any responsibility.

7. That period in my life was full of fun, happiness, and I had a lot of new experiences.

8. The candidate promised to create more jobs, to raise wages, to provide better schools, and at the same time he would lower taxes.

9. I like her soft voice, her willingness to listen, her refusal to criticize.

10. Erich Fromm said that loving takes concentration, patience, discipline, and it also takes a supreme concern.

☐EXERCISE 2

1. My first deep dive was exciting, but it took a lot of preparation.

2. I took lessons for a month, practiced every day in a pool, and of course I had to buy a lot of equipment.

3. Our instructor drilled us, tested us, and he also gave us encouragement.

4. Then finally he said that I was ready to make the plunge, ready to do what I had wanted to do for years.

5. I got all my equipment together, reviewed my instructions, and then I phoned my diving buddy.

6. She said she was ready to go, had been hoping I'd call, and that she would meet me at the dock.

7. In the dock dressing room I put on my wet suit and safety vest, slid my arms through the straps of my air tank, put on my mask, and I had to make sure I had my snorkel.

8. When I got down to the water's edge, I balanced on one foot to put on my fins, and then my buddy gave me the nod.

9. I plunged into the water, moved away from the shore, and I actually made my first dive.

10. A whole new world unfolded before me, and I realized that the lake would never be the same for me again.

□EXERCISE 3

1. In the days of Mark Twain, the Mississippi was simply a muddy river shining in the sun, rolling along between small towns, and it carried steamboats down to New Orleans.

2. The Mississippi starts in a tiny stream out of Lake Itasca in northern Minnesota, wanders 2,300 miles, and it empties into the Gulf of Mexico.

3. In Mark Twain's day there were beautiful vistas along the river, but to-day the banks are marred by old tires, rusty buckets, and there are junked cars here and there.

4. Today the river is a crowded thoroughfare with barges and towboats carrying cargo down the river, maneuvering between the channel mark-ers, and they try not to ram each other.

5. Along the last 120 miles, the riverbanks that used to display old man-sions are now crowded with chemical plants, cement works, power sta-tions, and there are granaries too.

6. The river is so crowded in this area that hundreds of barges, towboats, tugs, and freighters seem in constant danger of collision.

7. The boats are safer today, however, because of radar, sonar, short-wave radio, diesel engines, and up-to-date fire controls help avoid accidents.

8. People living near the Mississippi often can't see the river because of the flood-control levees, which are as much as 300 feet wide, may be 30 feet in height, and stretch along the river for 1,600 miles.

9. But a few places along the bends of the river seem unchanged from Mark Twain's day with their low mud flats showing cottonwoods, willows, and old stumps of trees.

10. In these mud flats, racoons, hawks, and snapping turtles can be seen, and sometimes even deer and bald eagles.

☐EXERCISE 4

1. Thanks to the foresight of early conservationists, many of our natural wonders have been preserved in national parks for the enjoyment, recreation, and also for the education of the American people.

2. The National Park Interpretive Services include exhibits, illustrated lectures, campfire programs, and there are also guided tours.

3. The park brochure of each park tells visitors where to stay, where to eat, and what to see.

4. Last summer my buddy and I took a long motor trip, visited two national parks, and we learned a great deal from the experience.

5. We first visited Canyonlands National Park in Utah, where the air cools quickly after sundown, drops to a low shortly before sunup, and then it warms rapidly as the sun rises.

6. Since we were camping out, we were aware of these changes in temperature and had to adjust to them.

7. At Canyonlands we saw rabbits, ground squirrels, kangaroo rats, and also we saw one of the few remaining populations of desert bighorn sheep.

8. After five days there, we drove north to Wyoming to Grand Teton National Park, which we had heard a lot about, which we had both always wanted to see, and it is just south of Yellowstone.

9. In Grand Teton are more than 200 species of birds, including herons, Canada geese, bald eagles, osprey, and sometimes the rare trumpeter swan can be seen.

10. We'd like to have gone on north to Yellowstone, but we decided that we had learned enough, that we should get back to our jobs, and so we decided that we'd save Yellowstone for another trip.

☐EXERCISE 5

1. Last night I heard a lecture on South Africa that was dynamic, interesting, and it enlightened everybody.

2. The speaker described conditions there, explained what he thought should be done, and then he asked us to support his efforts.

3. He said it's up to us to make the problems known, to urge our lawmakers to take action, and that we must get the newspapers interested.

4. I liked his ready wit, his sense of humor, and the fact that he is a keenly intelligent person.

5. He lived in South Africa for a number of years, taught in a university there, and now he spends his time lecturing in the United States.

6. He asked us to publicize the problems, write to our legislators, and that we should discuss the issues among ourselves.

7. At the end, he got a standing ovation, cheers, and he also got handshakes from lots of students.

8. I decided to read about South Africa, inform myself about the issues, and then I would write my sociology term paper on the problems.

9. I was surprised to find so many newspaper articles, magazine articles, and I even found some books on the subject.

10. After I wrote my paper, I felt proud of my efforts, pleased with the result, and I also felt pretty knowledgeable.

Correct the sentences that lack parallel construction.

☐EXERCISE 6

The town of Waterton Park, Alberta, which is just across the Canadian border from Glacier National Park, is populated not only by people but by dozens of mule deer. The citizens of Waterton have learned to live with the deer that come into town for the winter, take shelter on the porches, graze on the lawns, and they also devour the shrubbery. The town is an ideal place for the deer to spend the winter because coyotes and mountain lions, which kill deer elsewhere, don't come into the town. The deer have become quite tame and remain tame even when they leave the town in the summer. And they have learned to tolerate people. Visitors come to Waterton to watch the deer, to feed them, and they also photograph them. The deer will come close to the visitors for handouts, but they may strike with a front hoof if they don't receive the expected tidbit.

☐EXERCISE 7

In tropical forests gorillas are peaceful animals weighing 600 pounds, living in groups, and foraging for ginger root and wild berries. But until recently the gorillas in captivity lived in bare cages, lacked companionship, and they missed their natural environment. They became inactive, lost many of their wild characteristics, and failed to reproduce. Then the San Diego Zoo, which was the first to realize that gorillas have social and environmental needs, started the trend toward "open zoos." Now zoos are building pavilions that have waterfalls, trees, and there are even patches of bamboo. Amid these more natural surroundings the gorillas now beat their chests, show affection for their mates, and produce young gorillas. Since the number of gorillas in the wild is decreasing because habitats are being taken over by agriculture and urbanization, it is important for the survival of the species that the gorillas in zoos do reproduce.

Make the supporting points of these thesis statements parallel.

☐EXERCISE 8

1. Getting a college education is important to me.
   1. It will prepare me for a job.

   2. It will help me become an educated person.

   3. Have a good time.

2. Knowing how to write clearly will be of value after college.
   1. It will help me think clearly.

   2. Satisfaction is knowing how to write.

   3. It will be useful in most jobs.

3. The 55 mph speed limit should be retained nationally.
   1. It has caused the accident rate to decrease.

   2. It has decreased gasoline consumption.

   3. Pleasanter motoring.

4. I've decided to major in biology.
   1. I've always been interested in birds and animals.

   2. Jobs available.

   3. It will be good preparation if I go into medicine.

JOURNAL WRITING

Write a sentence with parallel construction telling how you spend your leisure.

CORRECTING SHIFT IN TIME

If you begin writing a paper in past time, don't shift now and then to the present; and if you begin in the present, don't shift to the past. In the following paragraph the writer starts in the present and then shifts to the past.

> In *The Old Man and the Sea*, the Old Man has to fight not only the marlin and the sharks but also the doubts in his own mind. He wasn't sure that he still had the strength to subdue the giant marlin.

It should be all in the present:

> In *The Old Man and the Sea*, the Old Man has to fight not only the marlin and the sharks but also the doubts in his own mind. He isn't sure that he still has the strength to subdue the giant marlin.

Or it could be all in the past:

> In *The Old Man and the Sea*, the Old Man had to fight not only the marlin and the sharks but also the doubts in his own mind. He wasn't sure that he still had the strength to subdue the giant marlin.

EXERCISES

These sentences have shifts in time, either from past to present or from present to past. Make all the verbs in each sentence agree with the first verb used. Cross out the incorrect verb and write the correct one above it.

☐EXERCISE 1

1. It is a good play, but it didn't have a happy ending.

2. In the movie the heroine faced one tragedy after another, but of course everything comes out all right in the end.

3. The book gives an account of the life of John Kennedy, but it didn't tell much about his writing.

4. Gesell's book shows the stages of child development and gave methods of training for each stage.

5. In *Future Shock,* Toffler predicted what life will be like in the future, and he explains how technology must be controlled for the social good.

6. The candidate spoke briefly and then ends with a plea for votes.

7. I thought I had given a good report, but then someone asks for my sources, and I became flustered.

8. He intended to come back to college, but then a job opens up and he takes it.

9. I went to college for a year, but then I come back to help in the family business.

10. Tension was high during the last few minutes of the game; then a touchdown gives us the victory.

The following selections from student papers shift back and forth between past time and present. Change the verbs to agree with the first verb used, thus making the entire selection read smoothly.

□EXERCISE 2

I was lucky. I saw the Edmonton Oilers play the Philadelphia Flyers in 1981 when Wayne Gretzky made five goals in one game and established a world record in hockey of 50 goals in 39 games. When he made his fifth goal in the game, the fans give him a standing ovation and begin to yell, "Gretzky, Gretzky, Gretzky." It was only his third season in the National Hockey League, and the 20-year-old Canadian had become the greatest scorer in hockey history. I was lucky that I saw the Great Gretzky make his first world record.

□EXERCISE 3

Yesterday I went to a hardware store to buy a thingamajig to connect my TV set to the antenna cable. What I wanted was just a simple little doohickey, but the clerk didn't seem to know what I'm talking about. He offers me one of those whatchamacallits that plug into a regular electric socket. Dumb clerk.

☐EXERCISE 4

After spending a day at the beach, I stopped to buy a snack on my way home. But when I reach for my wallet, it wasn't there. I check my other pockets and the car and then headed back to look at the beach. My driver's license, my ID card—my mind was racing through all the things I'd lost, and I felt rotten. A search of the beach and parking lot proved fruitless, so I headed home. I tried to forget it because there was nothing I could do, but I was mad at myself for losing it. After dinner while I'm sitting watching TV and trying to forget, the phone rings, and a voice says, "Did you lose a wallet? I found it on the beach." What a great feeling that gave me—not only for my luck but for my faith in all humanity!

☐EXERCISE 5

I LEARNED A LOT

I was 13 when I got my first summer job. I was a stock boy in a hardware store and did everything from sort merchandise to sweep floors. I was proud to have a job and was excited about working. Of course sometimes the work was really hard or dirty, but I always felt good when I finish each little project. Even the things I didn't want to do give me a feeling of satisfaction after I'd finish them.

I learn a lot that summer. I learn that every Friday was payday. I learn how long a day can be when you're bored. I learn that my bike went slower in the afternoons than it did in the mornings. I learn that the customer is always right. And I learn to drink coffee.

I must have done all right because the next summer I got a better job at the same store.

☐**EXERCISE 6**

PIGGLY WIGGLY

I was surprised to learn that there haven't always been supermarkets in this country. Before 1916 there were only small individually-owned grocery stores, where customers give a list of their needs to a clerk. The clerk then gets the items from the shelves, makes out a charge slip, packages the items, and gives the package to a delivery boy to take to the customer's house. But in Memphis in 1916 a "self-serving" store was opened in which customers could select their own groceries from the shelves. With a turn-style at the entrance and a checkout counter at the exit, where customers pay cash, the store was a big change, and people did not take to it readily until they found that the prices were lower. By having a low margin of profit and a high volume of sales, the store was able to cut prices and still make money. The store was called Piggly Wiggly, and soon there were 3,000 Piggly Wiggly stores across the United States. By 1930 Krogers, Safeway, and A & P were all following the trend toward self-service. Then in 1936 a store manager noticed that women tended to quit shopping when the baskets they are carrying get too heavy or too full. Thus was born the shopping cart, and the country has never been the same since.

Source: *American Heritage,* Oct.–Nov. 1985

JOURNAL WRITING

Write a brief paragraph describing how you did your homework each evening in high school. Then write another paragraph describing how you study each evening in college.

CORRECTING SHIFT IN PERSON

You may write a paper in

First person—*I, we*
Second person—*you*
Third person—*he, she, they, one, anyone, a person, people*

but don't shift from one group to another.

Wrong: In doing chemistry experiments, *one* should read the directions carefully. Otherwise *you* may have an explosion.

Right: In doing chemistry experiments, *one* should read the directions carefully. Otherwise *one* may have an explosion.

Right: In doing chemistry experiments, *you* should read the directions carefully. Otherwise *you* may have an explosion.

Wrong: Few *people* get as much enjoyment out of music as *they* could. *One* need not be an accomplished musician to get some fun out of playing an instrument. Nor do *you* need to be very far advanced before joining an amateur group of players.

Right (but stilted):   Few *people* get as much enjoyment out of music as *they* could. *One* need not be an accomplished musician to get some fun out of playing an instrument. Nor does *one* need to be very far advanced before joining an amateur group of players.

(Too many *one*'s in a paragraph make it sound stilted and formal. Sentences can be revised to avoid using either *you* or *one*.)

Better: Few *people* get as much enjoyment out of music as *they* could. It's not necessary to be an accomplished musician to get some fun out of playing an instrument. Nor is it necessary to be very far advanced before joining an amateur group of players.

Also, too frequent use of the expressions *he or she* and *him or her* can make a paper sound awkward. Turn back to page 117 to see how a sentence can be revised to avoid sex bias without using those expressions.

Wrong:	A student should take part in some extracurricular activity; otherwise *you* miss something.
Right (but awkward):	A student should take part in some extracurricular activity; otherwise *he or she* misses something.
Better:	Students should take part in some extracurricular activities; otherwise *they* miss something.

Often students write *you* in a paper when they don't really mean *you, the reader*.

You could tell that she hadn't been expecting callers.

Such sentences are always improved by getting rid of the *you*.

Obviously she hadn't been expecting callers.

Sometimes, however, a shift to *you* is permissible. The paper on pages 200–201 shifts quite logically to *you* in the last two paragraphs because the writer wants to talk directly to the reader. Similarly, the paper on pages 225–26 ends with a question to *you, the reader*.

As a rule, though, a shift in person should be avoided.

EXERCISES

Change the pronouns (and verbs when necessary) so that there will be no shift in person. Cross out the incorrect words and write the correct ones above. Sometimes you may want to change a sentence from singular to plural to avoid using too many *one*'s or the awkward *he or she* (see p. 117). Sentence 7 is an example.

☐EXERCISE 1

1. When I gave my first oral report, I was nervous, but one soon gets over it.

2. A lot of people think that if they just get a college degree, you can always get a good job.

3. It's true that if one gets a college degree, you have a valuable asset.

4. But just because you have gone to college doesn't necessarily mean one will get a good job.

5. If one wants a career, you should get started on it early.

6. If anyone wants to be in the next dramatic production, you should sign up for tryouts.

7. A student should schedule certain hours for study. Otherwise you won't get all your work done.

8. I'm jogging every morning because you should get some exercise every day.

9. To keep one's figure, you have to watch what you eat.

10. I've rewritten my paper three times, and that gives you a feeling of accomplishment.

When students write *you* in a paper, they usually don't mean *you, the reader.* On a separate sheet rewrite these sentences eliminating the *you* and stating the sentences as simply as possible. Getting rid of the *you* will usually get rid of wordiness also.

□EXERCISE 2

1. You should have seen all the presents she received.
2. You have no idea how worried I was after his accident.
3. When I opened the hood of the car, you could see what was the matter.
4. A chipping sparrow lighted in front of us so close that you could see its white eye stripes.
5. You'll find that walking two miles a day is good for your health.
6. You can't expect to have a good garden without constant work.
7. You don't have to pick up your ticket until half an hour before the plane is scheduled to leave.
8. You can imagine how much his letter meant to me at that time.
9. When I opened the door, you could hear the commotion.
10. By the time we had gone a hundred miles, you could see the mountains.

Make the necessary changes in these student paragraphs so there will be no shift in person.

☐EXERCISE 3

I've just bought an Aerobie, a really exciting invention. When I tossed it out the window of the tallest building on campus, my buddy had to run a block after it. You can fling it farther than a Frisbie or a baseball, and it made the Guinness world record for a hand-thrown object when it was flung 1,114.5 feet. Its inventor, a Stanford University engineering lecturer, spent hundreds of hours behind a computer terminal to come up with the algebraic formula for the disc. Someone has said that if you tossed an Aerobie off Mt. Everest in good flying weather, it would travel 42 miles.

☐EXERCISE 4

One summer a friend and I went out to Boulder, Colorado, to the 1985 Coors International Bicycle Classic, which is the premier cycling event in the United States. We had never seen such racing before. The crowd was so great that you couldn't get near the finish line, but we were right beside the track. As the riders went by, you could feel the rush of wind from their speed. One of the races for men was 60 miles, and one for women was 34 miles. Poland, Brazil, East Germany, Russia, France, and lots of other countries sent entrants, but we were pleased that the final winner of the men's 60-mile race was an American. Just watching such a contest makes you realize the dedication it must take to prepare for it. We learned that 82 million Americans now own and ride bicycles and that 55 percent of all riders are women. Also for the first time since the turn of the century, more adults than children are riding bikes.

☐EXERCISE 5

I've finally found out what metamorphosis is all about. I used to dismiss it as just a big word, but now I know it means change—a change of physical form or structure. Many animals change their form and function as they go through life. When a caterpillar crawls out of its chrysalis skin and becomes a damp butterfly, that's metamorphosis. When a tadpole slowly changes into a frog, that's metamorphosis. It would be difficult to watch the slow metamorphosis of a tadpole, but you can easily see a butterfly crawl out of its chrysalis and spread its wings to dry.

Eliminate the *you* in the following selections, thus making each one a smooth third-person account.

□EXERCISE 6

In 1985 America's favorite toy had its one-hundredth birthday. Various forms of the horseless carriage were produced in Germany, France, England, and the United States from 1884 to 1886, but there were problems. There were few roads you could drive a car on, and in Britain a law required three persons to be with any "road locomotive" on public roads. One of the three had to precede the vehicle by not less than 60 yards carrying a red flag of warning. Also you could travel only 2 mph in the city and 4 mph in the country. In 1895 the first U.S. automobile race was run from Chicago to Evanston and back. The winner covered the 54 miles in eight hours. Then in 1903 the Ford Motor Company was organized, and Henry Ford built eight models before the Model T, which came out in 1908. By 1924 you could buy his Model T two-seater for $290.

□EXERCISE 7

The psychologist Carl Rogers suggests a way for two people in an argument to come to an understanding. The first thing you have to do is stop the discussion for a moment. Then each person must restate as accurately as possible the other person's ideas and feelings. Not until each has restated the other's ideas to the other person's satisfaction may the discussion continue. It is impossible not to understand a person better if you take the trouble to state that person's views. Often you'll find that there wasn't as much disagreement between you as you at first thought.

☐EXERCISE 8

The cicada has an unusual life. It lives for 17 years underground and then lives for five weeks in the sunlight. It is one of the longest-living insects. During its few weeks aboveground, you can hear its shrill call everywhere throughout its range in the Midwest. Only the males can make the ear-piercing calls. The noise is made by little drumlike plates at the base of the abdomen, which are vibrated rapidly by strong muscles. You can observe, during their five weeks aboveground, how the cicadas damage the orchards and forests by cutting egg pockets in twigs, thus causing the twigs and leaves to fall off the trees. After the five weeks, however, you'll hear the cicadas' rasping calls no more. The cicadas' lives are over.

☐EXERCISE 9

Many people think communication means talking together. But communication is, or should be, 50 percent listening. Poor listening is responsible for many difficulties in child-parent relationships, in marriage, in college, and in business.

If you don't listen, troubles may arise. Parents often continue with their own thoughts and ignore what their child is saying. Newlyweds are usually good listeners but become poorer as the years go by until finally lots of talking is going on but not much listening. College students often have problems because they don't listen to lectures intently but let their minds drift into daydreams. A study has shown that business executives consider the ability to listen the most important quality for an executive.

Listening is a learned rather than an innate behavior. By jerking your mind back each time it wanders, you can soon train it to stay with the speaker. Simply by recognizing the problem and working at it, you can become a good listener.

JOURNAL WRITING

1. Write a brief paragraph telling a friend how to proofread a paper. It will, of course, be a "you should" paragraph.

CORRECTING WORDINESS

Good writing is concise writing. Don't say something in ten words if you can say it as well, or better, in five. "In this day and age" isn't as effective as simply "today." "At this point in time" should be "at present" or "now."

Another kind of wordiness comes from saying something twice. There's no need to say "in the month of July" or "7 A.M. in the morning" or "my personal opinion." July *is* a month, 7 A.M. *is* morning, and my opinion *is* personal. All you need to say is "in July," "7 A.M.," and "my opinion."

Still another kind of wordiness comes from using expressions that add nothing to the meaning of the sentence. "The fact of the matter is that I'm tired" says no more than "I'm tired."

Here are more examples of wordiness.

WORDY WRITING	CONCISE WRITING
a person who is honest	an honest person
at that point in time	then
due to the fact that	because
each and every	each
enclosed herewith	enclosed
end result	result
free gift	gift
he is a person who	he
important essentials	essentials
in order to	to
in spite of the fact that	although
in the event that	if
new innovation	innovation
personally I think	I think
refer back	refer
repeat again	repeat
shorter in length	shorter
surrounded on all sides	surrounded
the field of electronics	electronics
there are many boys who	many boys
there is no doubt but that	no doubt
to my friend and myself	to my friend and me
usual custom	custom
we are in receipt of	we have received

EXERCISES

Cross out words or rewrite parts of each sentence to get rid of the wordiness. Doing these exercises can almost turn into a game to see how few words you can use without changing the meaning of the sentence.

☐EXERCISE 1

1. There are many students who are working their way through college.

2. Never in all my life before have I seen such an absolutely spectacular display of fireworks.

3. It seems to me that many of us use many more words than we really need in our writing.

4. For a period of 10 days in the month of February I couldn't get my car out of my driveway because of the deep snow.

5. Part of the problem she is faced with is the fact that never before has she had to take any responsibility on herself.

6. In my opinion most of the children in our country are spending entirely too much of their time watching programs presented on TV.

7. It is interesting to note that the kiwi bird, which is found in New Zealand, sleeps 20 hours out of the 24 hours every day.

8. Skiing is a sport that interests many people but that has never held any particular interest for me.

9. I read in the evening paper last night about another fatal killing.

10. With reference to your recent order, I beg to inform you that we no longer carry the tape recorder you requested.

☐EXERCISE 2

1. As I have said, this letter of mine may not bring any results at all.

2. Tomorrow morning the employees of this institution will all meet promptly at 11 A.M. in the staff lounge.

3. The planning for the party was left up to Jennifer and myself.

4. I won't be surprised if the supervisors revert back to the rules that were laid down back in 1978.

5. There was a strong protest that followed the announcement that was made by the president.

6. This directive is being sent to the various offices in this department to ask that each individual make an effort to conserve paper whenever possible both for economic reasons of saving money and for ecological reasons of saving our trees.

7. He is a man who does as much work on his vacation as he does when he is at his regular job.

8. I have decided to go into the field of law enforcement because it is a field that will offer me opportunities for advancement.

9. It is my personal opinion that with all the cures and things being discovered every day, soon most of the diseases that we now call fatal may be conquered.

10. I think it would be very valuable if we had national health insurance for everyone.

☐EXERCISE 3

1. My past experience has made me convinced of the fact that one has to be constantly on the lookout for new opportunities in investing money.

2. Therefore I have decided that I'm going to move my savings account from the People's Bank to the Citizens' Bank.

3. There is no doubt but that both of the banks are good and have always had excellent reputations in the past.

4. But the fact is that now the Citizens' Bank has a new plan in which they offer a free gift to anyone who opens a new account.

5. Therefore for that reason I made up my mind to shift my account and take advantage of this new innovation.

6. It just happened that I was in the neighborhood when that old building that used to be a warehouse was completely destroyed by fire.

7. During the time that the firefighters were attempting to put out the fire, the building was completely surrounded on all sides by onlookers.

8. I personally think the firefighters did all they possibly could do to save the building from destruction.

9. From the point of view of those who hope to rehabilitate that neighborhood, the loss may be a good thing.

10. Now in their future plans they won't have to consider what to do with that old building which was no longer in any condition to be used.

The following paragraphs are the introduction to a booklet on safety put out by a large U.S. organization. Can you cut the 128 words to about 38 for better effect? Rewrite on a separate sheet.

☐EXERCISE 4

This booklet was composed and published by the Accident Prevention Committee of our organization. The purpose of this booklet is to make new employees as well as present employees aware of the particular hazards that they may be exposed to while in the duration of completing their daily job functions. We, the Committee, feel employees will incur fewer accidents and injuries if each individual is aware and understands the necessary precautions to complete job functions in the safest and most professional means possible.

Usually, the majority of employees have to travel from one department or location to another. It is for this reason the Accident Prevention Committee recommends that you take your time to read this material thoroughly, as it was composed for your own safety and well-being.

AVOIDING CLICHÉS

A cliché is an expression that has been used so often it has lost its originality and effectiveness. Whoever first said "light as a feather" had thought of an original way to express lightness, but today that expression is outworn and boring. Most of us use an occasional cliché in speaking, but clichés have no place in writing. The good writer thinks up fresh new ways to express ideas.

Here are a few clichés. Add some more to the list.

at loose ends
blind as a bat
center of attention
cool as a cucumber
flat as a pancake
frightened out of my wits
happy as a lark
head over heels
keep a stiff upper lip
last but not least
played his cards right
ruled the roost
set the world on fire
sigh of relief
through thick and thin

to make a long story short
turn a deaf ear
walking on air
worn to a frazzle

Clichés are boring because the reader always knows what's coming next. What comes next in these expressions?

all good things must . . .
cry over spilled . . .
don't count your chickens . . .
easy as . . .
honesty is the . . .
let your conscience . . .
lived from hand to . . .
save wear and . . .
swim like a . . .
take the bull by the . . .
the straw that broke . . .
white as . . .
work like . . .

EXERCISES

On a separate sheet rewrite these sentences to get rid of the clichés.

☐EXERCISE 1

1. I've been trying to help my small son with his homework, but it's easier said than done.
2. He's smart as a whip, but he beats a hasty retreat every time I mention schoolwork.
3. If I do get him to sit down in front of his books, he'll work like a dog for five minutes and then, quick as a flash, run for the door.
4. If I catch him, he says that schoolwork is a pain in the neck and that he's sick of all work and no play.
5. I tell him that when I was his age I was frightened out of my wits by teachers and barely made it through school by the skin of my teeth.
6. I tell him that in this world it's sink or swim, but I might as well save my breath.
7. I fear he'll be sadder but wiser one of these days.
8. Last night I got him to write out all his math problems, but soon his eyes were heavy as lead, and I had to call it quits.
9. It goes without saying that I'm fighting a losing battle.
10. But maybe he'll grow up to be a great success, and then he'll have the laugh on me.

WRITING ASSIGNMENT

One way to become aware of clichés so that you won't use them in your writing is to see how many you can purposely put into a paragraph. Write a paragraph describing your difficulties in trying to register for the next semester. You might begin something like this: "I got up at the crack of dawn and stood in line for hours. . . ." Use all the clichés you can while still keeping your account smooth and clear. What title will you give your paragraph? Why, a cliché of course. Writing such a paragraph should make you so aware of clichés that they'll never creep into your writing again.

Review of Sentence Structure

Only one sentence in each pair is correct. Read both sentences carefully before you decide. Then write the letter of the *correct* sentence in the blank. You may find any of these errors:

run-together sentence
fragment
wrong verb form
lack of agreement between subject and verb
wrong pronoun
faulty reference of pronoun
dangling modifier
lack of parallel construction
shift in time or person

_____ 1. A. There's nothing you can do it's too late now to help.
    B. My brother and I helped with the refreshments.

_____ 2. A. The coach gave jobs to both Greg and me.
    B. He told the boss that it was his fault.

_____ 3. A. Most of the students in this class will do well on the tests.
    B. I was intending to study, but I watch TV instead.

_____ 4. A. She likes math she doesn't like history.
    B. She has always been a good student but has never made A's.

_____ 5. A. If one wants an exciting book, you couldn't find a better one.
    B. Our team was good but not as good as our opponents' team.

_____ 6. A. Skiing down the steep slope, a pine tree in her path caused her fall.
    B.. I always work until midnight and even then don't finish.

_____ 7. A. Each of my brothers have their own car.
    B. Getting my own car pleased me and made me feel mature.

_____ 8. A. The manager is forceful, efficient, and is kind to everyone.
    B. That lot in the subdivision belongs to my fiancé and me.

_____ 9. A. Planning for years to be a coach and then finally landing just the job I wanted.
    B. I've done my exercises, written my papers, and passed my tests.

_____ 10. A. She was surprise to receive the award.
    B. They invited my husband and me to their cottage last summer.

_____ 11. A. He has walk two miles every day all winter.
    B. I like to play baseball, but golf and tennis bore me.

_____ 12. A. Each of the contestants is equally well prepared.
    B. Working hard almost all night, my term paper was ready to hand in.

_____ 13. A. The chairman asked Oswaldo and me to count the votes.
    B. We counted carefully, and then we realize something is wrong.

_____ 14. A. You was always good in chemistry, so you should get a good grade.
    B. We freshmen helped with the parking and the guided tours.

_____ 15. A. They invited Gary and me to their wedding.
    B. I can't decide whether to stay in college, get a job, or whether I should join the Marines.

_____ 16. A. He ask me to go to the play, and I accepted his invitation.
    B. Watch your step there.

_____ 17. A. One can't teach a person anything; you can only help him learn.
    B. I've worked hard all day and now am ready for a rest.

_____ 18. A. The program chairman asked Juanita and me to take charge of the May meeting.
    B. I can't decide whether to become a research chemist, a teacher, or go into commercial art.

_____ 19. A. Having given him a good lunch, I expected him to be satisfied.
    B. She told her mother that she had been late too many times.

_____ 20. A. Every one of these bananas are too ripe.
    B. They invited us to play tennis with them and to go out for dinner afterward.

_____ 21. A. One of my friends is planning to take a job next year.
    B. Because she needs the money and because she wants the work experience.

_____ 22. A. Hurrying down the steps, I slipped and dropped all my packages.
    B. You're suppose to have your paper finish by Friday.

_____ 23. A. Because she had decided to run for student body president and was hoping to win.
    B. She won the oratory contest and now will go to the nationals.

Proofreading Exercise

Can you find all eight errors? No answers are provided at the back of the book.

THOSE LITTLE FLEAS

I had to give a oral report last week, and I learned a lot. I learned that fleas have killed more people then all the wars that have ever been fought throughout the world.

Fleas are amazing creatures. A flea can jump 150 times it's own length. That's equal to a person jumping nearly a thousand feet. It can live for months without food. It can accelerate faster then the space shuttle and it can remain frozen for a year and yet live.

Fleas are the carriers of the plague throughout the world. The plague is a disease of rats, and the fleas pick up the plague germ from the rats and carry it to people. But for centuries people didnt know how they got the plague.

The plague started in Africa in A.D. 541 and then crossed the Mediterranean on ships to Constantinople. There 10,000 people died every day. For 200 years the disease continued and then miraculously disappeared. But in 1347 it appeared again when ships sailed into Sicily with crews dying from the mysterious disease. Within five years 25 million people died in Europe. One father wrote, "I buried my five children with my own hands."

In the late 1800s the plague again spread around the world but in 1894 a scientist discovered that the plague germ was carried from infected rats by fleas. From then on their were fewer deaths, but still in 1986 there were 1,003 cases reported throughout the world, mainly in developing countries, where rats infest crowded houses. Even in 1987 in the United States, 12 cases were reported, and two people died.

And it's all because of those little fleas.

Source: *National Geographic,* May 1988

Punctuation
and
Capital
Letters

3 Punctuation and Capital Letters

PERIOD, QUESTION MARK, EXCLAMATION MARK, SEMICOLON, COLON, DASH

Every mark of punctuation should help the reader. Just like Stop and Go signals at an intersection, marks of punctuation will keep the reader, like the traffic, from getting snarled up.

Here are the rules for six marks of punctuation. The first three you have known for a long time and have no trouble with. The one about semicolons you learned when you studied independent clauses (p. 72). The one about the colon may be less familiar.

Put a period at the end of a sentence and after most abbreviations.

Mr.	A.D.	Dr.	Wed.	sq. ft.
Ms.	etc.	Jan.	P.M.	lbs.

Put a question mark after a direct question (but not after an indirect one).

"Who's there?" he asked. (the exact words of the speaker)
He asked who was there. (not the exact words of the speaker)

Put an exclamation mark after an expression that shows strong emotion.

Wow! You aced that exam!

Put a semicolon between two closely related independent clauses (unless they are joined by one of the connecting words *and, but, for, or, nor, yet, so.* (Refer to pp. 72–73 for a review of the semicolon.)

> The blizzard continued; the drifts piled higher.
> No one came to the meeting; therefore we left.

Actually you can write quite acceptably without ever using semicolons because a period and capital letter can always be used instead of a semicolon.

> The blizzard continued. The drifts piled higher.
> No one came to the meeting. Therefore we left.

Put a colon after a complete statement when a list or long quotation follows.

> We took the following items: hot dogs, fruit, and coffee. (*We took the following items* is a complete statement. You can hear your voice fall at the end of it. Therefore we put a colon after it before adding the list.)
>
> We took hot dogs, fruit, and coffee. (Here *We took* is not a complete statement; it needs the list to make it complete. Therefore, since we don't want to separate the list from the first part of the sentence, no colon is used.)

> The speaker closed with a quotation from Benjamin Franklin: "Dost thou love life? Then do not squander time, for that is the stuff life is made of." (*The speaker closed with a quotation from Benjamin Franklin* is a complete statement. Therefore we put a colon after it before adding the quotation.)
>
> Benjamin Franklin said, "Dost thou love life? Then do not squander time, for that is the stuff life is made of." (*Benjamin Franklin said* is not a complete statement. Therefore we don't put a colon after it.)

Use a dash to indicate an abrupt change of thought or to throw emphasis upon what follows. Use it sparingly.

> The little old lady sat in front of her spinning wheel—in Las Vegas.
> And the dash—well, don't use it too often.

EXERCISES

Add to these sentences the necessary punctuation—period, question mark, exclamation mark, semicolon, colon, dash. Not all sentences require additional punctuation. Also your answer may differ from the one at the back of the book because either a semicolon or a period with a capital letter may be used between two independent clauses.

☐EXERCISE 1

1. We wanted to go to the big game however we couldn't find a ride.
2. Finally my brother came home he agreed to take us.
3. We were late luckily, however, we were able to get seats.
4. The Cornhuskers had the ball then the Sooners of Oklahoma recovered a fumble.
5. Oklahoma's top line offense blends with their excellent defense consequently they are a threat to any team they play.
6. They average a lot of fumbles per game nevertheless they are a powerhouse of college football.
7. They employ the wishbone it's the most exciting offense in college ball.
8. I play on our second string team therefore seeing a big game is really exciting for me.
9. In the last 30 seconds Oklahoma scored a touchdown thus they made the score 6 to 3 in favor of Oklahoma.
10. It was one of the best games I've seen I'll never forget it.

☐EXERCISE 2

1. The earthworm is nature's farmer it turns the soil over and over just as a farmer does with a plow.
2. It eats the soil to get bits of leaves and animal matter thus it lets air and water get to the plant roots.
3. An acre may hold more than a million earthworms many tons of earth pass through their bodies in a year.
4. Earthworms dig burrows about 12 inches below the surface however they may burrow as deep as 8 feet.
5. An earthworm has no eyes but can tell light from dark also it can feel the lightest touch because it has "sense cells" on its body.
6. Do you know what happens if a robin eats a few segments of an earthworm.
7. The remaining portion simply grows new segments to replace those lost this process is called regeneration.
8. On our walk this morning we identified the following plants trillium, bunchberry, devil's paintbrush, and heal-all.
9. We failed to see any buttercups, violets, or blue-eyed grass.
10. I like learning about nature it makes my walks more interesting.

☐EXERCISE 3

1. Isn't it surprising that foreign students don't have more trouble with our language.
2. How can they cope with all our inconsistencies.
3. Much of our spelling is inconsistent much of our pronunciation is too.
4. Note the pronunciation of the following words *rough, cough, through, dough, bough, hiccough*.
5. They all end in *ough* however the pronunciation of each is different.
6. And look at these words *bird, curd, heard, herd, stirred, word*.
7. They all have the same sound nevertheless the sound is spelled differently in each word.
8. In 1906 Theodore Roosevelt wrote the Government Printing Office requesting them to use simplified spelling in all government publications Congress, however, passed a resolution forbidding any departure from standard spelling.
9. George Bernard Shaw left a large share of his estate to promote simplified spelling the British court broke his will on the grounds of impracticality.
10. The Chicago *Tribune* tried for years to spell many words more simply it finally was forced to give up the battle.

☐EXERCISE 4

1. Did you ever wonder why bulls are excited by the color red.
2. Bulls aren't excited by the color red bulls are color-blind.
3. Do you know what's the biggest animal that ever lived.
4. It's alive today it's the blue whale.
5. A blue whale may measure over 100 feet in length its weight can go over 100 tons.
6. Do you know what was the first helicopter.
7. The hummingbird is nature's helicopter it can hover and even fly backward.
8. Do you know a bird you shouldn't envy it's the male New Zealand kiwi.
9. The female kiwi gets off easy all she does is lay an egg.
10. The male kiwi sits on the egg for 80 days he loses half his weight during that time.

☐EXERCISE 5

1. I've been looking through a replica of a 1908 Sears, Roebuck Catalogue the prices are astounding.
2. Here are some of the prices kitchen chairs for 38 cents each, a brass bed for $3.10, a 56-piece china dinner set for $5.85, and a solid oak dining table for $6.95.
3. Some washing machines sold for $1.93 their best "Superba Ball Bearing Washing Machine," however, sold for $6.38.

4. The Superba was guaranteed for five years against all defects furthermore it was offered on six months' free trial.

5. Among all the fascinating things pictured are crank telephones, stereoscopes, buggies, surreys, and windmills.

6. In the clothing section, ladies' long underwear cost 24 cents per garment lace-trimmed "drawers" for summer were 21 cents.

7. Men's shirts cost from 48 to 89 cents men's fine linen collars were 7 cents.

8. Among the luxury items were the following ladies' fans for 23 cents, ladies' genuine leather bags for 49 cents, and jeweled hat pins for a quarter.

9. In the front of the catalogue is the following statement "Tell us what you want in your own way, written in any language, no matter whether good or poor writing, and the goods will be promptly sent to you."

10. On the back of the catalogue is this notice "We Have No Agents or Solicitors—Persons Claiming to be Our Representatives are Swindlers."

☐EXERCISE 6

1. Turtles have been around for 175 million years during that time dinosaurs came and disappeared.

2. The life of sea turtles remains a mystery they come to shore to lay their eggs then they disappear back into the water.

3. The female digs a two-foot hole, lays about 110 golf-ball-size eggs, and covers them with sand then she crawls back into the sea.

4. She is guided by instinct she was never taught how to make a nest or where to lay her eggs.

5. The baby turtles crawl into the water they are not seen again until, as adults, the females come ashore to lay their eggs.

6. The enemies of the young turtles are the following crabs, raccoons, human hunters, beach traffic, and washouts.

7. Many female turtles find their nesting places taken over by a parking lot they are going to need help to survive.

8. Now a group of people in Florida are tagging the sea turtles they hope to discover more about them.

9. At night during the nesting season, the taggers attach a metal tag to a front flipper of the female they also take a sample of marine vegetation from under her shell.

10. The taggers want to learn where the turtles go they also hope to learn how to protect this increasingly rare reptile.

☐EXERCISE 7

1. Two new highways to the Arctic have been built the Dalton Highway in Alaska and the Dempster Highway in Canada.

2. The Dalton Highway runs for 397 miles from Livengood to the oil fields of Prudhoe Bay the Dempster Highway runs 465 miles from Dawson in the Yukon to Inuvik on the Beaufort Sea.
3. The Dalton Highway, not open to the public, was built to transport workers, machines, and materials for the building of the Trans-Alaska Pipeline the Dempster Highway was built by the Canadian government to aid the development of the Yukon and the Northwest Territories.
4. The Dalton Highway runs for its entire length beside the pipeline the Dempster Highway, hundreds of miles farther east, runs about parallel to the Dalton Highway.
5. Both highways are made of dirt and gravel furthermore both are built about six feet above the terrain to avoid damaging the permafrost.
6. Travelers on the Dempster Highway will face difficulties snow in the winter, mud in the spring, and almost no roadside facilities.
7. Thus when one gets on the highway, one must keep going only in a very few spots on the Dempster Highway is it possible to pull off to the side of the road.
8. The Dempster Highway will bring tourists to these undeveloped lands it may, however, have a detrimental effect on the environment.
9. Along the highway, hunting and fishing may decrease the natural wildlife herds of caribou may also decrease if their migratory paths are disturbed.
10. Supporters of the highway say that tourists will bring in millions of dollars environmentalists say, however, that the money brought in will not make up for the loss of wildlife and wilderness.

□EXERCISE 8

1. Tribal peoples of the world are fast losing their land and their way of life civilization is taking over.
2. Industrial nations are moving into tribal lands in search of oil and mineral resources they often care little for native rights.
3. Developers are stealing native lands legally the ancient hunters and gatherers have nowhere to flee.
4. Losing their land is fatal to them it causes them to lose their ties and their personalities.
5. The Hill Tribes in the Philippines are faced with a development plan to build four hydroelectric dams the dams will flood their rice terraces and erase their way of life.
6. The greatest threat to tribal people is disease brought in by developers the tribes in the rain forests of Brazil are dying of diseases brought in by the builders of the new highways.
7. The tribal peoples are an endangered species most conservationists, however, seem more concerned about endangered plants and animals.

8. At first the tribes were helpless now they have taken a cue from the U.S. civil rights movement and are beginning to organize.

9. They are standing up to the developers and pressing for court action they are learning how to resist being uprooted from their lands and how to adjust to development.

10. Destroying these tribal cultures is destroying something of value to the world their knowledge of wildlife, ecology, and medicinal plants can enrich civilization.

☐EXERCISE 9

1. Forty years ago most U.S. workers were blue-collar today at least half the workers are white-collar.

2. Times are changing in other ways too the old work schedules for white-collar workers are now a thing of the past.

3. More and more companies are using flexible work schedules to make their white-collar employees more efficient some companies are even using the plan for technical workers.

4. The old work hours were based on tradition the new flexplan is based on employee satisfaction.

5. Flextime works this way an employee can begin work any day between 6:30 and 9:30 in the morning and quit between 3:00 and 6:00 in the afternoon.

6. How has the new plan worked.

7. Employees everywhere are enthusiastic managers like the plan too.

8. Companies find that it saves them money in two ways the problem of tardiness has been almost eliminated, and one-day absences have declined.

9. Employees discover that they also have two benefits they have more time before or after work for their own pursuits, and they can avoid rush-hour traffic.

10. Has the company you work for converted to flextime yet.

☐EXERCISE 10

1. A man in the Colony of Massachusetts made the first Colonial coins he was given one coin for every 40 he made.

2. Today all U.S. coins are made in a government mint in either Philadelphia or Denver.

3. The designs for the coins are chosen by the director of the mint with the approval of the secretary of the treasury the designs may not be changed for 25 years without congressional approval.

4. The motto "In God We Trust" first appeared on a two-cent coin in 1864 in 1955 Congress ruled that the motto be on all new U.S. money.

5. Some coins minted at various times but no longer made are the following half-cent, two-cent, three-cent, and twenty-cent pieces.

6. Myths are similar all over the world the same story is often told in widely separated countries.
7. For example, the story of a flood was told by the Greeks a similar story was told on the other side of the world by the Algonquin Indians.
8. The Greek version said that Zeus poured a great rain from the sky all people perished except a few who fled to the mountains.
9. The Algonquin story said that a great flood covered the earth only a few people saved themselves by jumping on the back of a huge turtle.
10. Mythology, especially Greek mythology, has had a great effect on our culture its influence is evident in our language, our arts, and our architecture.

JOURNAL WRITING

Write two sentences, the first requiring a colon and the second not requiring a colon, in which you list some of the things you plan to do during your next vacation. Make sure, of course, that the items are parallel.

Proofreading Exercise

Can you find all six errors in this paragraph? No answers are provided.

HE MAKES ME MAD

Ive just read an article by a psychologist entitled "He Makes Me Mad." The author points out that nobody can make you mad. Only you can decide to be mad. Anger isnt something like toothache that invades you without your willing it you simply decide to be angry because you have trained yourself to be angry in certain situations. Do you get angry at your boss. No, you restrain your anger. But with friends or family you let the anger roll. Its a matter of training yourself just as it's a matter of training yourself to stand up straight or to use the correct fork. No one can make you use the wrong fork. Only you can decide to use the wrong fork and only you can decide to be angry.

COMMAS (RULES 1, 2, and 3)

Students often sprinkle commas through their papers as if they were shaking pepper out of a pepper shaker. Don't use a comma unless you know a rule for it. But commas are important. They help the reader. Without them, a reader would often have to go back and reread a sentence to find out what the writer meant.

Actually you need only six comma rules, MASTER THESE SIX RULES, and your writing will be easier to read. The first rule you have already learned (p. 73).

1. Put a comma before *and, but, for, or, nor, yet, so* when they connect two independent clauses.

> We lost our oars, and that was the end of our boating.
> We may leave Friday, or we may wait until Monday.

But be sure such words do connect two independent clauses. The following sentence is merely one independent clause with one subject and two verbs. Therefore no comma should be used.

> I wanted to go but couldn't get my car started.

2. Put a comma between items in a series.

> Hurrah for the red, white, and blue.
> She put down the phone, picked up her purse, and left.

Some words "go together" and don't need a comma between them even though they do make up a series.

> The dear little old lady
> The eager little boy
> The dilapidated old building

The way to tell whether a comma is needed between two words in a series is to see whether *and* could be used naturally between them. It would sound all right to say *red and white and blue;* therefore commas are used. But it would not sound right to say *dear and little and old lady* or *eager and little boy;* therefore no commas are used. Simply use a comma where an *and* could be used. (It's permissible to omit the comma before the *and* connecting the last two members of a series, but more often it's used.)

If an address or date is used in a sentence, treat it as a series, putting a comma after every item, including the last.

> He was born on May 17, 1962, in Bowling Green, Kentucky, and grew up there.
> She lived in Garden City, New York, for two years.

When only the month and year are used in a date, the commas are omitted.

> In May 1980 he moved to Bellingham, Washington.

3. **Put a comma after an introductory expression that doesn't flow smoothly into the sentence, or before an afterthought that is tacked on.** It may be a word, a group of words, or a dependent clause.

> Yes, I'd like to go.
> Well, we'll try again.
> Moreover, the umpire agreed with me.
> Keeping a steady gait, she won the race.
> It's too late to register now, isn't it?
> When I entered, the auditorium was packed.

When you studied dependent clauses, you learned that a dependent clause at the beginning of a sentence needs a comma after it. In the last sentence above, you can see that a comma is necessary. Otherwise the reader would read *When I entered the auditorium . . .* before realizing that that was not what the writer meant. A comma prevents misreading.

EXERCISES

Punctuate these sentences according to the first three comma rules.

☐EXERCISE 1

1. Because I had three weeks' vacation I decided to drive to Minnesota.
2. I was impressed with the lakes the forests and the clean cities.
3. My cousins have lived in Duluth Minnesota for a year.
4. Because I had no idea how to get to their house I had to stop for directions.
5. After making several wrong turns I finally found their place.
6. They bought a house with eight rooms a two-car garage and a quarter-of-an-acre garden.

7. In that garden they raise all their own vegetables enough fruit to give away and an abundance of flowers.
8. As soon as they come home from their jobs my cousins put on their work clothes and go to work in the garden.
9. When they bought the place they didn't know how much time the garden would take.
10. They spend a lot of time there but they say it's worth all the work.

☐EXERCISE 2

1. When I visited Minneapolis last summer I was impressed with Nicollet Mall.
2. It's the longest pedestrian strollway in the United States and is interesting both in summer and winter.
3. In summer it's perfect for a leisurely walk among the trees flowers and fountains and in winter it's a spectacle of lights during the holiday season.
4. Along this tree-flanked avenue no auto traffic is allowed except buses and cabs.
5. While I was in Minneapolis I also visited the University of Minnesota.
6. With an enrollment of over 43,000 it's the largest university on one campus in the United States.
7. The city is famed for the 22 lakes and lagoons within its boundary and it is also famed for its system of pedestrian skyways.
8. Heated in winter and air-conditioned in summer the skyways connect most of the major buildings downtown.
9. With an observation tower on the 51st floor the Investors Diversified Services skyscraper is one of the most interesting spots in the city.
10. Its glass walls shine in the daytime and are artistically lighted in zigzag patterns at night.

☐EXERCISE 3

1. I've just read that the Pyramids are crumbling and Egypt's archeological treasures may soon be lost.
2. Rubble and rock dust falling from the Pyramid of Chephren have accumulated in piles on its lower levels.
3. The Sphinx has lost a 600-pound chunk from its right shoulder and the neck is so weak that the statue's massive head is in danger of falling off.
4. Three thousand people a day go into King Tut's tomb and they are causing some of the trouble.
5. They sweat and that moisture is destroying paintings in the tomb.
6. Tourists climb the pyramids regardless of signs prohibiting climbing and they touch the fading and crumbling paintings and inscriptions.
7. While the Egyptian government is aware of the restorations needed it has little money for such an enormous project.

8. Part of Egypt's problem is the ludicrously low entrance fees. Visitors to the pyramids are charged only about $1.50 and entrance to many of the tombs is free.
9. Since a developing country like Egypt cannot undertake the massive restorations needed other governments will have to increase their aid.
10. If the monuments of one of the world's most ancient civilizations are allowed to crumble the entire world will feel the loss.

Source: *Time*, May 15, 1989

□EXERCISE 4

1. While I was waiting for my appointment I read an article on the life of ants.
2. Ants live in the Arctic in tropical forests in deserts on mountains and along seashores.
3. They build their nests under city pavements in cornfields and under logs and leaves in the woods.
4. Although most anthills are small some ants build hills that are three feet high and six feet across.
5. In the southwestern states the harvester ants gather seeds and the honey ants live on a sweet liquid from oak galls and aphids.
6. Because the ant has exceptionally strong jaws it can carry a load almost as big as itself.
7. Since an ant can swallow nothing but liquids it has a storage pocket behind the jaw for storing solid food.
8. As soon as the ant's strong saliva breaks down the solid food the ant can eat.
9. It swallows the liquid part of the food and spits out the solid part.
10. Watch a colony of ants sometime and you'll be surprised at what goes on.

□EXERCISE 5

1. Penguins are probably the most commonly recognized of all birds for their white breasts and black coats make them distinctive.
2. In prehistoric times penguins could fly and some penguins stood six feet tall.
3. Because the penguins had few enemies in the Antarctic they did not need to fly and during the long process of evolution their wings became useless.
4. Today they use their wings only to help them swim and most penguins stand no more than 3½ feet high.
5. Of all birds they are the most fully adapted to water and extreme cold.
6. They are clumsy on land but at home in the water and they may stay at sea for weeks at a time.
7. Penguins are extremely sociable and nesting rookeries may contain thousands of birds.

8. The young are born blind and are fed by the parents for an unusually long time.
9. Following their sociable tendency the penguins tend large numbers of half-grown young as a group.
10. Penguins will bite if molested but they have little fear of people are easily trained and show considerable intelligence.

☐EXERCISE 6

1. When first discovered America was a land of incredibly rich natural resources.
2. Early explorers were awed by the beauty of its landscape and the abundance of its plants and animals.
3. Then colonization transformed the continent and more and more natural areas were converted to human uses.
4. Human activities such as agriculture timbering mining and transportation destroyed much of the natural landscape.
5. Because their natural habitats were disturbed or destroyed many plants and animals died.
6. The early developers laid down highways cut forests dammed rivers and drained swamps with no thought of environmental consequences.
7. In the early years of this century thousands of square miles of pine oak and other valuable timber species were destroyed.
8. In Ohio 99 percent of the land has been altered from its original state and many other states have lost much of their natural land.
9. Illinois has only 1,000 tracts of relatively undisturbed land remaining and they are being destroyed at the rate of 15 percent annually.
10. In Wisconsin the wetlands have decreased from 7 million to 1.5 million acres and in Tennessee only 72 percent of the native plant communities still exist.

☐EXERCISE 7

1. The country's few remaining virgin forests are found mainly in the Northwest and in Alaska.
2. With the tremendous growth in development and in agriculture today these few remaining forests are threatened.
3. The bulldozers continue to clear the way for more highways shopping centers and urban sprawl.
4. With the destruction of the natural land hundreds of plants and animals are no longer able to survive.
5. Since America was first settled about 500 species of plants and animals have become extinct and today the U.S. Fish and Wildlife Service lists 177 animals as endangered species.
6. Unless a program is designed to counteract the loss of natural lands future generations will be deprived of a natural resource of great value.

7. A number of conservation organizations are working to increase public awareness to reassess national values and to prod the government into taking greater action.
8. Since it is estimated that 1.25 million acres are being converted to more intensive use each year a number of states have started programs to inventory and protect their natural resources.
9. New development projects are being located where nature reserves will not be harmed.
10. With foresight and planning the country's remaining natural resources may yet be saved.

☐EXERCISE 8

1. If one is considering the valuable resources of the earth topsoil is the most important single resource.
2. It is more important even than oil and that means it's very important.
3. It takes 500 years of wind weather life death and geological activity to create one inch of topsoil.
4. Topsoil is necessary to produce the corn wheat beans and other products that make up the greatest wealth of our country.
5. Our wealth is washing away and many of us are unaware of the loss.
6. Unknown to most people some 13 tons of topsoil per acre of farmland are washing away every year.
7. According to the experts not more than five tons would be tolerable.
8. If nothing is done to stop this loss our greatest national resource will be gone in 50 years.
9. In Guatemala the Mayan civilization developed for 17 centuries and then it suddenly disappeared.
10. Modern analysis found that the Mayan civilization collapsed because their topsoil ran out.

Source: "Pay Heed to the Prairie" by Hugh Sidey in *Time*, Sept. 10, 1984

☐EXERCISE 9

1. Houseflies were once considered merely a harmless nuisance but now they are known to be one of humanity's worst enemies.
2. The housefly can walk on vertical windowpanes or upside down on a ceiling because of a secretion produced by tiny glandular pads on its feet.
3. Its feet may also carry millions of microorganisms that can cause disease and thus flies cause thousands of deaths a year.
4. Screens insecticides and various sprays have been used to try to control the flies.
5. In spite of all such attempts we have not rid ourselves of this death-carrying enemy.

6. A single female fly deposits more than 100 eggs at a time and she may lay more than 2,700 eggs in a 30-day period.
7. The eggs take only 12 to 24 hours to hatch and the reproductive process begins all over again.
8. One female fly could have 190 quintillion descendants a year if all her offspring lived but of course that doesn't happen.
9. To keep down the number of flies it is necessary to prevent breeding.
10. If all garbage could be destroyed twice a week houseflies could be controlled.

☐EXERCISE 10

1. Last summer I went racing in my Hobie Cat sailboat.
2. Since I had had my boat for a year and could sail really fast I felt that I was ready to race.
3. The race course was triangular with inflated buoys marking the three corners and we had to sail around it twice.
4. Each of the 20 boats had two sailors and my buddy and I set our sails as best we could.
5. Most of the boats, however, pulled ahead of us and I began to notice the set of their sails.
6. I immediately copied the way the fastest boats had their sails set and that improved our speed.
7. Suddenly I remembered something my grandfather used to say: "It's the set of the sails and not the gales that determines how we'll go."
8. For the first time I realized how much faster a boat can go if the sails are set perfectly.
9. By the middle of the race, however, the fastest boats were too far ahead even to be seen and I realized that I had a lot more to learn.
10. Even so we didn't come in last—just next to last.

JOURNAL WRITING

In your journal write the first three comma rules. Then write a sentence to illustrate each.

COMMAS (RULES 4, 5, AND 6)

4. Put commas around the name of a person spoken to.

> I think, Sylvia, that you are absolutely right.
> Kim, how about a game of tennis?
> I've finished washing the car, Jay.

5. Put commas around an expression that interrupts the flow of the sentence (such as *however, moreover, finally, therefore, of course, by the way, on the other hand, I am sure, I think*).

> We knew, of course, that we were late.
> We didn't expect, therefore, to get seats.
> She should, I think, take a vacation.

Read the preceding sentences aloud, and you'll hear how those expressions interrupt the flow of the sentence. Sometimes, however, such expressions flow smoothly into the sentence and don't need commas around them. Whether an expression is an interrupter or not often depends on where it is in the sentence. If it's in the middle of a sentence, it's more likely to be an interrupter than if it's at the beginning or the end. The expressions that were interrupters in the preceding sentences are not interrupters in the following sentences and therefore don't require commas.

> Of course we knew we were late.
> Therefore we didn't expect to get seats.
> I think she should take a vacation.

Remember that when one of the above words like *however* comes between two independent clauses, that word always has a semicolon before it. It may also have a comma after it, especially if there seems to be a pause between the word and the rest of the sentence. (See p. 72).

> I overslept; however, I still got to class on time.
> I didn't want to volunteer; furthermore, I was too busy.
> I wanted to learn; therefore I worked hard.
> I didn't study in high school; now I do.

Thus a word like *however* or *therefore* may be used in three ways:

1. as an interrupter (commas around it)
2. as a word that flows into the sentence (no commas needed)
3. as a connecting word between two independent clauses (semicolon before it and often a comma after it)

6. Put commas around nonessential material.

Such material may be interesting, but the main idea of the sentence would be clear without it. In the following sentence

Dorothea Marks, who is running for mayor, will speak tonight.

the clause *who is running for mayor* is not essential to the main idea of the sentence. Without it we still know exactly who the sentence is about and what she is going to do. Dorothea Marks will speak tonight. Therefore the nonessential material is set off from the rest of the sentence by commas to show that it could be left out. But in the following sentence

The woman who is running for mayor will speak tonight.

the clause *who is running for mayor* is essential to the main idea of the sentence. Without it the sentence would read: The woman will speak tonight. We would have no idea which woman. The clause *who is running for mayor* is essential because it tells us which woman. It couldn't be left out. Therefore commas are not used around it. In this sentence

Our Volkswagen, which we bought last year, is now a wreck.

the clause *which we bought last year* could be left out, and we would still know the main meaning of the sentence: Our Volkswagen is now a wreck. Therefore the nonessential material is set off by commas to show that it could be left out. But in this sentence

The Volkswagen that we bought last year is now a wreck.

the clause *that we bought last year* is essential. Without it, the sentence would read: The Volkswagen is now a wreck. We'd have no idea whose Volkswagen. Therefore the clause couldn't be left out, and commas are not used around it.

The trick in deciding whether material is essential is to say, "Interesting, but is it necessary?"

EXERCISES

Punctuate these sentences according to Comma Rules 4, 5, and 6.

☐EXERCISE 1

1. The book that I read last week didn't interest me at all.
2. *Oliver Twist* which I'm reading now is interesting.
3. I saw the movie *Oliver* which was here a few years ago, and I decided to read the book.
4. Charles Dickens the author gives a realistic picture of the underworld of London in the nineteenth century.
5. Oliver Twist the hero of the novel was born in a workhouse.
6. He ran away to London and fell into the hands of Fagin and Bill Sikes who were thieves.
7. Many adventures befell Oliver who kept trying to get out of the clutches of Fagin and Sikes.
8. This is the first Dickens novel that I have read.
9. I'd now like to read *David Copperfield* which is another famous novel by Dickens.
10. Have you ever read any novels by Dickens Lisa?

☐EXERCISE 2

1. Whales most people assume are nonvocal mammals.
2. But one whale the humpback emits a "song."
3. By "song" is meant a regular sequence of repeated sounds that are organized into patterns like the calls made by birds.
4. Unlike birdsongs which are high-pitched and last only a few seconds humpback songs vary in pitch and last between six and thirty minutes.
5. The amazing thing about the humpback whale's song however is that it is constantly changing.
6. All the whales in one locality sing the same song in any one year. The following year however their song will be slightly different.
7. The whales compose it seems as they go along, and they incorporate new elements into their song of the previous year.
8. All the whales in Bermuda waters for example will sing the same song in any one year while all the whales in Hawaii waters will be singing a slightly different tune.
9. The following year however each group will alter its song slightly.
10. This astonishing fact moreover sets these whales apart from all other mammals because no other mammal except man has the ability to vary its song.

☐EXERCISE 3

1. The whales' ability to compose new songs by improvising on the old ones would it seems indicate an unusual intelligence.

2. They sing solos, or they may sing duets or trios or even choruses which are made up of interweaving voices.
3. All are singing the same song; no one however is exactly in unison with the others.
4. Each it seems is doing its own composing.
5. The songs of the humpback whales have been recorded by hydrophone which is a kind of underwater microphone.
6. The songs have furthermore been sent into space.
7. *Voyagers 1* and *2* carried into space some recordings including a section entitled "Sounds of Earth."
8. On that recording delegates from the United Nations offered a greeting in 55 languages followed by a "greeting" by a humpback whale which had been recorded off Bermuda in 1970.
9. Perhaps a billion years from now someone in outer space may come upon this record of the song of the humpback whale which is probably the longest, loudest, and slowest song in nature.
10. It is a song moreover that few people on earth have ever heard.

Source: *National Geographic,* January 1979

☐EXERCISE 4

1. Automobile racing is for many the most exciting of all spectator sports.
2. The most popular race is the 500-mile race at Indianapolis which is held on Memorial Day.
3. It's attended by more than 250,000 people and attracts visitors from every state.
4. In the first Indianapolis race which was held in 1911 the winning car went 75 miles an hour.
5. In 1986 the winning car averaged 170.722 miles an hour which is the record speed.
6. The typical car entered in the race is built primarily for that race and weighs only 1500 pounds which is less than the weight of an ordinary small car.
7. Another kind of race is the stock-car race which is run by standard automobiles that reach speeds of about 150 miles per hour.
8. Stock-car races which are run on racetracks and also on roads show which model can get the best mileage.
9. In a drag race which measures acceleration the driver tries to cover one-quarter mile in the shortest possible time.
10. Automobile racing has come a long way since the first race which took place in France in 1895 when the average speed was 15 miles an hour.

☐EXERCISE 5

1. The monarch butterflies that fly from Canada to Pacific Grove, California, every October have made that city famous.

2. The monarchs travel up to 80 miles a day or 2,000 miles in all, but their ability to soar on wind currents aids them.

3. All winter about two million monarch butterflies cover the branches of six acres of pines which protect them from the wind.

4. The same trees are chosen year after year because certain trees it is surmised offer the greatest protection.

5. Each October the schoolchildren of the town have a parade to celebrate the arrival of the monarchs.

6. The thousands of tourists who come to see the monarchs are directed by street signs to the butterfly trees.

7. On warm, sunny days the monarchs fly to nearby gardens where they feed on the nectar of flowers.

8. The monarchs which are short-lived could not possibly live long enough to make the journey from Canada to California twice.

9. How then one wonders can they find their way over such great distances without guideposts?

10. It is the same question as the one concerning the migration of birds which has puzzled naturalists for years.

☐EXERCISE 6

1. The winter of 1988–89 was I think one of the most unusual in history.

2. For a whole month the entire state of Alaska was gripped by one of the fiercest Arctic cold waves on record.

3. Some towns in the interior it is reported registered temperatures as low as −75°F for days at a time.

4. The Kusko 300 which is one of the state's major dog-mushing events had to be postponed.

5. Why was it so cold? Winters are always frigid in Alaska; the cold however is usually relieved by warm winds from the Pacific.

6. This year though a mass of cold air blew in from Siberia and stayed put over Alaska keeping out the warming Pacific winds.

7. Finally at last the icy air roared out of Alaska and across western Canada.

8. Driven by 100 mph winds, the frigid front dropped temperatures by as much as 70° in a matter of hours.

9. The worst snowstorm in Edmonton since 1885 brought the city to a standstill, and in Calgary the windchill factor reached −67°F a level at which exposed flesh freezes in less than a minute.

10. Then as we know Max the frigid weather crossed into the American Midwest.

Source: *Time* Feb. 13, 1989

☐EXERCISE 7

1. The nation's Capitol Building which was the first public building constructed in Washington has come to be a symbol of the United States.
2. George Washington had chosen the site for the city and had asked Pierre Charles L'Enfant a French-born engineer to plan it.
3. The design of the Capitol Building was decided in a contest that offered the winner $500 and a city lot.
4. The winner was Dr. William Thornton a physician who had just come to this country from Paris.
5. Thornton's design of a stately building with two wings joined by a domed center was praised by Thomas Jefferson who was then Secretary of State.
6. Construction was slow however because men and materials were scarce.
7. By 1800 the north wing was completed, and the House, the Senate, and the Supreme Court which had all been in Philadelphia crowded in.
8. By 1810 the second wing was completed under the supervision of Benjamin Latrobe the first important professionally trained architect to practice in the United States.
9. In 1814 however the British invaded Washington and burned the Capitol which was saved from total destruction only by a sudden rainstorm.
10. After the War of 1812 was over, the Capitol Building was rebuilt under the direction of Charles Bulfinch of Boston the first U.S.-born architect to direct work on it.

☐EXERCISE 8

1. In 1850 Congress decided to make a massive enlargement that called for the existing wings of the Capitol to become mere links between the two new additions and the rotunda.
2. The Capitol which increased almost threefold in size was about to become the building we know today.
3. Construction was started and continued even during the Civil War.
4. During the war the great new dome which was an engineering masterpiece was constructed while the rotunda was being used as a hospital.
5. In 1863 "The Statue of Freedom" a 19½-foot sculpture was raised to the top of the dome.
6. Each year about 1.5 million people visit the Capitol which is open seven days a week.
7. Crowds which swell to 11,000 a day in the spring and summer are given free guided tours through the building.
8. The Capitol which has 540 rooms covers 16½ acres.
9. It is lavishly furnished with works of art that reflect U.S. history.

10. Especially interesting are the frescoes by the Italian-born artist Constantino Brumidi who spent a quarter of a century "to make beautiful the Capitol of the one country on earth in which there is liberty."

☐EXERCISE 9

1. My sister and I decided to visit Enchanted Rock the largest granite dome between the Rockies and the Appalachians.
2. Located near Fredericksburg, Texas, it covers more than a square mile. One doesn't realize its enormous size however until one gets close.
3. "Hey Sis," my sister called to me from the top of the rock, "I feel as if I'm on top of the world."
4. The pink granite mass which is more than a billion years old is covered in spots with lichens that attach themselves to its surface and give it various colors.
5. The rock appears to be blue, yellow, sea green, and gray in small patches where the lichens grow.
6. Enchanted Rock is interesting furthermore because of its archeological history.
7. Prehistoric Indians who lived beside the rock before Europeans came to this country left at its base the remains of an Indian culture dating back some 8,000 years.
8. These archaic remains which have added to our knowledge of prehistoric people include fire pits, dart points, potsherds, stone tools, and animal bones.
9. Enchanted Rock is important furthermore as the home of various plants, ferns, and grasses that once were in danger of becoming extinct.
10. They are in danger no longer however because the rock has been placed under the management of the Texas Parks and Wildlife Department, and the vegetation will be protected.

JOURNAL WRITING

Write six sentences using the six comma rules given in the following box.

Review of the Comma

The Six Comma Rules

1. Put a comma before *and, but, for, or, nor, yet, so* when they connect two independent clauses.
2. Put a comma between items in a series.
3. Put a comma after an introductory expression or before an afterthought.
4. Put commas around the name of a person spoken to.
5. Put commas around an interrupter, like *however, moreover,* and so forth.
6. Put commas around nonessential material.

Add the necessary commas to these sentences.

1. In 1979 *Voyager 1* and *Voyager 2* satellites sent back to earth pictures of Jupiter which is the sun's largest planet.
2. The pictures showed that Jupiter is surrounded by at least 13 moons and there may be a 14th.
3. The four largest moons are named Io Europa Ganymede and Callisto.
4. Because they were discovered by Galileo they are called Galilean moons.
5. They are large enough to be called small planets but they have never been seen clearly through earthbound telescopes.
6. Now however the *Voyager* cameras have shown that these four moons are all different in age composition and appearance.
7. The surface of Callisto the outermost of these moons has craters apparently made by the pummeling of meteorites.
8. Ganymede has a cracked cratered icy crust which may indicate moonquakes and Europa has an intricate latticework of lines on its surface.
9. Io the innermost of the Galilean moons is a brilliant orange-red and is scarred with plateaus dry plains highlands fault lines and eight volcanoes.
10. Because of these colors and scars scientists have called Io the pizza of the sky.
11. The most surprising discovery of *Voyager 1* however was a ring around Jupiter.
12. Thus it is now known that Saturn Uranus and Jupiter all have rings.
13. During the tense hours of the close encounters with Jupiter *Voyager 1* and *Voyager 2* performed almost flawlessly.
14. *Voyager 2* then went on to take pictures of Saturn in 1980 reached Uranus in 1986 and Neptune in 1989.

15. Triton Neptune's largest moon is the coldest body ever measured in the solar system—minus 400°.

16. Voyager I sent back pictures of Saturn in 1981 but then headed out of the system to wander aimlessly among the stars.

17. Now a new Space Age is beginning with the launching of unmanned spaceships that will go where manned spaceships cannot go.

18. For example astronauts can someday land on Mars but they can never land on Venus where daytime temperatures reach 900°F.

19. Robotic voyages began in 1989 with the launching of the spacecraft Magellan which went on a 15-month trek to Venus.

20. Robots will try to puzzle out the origin and evolution of the solar system and they will also probe our universe.

21. Besides giving us data about our universe these robotic voyages are going to be early tests of Soviet-American space cooperation.

QUOTATION MARKS

Put quotation marks around the exact words of a speaker (but not around an indirect quotation).

> He said, "I will go." (his exact words)
> He said that he would go. (not his exact words)

Whenever *that* precedes the words of a speaker (as in the last example), it indicates that the words are not a direct quotation and should not have quotation marks around them.

If the speaker says more than one sentence, quotation marks are used only before and after the entire speech.

> He said, "I will go. It's no trouble. I'll be there at six."

The words telling who is speaking are set off with a comma unless, of course, a question mark or exclamation mark is needed.

> "I will go," he said.
> "Do you want me to go?" he asked.

Every quotation begins with a capital letter. But when a quotation is broken, the second part doesn't begin with a capital letter unless it's a new sentence.

> "Genius," said Carlyle, "is the art of taking infinite pains."
> "Don't be afraid to take a big step if one is indicated," said David Lloyd George. "You can't cross a chasm in two small jumps."

Begin a new paragraph with each change of speaker.

> "May I have the car?" I asked.
> "What for?" Dad said.
> "To go see Kathy," I replied.

Put quotation marks around the name of a short story, poem, song, essay, TV program, radio program, or other short work. For a longer work such as a book, newspaper, magazine, play, album, or movie, use underlining, which means it would be italicized in print.

> I like Robert Frost's short poem "Fire and Ice."
> The movie *Gone with the Wind* has been the greatest box office success of all time according to *Newsweek*.

Rachel Carson's essay "And No Birds Sing" is found in her book *Silent Spring.*

Michael Jackson's albums *Off the Wall, Thriller,* and *Bad* have been enormously successful.

Indent and single space, without quotation marks, all quotations of more than five lines.

The great German composer and pianist Johannes Brahms gave the following advice to a young composer:

It seems to me you are too easily satisfied. Let it rest, let it rest, and keep going back to it and working at it again and again, until it is completed as a finished work of art, until there is not a note too much or too little, not a bar you could improve upon. I am rather lazy, but I never cool down over a work once begun until it is perfected, unassailable.

EXERCISES

Punctuate the quotations, and underline or put quotation marks around each title.

☐EXERCISE 1

1. When James Garfield was president of Hiram College in Ohio, a father once said to him I want to talk to you about my son.

2. Yes? said President Garfield.

3. I want to know said the father whether there is not some way my son can get through college in less than four years.

4. Certainly replied Garfield but it all depends upon what you want to make of your boy.

5. What do you mean the father asked.

6. Well said Garfield when God wants to make an oak tree He takes a hundred years but when He wants to make a squash He takes only two months.

7. Woody Allen says that the toughest writing is going from nothing to the first draft.

8. Simplify, simplify said Henry David Thoreau.

9. I wish I was as sure of anything as he is of everything said Thomas Macaulay.

10. If in the last few years said Gelett Burgess you haven't discarded a major opinion or acquired a new one, check your pulse. You may be dead.

☐EXERCISE 2

1. Flammable means the same as inflammable; valuable means the same as invaluable; and ravel means the same as unravel Arthur B. Myers points out.

2. A young man filling out a job application came to the question about marital status and wrote Eligible.

3. I never understand anything wrote Hugh Walpole until I have written about it.

4. In Japan, where families still arrange marriages for some young people, a young man said we may not marry the girl we love, but we love the girl that we marry.

5. A. A. Milne's children's books include Winnie the Pooh, The House at Pooh Corner, When We Were Very Young, and Now We Are Six.

6. Children need love says Harold S. Hulbert especially when they do not deserve it.

7. Mozart was not an accomplished pianist at the age of eight as the result of spending his days in front of a television set says Seymour St. John.

8. The guidebook to the Shenandoah National Park says The candy bar you take into the woods should provide at least the energy needed for bringing the wrapper out.

9. You can think without writing my instructor says but you can't write without thinking.

10. My instructor says that learning word roots is the quickest and most interesting way to improve one's vocabulary.

Some of the following exercises are dialogues such as you might find in a story. Even though the "he said" or "she said" is not repeated in every line, the sense of the material will let you know who is speaking, and of course you should punctuate each such line as a quotation.

☐EXERCISE 3

1. Will it take you long to check the reference she asked.

2. I'll do it as quick as a wink he replied.

3. How quick is that?

4. Well physiologists of the eye tell us it's between .3 and .4 of a second he said.

5. You do know a lot she said.

6. And if it interests you, skin deep is from $\frac{1}{16}$ to $\frac{1}{8}$ of an inch deep.

7. Really! Now I wonder if you can tell me how fast a snail's pace is.

8. Oh, that's easy he said a snail travels about two inches in a minute.

9. What you know astounds me!

10. Oh, I may know a few facts he said but you are worth your weight in gold. And that makes you worth about $500,000.

☐EXERCISE 4

1. I've discovered some word games said Cindy do you know what a palindrome word is?

2. Nope said Pete never heard of it what is it?

3. It's a word that can be written either forward or backward. *Eye, level, radar,* and *rotator* are examples.

4. I can think of some more said Pete how about *deed* and *bob*?

5. Yes said Cindy there are lots of them but palindrome sentences are harder to find.

6. Do you know any asked Pete.

7. Yes, here's one that Adam is supposed to have said to Eve: *Madam, I'm Adam.*

8. How is that a palindrome sentence?

9. Well, try spelling it backward, and you'll see that it comes out just the same as spelling it forward.

10. Sure enough it does said Pete do you know any more?

☐EXERCICE 5

1. Yes, here's another palindrome sentence: *Was it a cat I saw*?

2. You're right. It does spell backward the same as forward said Pete.

3. Here's one more: *Dennis and Edna sinned.*

4. Amazing said Pete. I'll have to see if I can make one up.

5. It's not easy said Cindy.

6. When Le Baron Russel Briggs was dean of Harvard College, he once said to a student why did you not finish your assignment?

7. I wasn't feeling very well, sir the student replied.

8. I think said the dean that in time you may perhaps find that most of the work of the world is done by people who aren't feeling very well.

9. Having the right to do it doesn't mean that it's right to do it said Frank A. Clark.

10. Why is it L. L. Levinson asks that goods sent by ship are called cargo while goods that go in a car are a shipment?

☐EXERCICE 6

1. In our modern American literature course each student had to give a five-minute talk on the subject My Favorite Author.

2. I chose Carl Sandburg and read his poem Chicago from his book Chicago Poems.

3. One student discussed Robert Frost's interest in the people of New Hampshire and read his poem Mending Wall.

4. Another student told about Frost's interest in nature and read the short poem Dust of Snow.

5. Someone talked about Hemingway and gave an analysis of the short story The Killers, which we had read in class.

6. The person who talked about Vachel Lindsay gave an excellent reading of his poem The Congo.

7. Another poem that was read was Patterns by Amy Lowell.

8. The only play discussed was Our Town by Thornton Wilder.

9. And the only novel presented was Mark Twain's Tom Sawyer.

10. The talk that interested me most, however, was one on Henry David Thoreau's book Walden.

☐EXERCISE 7

1. Character my dad used to say is the ability to eat only one salted peanut.

2. Oliver Wendell Holmes wrote many people die with their music still in them.

3. Education said Robert Frost is the ability to listen to almost anything without losing your temper or your self-confidence.

4. Golf is a good walk spoiled said Mark Twain.

5. Control smoking, alcohol, handguns, overeating, and seat belts, says James Speer, a professor of biomedical history at the University of Washington, and that would be a new world.

6. There is at least one TV in 94 percent of U.S. homes the lecturer said but there are bathtubs in only 85 percent of homes. Perhaps more brains are being washed than bodies.

7. I never lose sight of the fact said Katherine Hepburn that just being is fun.

8. Some days the only good things on TV are the vase and the clock says Laurence J. Peter.

9. After three days fish and visitors begin to stink said Benjamin Franklin.

10. In his novel Heart of Darkness, Joseph Conrad said that we live as we dream—alone.

□EXERCISE 8

1. Do you know who was the first American to make a flight into space Cheryl asked.

2. Sure, it was Alan Shepard I said.

3. Wrong Cheryl said. It was a chimpanzee named Ham. He made his flight on January 31, 1961, just before Alan Shepard made his.

4. I didn't know that I said.

5. Few people do Cheryl responded and do you know who was the first American to orbit the earth?

6. John Glenn I said.

7. No, it was Enos, another chimp, who circled the earth two times on November 29, 1961, just before John Glenn made his orbit.

8. Why did the chimps go first I asked.

9. NASA administrators wanted to test their space technology on chimpanzees before sending human astronauts up. Both chimps survived their flights and furnished NASA with valuable information.

10. That's interesting I said.

□EXERCISE 9

Sir Christopher Wren, one of the greatest of English architects, walked one day unrecognized among the workmen building St. Paul's Cathedral, which he had designed.

What are you doing he asked one laborer.

The man answered I am cutting a piece of stone.

He asked the same question of another man and received the reply I am earning five shillings twopence a day.

But a third man, in answer to his inquiry, said I am helping Sir Christopher Wren build a beautiful cathedral.

JOURNAL WRITING

To practice using quotation marks, write a conversation that might be heard at your breakfast table any morning. Remember to start a new paragraph with each change of speaker.

CAPITAL LETTERS

Capitalize

1. The first word of every sentence.

2. The first word of every direct quotation.

> He said, "You've won."
> "I've done my best," he said, "and I can do no more." (The *and* is not capitalized because it does not begin a new sentence.)
> "Why do you worry?" she said. "You've done well." (*You* is capitalized because it begins a new sentence.)

3. The first, last, and every important word in a title. Don't capitalize prepositions, short connecting words, the *to* in front of a verb, or *a, an, the*.

> *What a Property Owner Needs to Know*
> "The Day the Saucers Flew By"

4. Names of people, places, languages, races, and nationalities.

> Grandfather Horton   Japan   Chicano
> Uganda   English   Indian

5. Names of months, days of the week, and special days, but not the seasons.

> February   Fourth of July   spring
> Wednesday   Thanksgiving   summer

6. A title of relationship if it takes the place of the person's name. If *my* (or *your, her, his, our, their*) is in front of the word, a capital is not used.

> I think Mother will come.   *but*   I think my mother will come.
> She visited Aunt Margarita.   *but*   She visited her aunt.

7. Names of particular people or things, but not general ones.

> I spoke to Professor Haviland.   *but*   I spoke to the professor.
> We sailed on the Hudson River   *but*   We sailed on the river.
> Are you from the Midwest?   *but*   We turned west.
> I take Art 300 and French 101.   *but*   I take art and French.
> I go to St. Joseph's High School.   *but*   I'm in high school now.
> He goes to Eldorado College.   *but*   He goes to college now.

EXERCISES

Add the necessary capital letters.

☐EXERCISE 1

1. Last summer my parents and I took a long motor trip through the mid-west and the west.
2. Mother and dad had never had a real vacation before.
3. I had never gone sailing on a river until I sailed on the Red river.
4. We visited the Badlands of South Dakota, but we missed seeing mount Rushmore.
5. My mother particularly enjoyed seeing Yellowstone national park.
6. I'm impressed with all the national parks in our country.
7. My dad liked the drive through the groves of redwood trees in California.
8. Both mother and dad enjoyed walking along the Pacific ocean.
9. Then we left Marin county and drove across the golden gate bridge.
10. I like the climate of the west coast, but my summer job is in the east.

☐EXERCISE 2

1. All of us children except my brother Ned will be in college this fall.
2. Ned graduated last spring from Wichita state university in Kansas.
3. Last summer he worked for the Ford motor company but was not there long enough to receive any company benefits.
4. Now he works for a refinery of the Mobil oil company, which is 10 miles from our house.
5. "I need a motorcycle," he said, "and I'm going to buy one."
6. He asked dad for advice about buying a motorcycle.
7. "You know more about them," dad said, "than I do."
8. Ned then went to the public library and found an article entitled "How to buy your first motorcycle."
9. He looked at motorcycles all summer.
10. Then he finally bought one and now rides to work each day.

☐EXERCISE 3

1. My sister Sal is going to the college of San Mateo, which is where my mother went years ago.
2. My older sister is a sophomore at Purdue university in Indiana.
3. I'm a freshman at southwest state university in Marshall, Minnesota.
4. Now that I'm in college I'm working harder than I did in high school.
5. When I signed up for English 101 and History 211, I had no idea that english would be so easy and history so difficult.
6. As for math and economics, I don't find them difficult.
7. I've always liked math, and economics is related to it.

8. I think I'll enjoy the course in business administration, for I'd like to work for the Addison accounting firm.
9. Dad and mother say the house is unbearably quiet this fall.
10. Most of us were home for thanksgiving day though.

☐EXERCISE 4

1. It's my oldest brother Dick who has really had a wide college experience.
2. First he went to a community college for a year.
3. Then he decided he wanted to go really far from home.
4. For his sophomore year he registered at Sheldon Jackson junior college in Sitka, Alaska.
5. He enjoyed Sitka, but then he made a still bigger jump and now is in Windward community college in Hawaii.
6. He wrote recently that he has had enough traveling and has registered at the university of Montana at Missoula for his third year.
7. Now that we are all settled in our colleges, dad and mom have announced that they are going to college too.
8. They are going to take some courses at the local community college.
9. Dad wants to take a course in woodworking, and mom would like to learn to use our computer.
10. So our house will be a hangout for college students for some time to come.

☐EXERCISE 5

1. I've been taking an interesting course in art history.
2. We are studying a bit about architecture.
3. The grace lutheran church is the most architecturally interesting church in our city.
4. The Woolworth building is one of the most interesting commercial buildings.
5. Besides working on my regular courses, I now have a part in a play the drama department is putting on.
6. I think dad is coming to the play, and perhaps my cousin and my sister will come too.
7. I'm so much interested in drama that I'd like to go to graduate school next year and get a master's degree in the history of drama.
8. I'll need to make some money this summer if I stay in college another year.
9. I've applied for a job at central Illinois public service company for the summer.
10. The only vacation I'll have will be the fourth of July.

☐EXERCISE 6

1. My aunt and uncle have a cottage in northern Michigan.

2. Each summer aunt Cleo invites us to visit her and uncle Bart for a week.
3. The cottage is on a small lake not far from lake Superior.
4. The area is populated mainly by norwegian and finnish people.
5. My other aunt lives in Houston, Texas, which is the south's largest city.
6. Its business district starts at the south bank of buffalo bayou.
7. To the east is Galveston bay, an inlet of the gulf of Mexico.
8. To the northeast flows the Trinity river. To the southwest is the Brazos river.
9. The port of Houston ranks second in commerce among U.S. ports.
10. I always enjoy my visits to the city of Houston.

☐EXERCISE 7

1. My dad and I were traveling through an unfamiliar city.
2. "I think you should have turned south at that intersection," I told him.
3. "We'll turn at the next avenue and get to main street just the same," he said.
4. "Doesn't main run north and south?" I asked.
5. After a few wrong turns we finally got to the century museum.
6. Ever since his college days, dad had wanted to see that museum.
7. He said that professor Scott had often talked about the museum's fossil collection.
8. Most of the specimens were from the west and the midwest.
9. We took time to see some roman sculptures too.
10. Then we had lunch in the museum cafeteria before starting again for the west coast.

Review of Punctuation and Capital Letters

Punctuate these sentences and paragraphs. They include all the rules for punctuation and capitalization you have learned. Correct your answers carefully by those at the back of the book. Most sentences have several errors.

☐EXERCISE 1

1. Should people be allowed the unrestricted use of their national parks.

2. Many say that it is their right to enjoy their parks but the environmentalists say that the natural state of some of the land should be preserved for future generations as well.

3. Sailing down the Colorado river through the Grand canyon for example is one of the most spectacular river trips in the world.

4. More than 16,000 people take the trip every year and there is often a waiting list.

5. Strapped to rubber rafts, the riders shoot the rapids then they float between the canyon walls which are more than two billion years old.

6. Some go in oar-rigged rafts others go in motorized rafts.

7. The environmentalists say the trip should be made silently in oar-rigged rafts, but some commercial boaters say many people do not have time to go in oar-rigged rafts.

8. The voyagers used to leave behind them garbage and trampled vegetation but now that has changed.

9. The National park service has taken control and the area today is one of the cleanest anywhere.

10. The problem of park use is not new it is faced by all national parks.

☐EXERCISE 2

1. Rochester New York used to be called the flour city because it had so many flour mills now it is called the flower city because of its many varieties of lilacs.

2. The most frequently sung songs in english are Happy Birthday to you For he's a jolly good fellow and Auld lang Syne.

3. George Bernard Shaw wrote the test of a man's or a woman's breeding is how they behave in a quarrel.

4. Did you know that Charles Darwin and Abraham Lincoln were born on the same day—February 12, 1809.

5. In 1968 the London Bridge was sold to the McCullough Oil corporation of Los Angeles for $2,460,000 it was transported and reassembled at Lake Havasu City Arizona.

6. A sentence containing 1,300 words appears in Absalom, Absalom a novel by William Faulkner.

7. Love is like the moon when it doesn't increase it decreases.

8. Gandhi had this sign on the wall of his home when you are in the right you can afford to keep your temper and when you are in the wrong you cannot afford to lose it.

9. Love does not consist said Antoine de Saint-Exupéry of gazing at each other but of looking outward together in the same direction.

10. A nickel goes a long way these days you can carry it a long way before finding anything you can buy with it.

☐EXERCISE 3

1. Many things that we consider modern were really discovered by the early Greeks Democritus in the fifth century B.C. developed an atomic theory spoke of a number of universes spoke of mountains on the moon had a theory of evolution and knew that color is not inherent in things Pythagoras in the sixth century B.C. said the earth was not the center of the universe.

2. In the fifth century B.C., Socrates said Children now love luxury they have bad manners and contempt for authority children are now tyrants, not the servants of their households they contradict their parents chatter before company gobble up dainties at the table and tyrannize their teachers.

3. Athletics have become professionalized said Socrates in the fifth century B.C.

4. The first of June and nothing has been done by the Senate wrote Cicero in the first century B.C.

5. I am in difficulty both summer and winter about my salary said an Egyptian letter written in 256 B.C.

☐EXERCISE 4

Psychologists say that how you write your name can be revealing. If you write your name clearly you probably have nothing to hide. You are likely reasonably satisfied with yourself and sincerely want to communicate with other people. If on the other hand your signature is simply an unreadable scrawl you may be ashamed of your name or of what you have written. Or you may be afraid to communicate with others or feel so inferior that you have to pretend you're a big shot with a scrawl for a signature. You should remember however that a big shot always has a secretary to type a name underneath the scrawl. So if you want to use a big-shot scrawl on your papers make sure you type or print your name underneath.

☐EXERCISE 5

The Old State House in Hartford Connecticut which is the nation's oldest statehouse was in danger of being demolished to make way for office buildings local residents formed the old state house association and organized a drive to get funds for restoration. Although large corporations donated the bulk of the money the association wanted to get more people involved they decided upon an unusual mode of taxation each window with a view of the Old State House was taxed $5 the citizens responded enthusiastically and the windows tax brought in $8,700 the Old State House was restored and Hartford had saved an important historic landmark.

That was in 1975. In 1989 it was decided to ask for a voluntary fee of $10 per window to help with the upkeep of the State House which has now been turned into a museum the companies and individuals with a view responded gladly.

Proofreading Exercise 1

This student paper has 10 errors. Try to find all 10. This is the kind of careful proofreading you should do before you call your own papers finished. No answers are provided at the back of the book for this exercise.

LADYBUG, LADYBUG

Stop. Don't squash that bug. Dont you no that not all bugs are harmful. Some bugs are actually helpful and the ladybug is that kind. Ladybugs eat the aphids that destroy gardens. Farmers and gardeners pay up to $20 a quart for those little bugs.

From the time of the Middle Ages the ladybug has been admired. Northern Europeans thought that if a ladybug crept across a young girls hand, her chances of matrimony would improve. A century ago an insect pest threatened the entire fruit crop of California ladybugs were brought in and saved the crop. Ladybugs have even been immortalized in the childrens poem "Ladybug, Ladybug, Fly away Home," and now New York State has made that little orange and black bug it's official insect.

So dont squash that little ladybug. Carry it into your garden.

Source: *U.S. News and World Report,* Aug. 7, 1989

Proofreading Exercise 2

Here is another student paper to proofread. This one has eight errors (the shift to *you* in the second half of the paper is not considered an error because the writer seems to be having a conversation with *you,* the reader). No answers are provided at the back of the book for this exercise.

NOW IF YOU HAVE AN HOUR OR TWO . . .

Last summer I finally did it. I went to Europe. I remember how excited I was when I made up my mind to go and sent in my nonrefundable deposit for my air ticket. I was glad the deposit had me hooked. I knew that as the trip drew nearer and the fear of going so far away increase, I might find it to easy to create some little excuse to back out. But that deposit held me committed. Losing the deposit was unthinkable. I can't stand to loose money.

I grew excited about it and spent hours reading travel books and making plans. I developed a casual way of mentioning my plans in conversation as though I always did that sort of thing it felt good.

I discovered there are two types of people—those who have been to Europe and those who haven't. You can tell them apart when you explain that your planning to go. The first type immediately begins to tell you the things you absolutely must do and the things you positively shouldn't miss. They often go on for an hour or two boring you with there experiences. The second type is really impressed by your plans but practices a little one-upmanship by saying that when they go, it won't be for just a month. They'll go for a year or two and really see all that's to be seen.

Well, now I've been to Europe I had a really great time. And, by the way, if you think you might go someday I can tell you some things you absolutely must do and some things you positively shouldn't miss.

Proofreading Exercise 3

Proofread this student paper. You will find only a few errors—11 in fact—but correcting those few errors will improve the paper. You may have to go through the paper several times to find all 11 errors. Challenge your instructor to find all 11 on the first try! No answers are provided.

IT'S EASY

After watching for hours, I went down the beach to talk to the fellow who owned the windsurfer. He had made windsurfing look so easy as he just stood on the surfboard holding up the sail and letting the wind do the rest.

"Windsurfing is easy," he said, "once you get the hang of it."

Yes, I thought, especially on a day like this with a brisk breeze blowing. What I really wanted, of course, was to borrow his windsurfer and sail off, letting the wind skim me over the water like a water strider.

After I had talked to him for a few minutes he couldn't ignore my enthusiasm any longer and offer to let me try his windsurfer.

"Great," I said. And after a minute's basic instruction, I pushed the windsurfer into the water and climbed on.

"Now pull up the sail, and remember what I said," he yelled.

Standing on a surfboard in the water is not the easiest thing to do and then holding a sail up in the wind at the same time becomes really tricky. I was concentrating so hard on not falling forward that I fell backward with a splash.

"I must have slipped," I yelled as I climb on again—and promptly fell over sideways.

"No problem," I yelled as I tried again . . . and again . . . and again.

I spent more time in the water than on that crazy windsurfer. A small crowd had gather on the beach to watch the entertainment that I was providing I could hear their laughs each time I fell in.

I learned that its not as easy as it looks. It takes balance and agility. I wasn't a total failure though. Once or twice I actually got the wind in the sail and started moving forward for a few moments—before I fell off again. That little bit of success on my first day was enough to make me try again on other days. Until I could really sail.

Now on hot summer afternoons I bring my own windsurfer onto the beach and sometimes someone will ask me about it. I smile and say, "Its easy once you get the hang of it." Soon he's trying it, and I stand back on the beach and watch and laugh, knowing I must have look just that silly when I was learning.

Comprehensive Test on Entire Text

In these sentences you will find all the errors that have been discussed in the entire text. Correct them by adding apostrophes, punctuation, and capital letters and by crossing out incorrect expressions and writing the corrections above them. Most sentences have several errors. A perfect—or almost perfect—score will mean you've mastered the first part of the text.

1. She ask my sister and me to serve the dessert we was glad to help.

2. If a person is serious about getting an education you can get one.

3. Because I had done the very best I could all semester in my math course.

4. Its not my fault that hes not here he should be coming soon.

5. While they were on there way they lost they're keys.

6. I can't decide whether to study math, write my paper, or whether I should just watch television tonight.

7. I'll stay at home Michelle if you're going to be hear to.

8. Your going to the game, aren't you.

9. We girls made a upside-down cake for desert everyone liked it.

10. I was quiet happy to hear about Sarahs promotion.

11. When we reached the main road we turn south and then West.

12. Which took us about five miles out of are way.

13. Its the Johnsons car but there letting me drive it.

14. Each of his trophies are displayed in the entrance hall.

15. Coming quickly to the boiling point, she turn down the burner.

16. That Honda belongs to my sister and me Robin said.

17. I think Kellys paper was more interesting then Kays.

18. I'm taking the following courses psychology history spanish and english.

19. The Cherry Orchard which I read last year is a play by Chekhov.

20. He told his brother his TV needed a new tube.

21. Two of my friends goes to Mt. Hood community college.

22. She was supposed to memorize the poem Birches from Robert Frost's book Mountain Interval.

23. They invited him and I to go with them.

24. We walked as far as we could and then we give up.

25. You are responsible for what happens in the future my counselor said no matter what has happen in the past.

26. I would have went to the parade if I had knowed you was going.

27. Dad gave my brother and me tickets to the final baseball game.

28. Last week I join a lawn crew and have all ready work four days.

29. My friend and I are hoping to get jobs for the summer.

30. If one has done all the exercises in this text, you'll do well on this test.

31. Did you know that the octopus of which there are about 150 species is the most intelligent of all invertebrates.

Writing

4

4 Writing

You learn to write by *writing*—not by reading long discussions *about* writing. Therefore the instructions in this section are brief. In fact, they are boiled down to just eight steps that you need to take to write good papers. Take these eight steps, one at a time, and you'll write more effectively and also more easily. Here are the steps:

EIGHT STEPS TO BETTER WRITING

    I. Do some free writing.
   II. Limit your topic.
  III. Write a thesis statement.
  IV. Support your thesis with reasons or points.
   V. Organize your paper from your thesis.
  VI. Organize each paragraph.
 VII. Write and rewrite.
VIII. Proofread ALOUD.

I. DO SOME FREE WRITING

"Writing is good for us," Oliver Wendell Holmes said, "because it brings our thoughts out into the open, as a boy turns his pockets inside out to see what is in them." Try "turning your pockets inside out" by writing as fast as you can for five minutes. Write anything that comes into your mind. Put your thoughts down as fast as they come. What you write may not make sense, but that doesn't matter. No one is going to read what you write. Write fast. Don't stop a moment. Don't even take your pen off the page. If you can't think of anything to write, just write, "I can't think of anything to write," over and over until something occurs to you. Look at your watch and begin.

This free writing should limber up your mind and your pen so that you'll write more freely.

Now try another kind of free writing—focused free writing. Write for five minutes as fast as you can, but this time stick to one subject— sports.

Look at your watch and begin.

Did you focus on sports that long? Did you think of sports your dad tried to interest you in as a child, of your struggles and failures with some sports, of your successes with others, of coaches who have influenced you, of spectator sports as well as those you have participated in?

You didn't have time to include all those things of course. Now write for 10 minutes and add more to your discussion of sports.

Focused free writing is a good way to begin any writing. When you are assigned a paper, try writing for 10 minutes putting down all your thoughts on the subject. It will let you see what material you have and will help you figure out what aspect of the subject (what topic) to write about.

II. LIMIT YOUR TOPIC

Finding the right topic is sometimes the hardest part of writing. For one thing, you need to limit your topic so that you can handle it in a paper of 300 to 500 words. The subject sports, which you used for free writing, was obviously too big. You could limit it by saying

Sports here at college
The importance of sports in my life
My favorite sport—table tennis

but even those topics are too big. Keep making your topic smaller

Being on the college table tennis team

and smaller

My first table tennis tournament

and smaller

My final game in the table tennis tournament

Now you have a topic limited enough to write about in a short paper.

Usually the more you limit your topic, the better your paper will be, for then you'll have room to add plenty of specific details. And it's specific details that will make your reader interested in what you are saying.

☐EXERCISE 1

Make each of these topics more and more limited until it would be a possible topic for a short paper. Then compare your topics with those suggested at the back of the book.

1. Music as a career

_____

_____

2. Refinishing furniture

_____

_____

3. My summer job

_____

_____

4. The house where I grew up

_____

_____

5. My elementary school

_____

_____

6. Cross-country skiing

_____

_____

The following two assignments emphasize the first two Steps to Better Writing—doing some free writing and limiting your topic. In these two assignments we are not going to worry about paragraph structure and many of the things we'll consider later. Just present your ideas the way you would if you were talking to someone.

Assignment 1   A Satisfying Moment

Describe a satisfying moment in your life. It might be a moment when you felt proud of yourself for something you did or a moment when something good happened to you. It need not be a dramatic moment; it might be a very simple one. First do some free writing to call to your mind specific details. You'll want to tell what you saw at that moment, what you heard, how you felt. If you are groping for details, remember your five senses—sight, hearing, smell, taste, and touch. Each of them may call forth some details you hadn't thought of before.

When you've done all the free writing you can, then make sure your topic is limited. If you are writing about winning a trophy, you won't tell about the entire season but only about actually receiving the award.

In the following paper on this assignment, the writer has used many details to set the scene and make the final moment effective.

A MOMENT OF REWARD

It was the evening of our annual spring concert. All of us in the choir had worked hard for this final event, and I was proud to be part of the group. Looking dignified in his green tuxedo, Conductor Williams stood at the podium while we choir members stood straight and tall behind him in our yellow and black evening wear.

What a thrilling performance we gave that night as we lifted our voices in praise! Never before had we sung so well. "John Saw Duh Numbuh" and "When the Saints Go Marching In" were the two numbers the audience seemed to like the most.

Then Professor Williams turned toward the audience, and as he stood behind the podium, there was a moment of stillness in the auditorium. He began a presentation, and I held my breath.

Then it happened. My name was called to receive the award as the "Most Outstanding Choir Member" of the year. I gasped. And my knees shook as I walked toward the podium, held out my hand, and said almost inaudibly, "Thank you." As I turned back to my place in the group, I suddenly realized that a few tears were rolling down my face.

Receiving this honor was indeed a moment of reward, but it was a moment of melancholy as well, for I knew that my days of performing and traveling with the group were now at an end.

Now write your paper for this assignment. Imagine you are telling someone about your satisfying moment, and write what you would say. Remember that fully as important as making your paper mechanically correct is making it so interesting that your readers will enjoy it.

Finally, spend some time thinking of a satisfactory title. Just as you're more likely to read a magazine article with a catchy title, so your readers will be more eager to read your paper if you give it a good title. Which of these titles from student papers would make you want to read further?

An Unusual Experience	Open Mouth; Insert Foot
Reach for the Sky!	An Excellent Movie
Monkey See, Monkey Do	Smoke Signals
My Favorite Class	Love at First Casserole

Your paper should be typed, double-spaced, or written legibly in ink on 8½-by-11-inch paper on one side only. An inch-and-a-half margin should be left on each side of the page for your instructor's comments. The beginning of each paragraph should be indented about five spaces.

Part of the success of a paper depends on how it looks. The same paper written sloppily or neatly might well receive different grades. If, however, when you do your final proofreading, you find a word repeated or a word left out, don't hesitate to make neat corrections in pen. So long as your paper gives a neat appearance, no one will mind a few minor corrections.

Assignment 2   A Place Important to Me

What place means more to you than any other place in the world? It might be a place you know now or one you knew in childhood—a playroom, your workshop, a backyard, your grandmother's kitchen, a locker room, a playing field . . .

Do some free writing to bring to your mind specific details that will help your reader see your place. Telling some things that happened there will also help your reader participate in your memory of it.

After you have done all the free writing you can, ask yourself whether your topic is limited enough. Take it through several steps of limiting to see whether you can turn it into a more manageable topic.

Before you begin to write, read this student paper—a third draft.

With each draft the writer kept adding specific details about what he saw, what he heard, what he did, and how he felt. Now you can visualize the place and understand how the writer feels about it.

MY PLACE

It was a mighty special place for a nine-year-old kid—just a little clearing on one side of a big-city ravine but still mighty special. The ravine itself—the scene of countless peashooter fights, secret club meetings, and hours of just plain exploring—was well know to all the kids in the neighborhood. But My Place was different.

And it really was My Place. Of course it wasn't hidden. It was right next to one of the main ravine paths, only on a slightly lower level. It was one of those places a person could walk by a hundred times and never notice. And although there were always people in the ravine, I never saw anyone else in My Place.

It wasn't more than 100 feet across and maybe half that deep. On three sides were steep tree-covered hills, and on the fourth some trees, the path, and then the stream. The trees weren't any particular kind, just big green protecting trees to a nine-year-old. They kept out almost all the sunlight and wind, creating a dim and comforting silence, broken only by the occasional chatter of a squirrel or the chirp of a bird. No matter what the time of day or the weather, in My Place nothing ever changed.

But the really wonderful part of My Place was my tiny pond—a puddle not more than five feet across and not very deep. Directly above it a long tree limb forked at just the right spot so that I could lie on my back on it and look up at the trees and flecks of sky, and at the same time dip my hand into the cold water of the pond below. The pond was always perfectly clear and calm, with leaves on the bottom but no sign of life. After a few minutes, though, if I kept still, the little water striders would come and play around my hand.

I could lie on that limb over the tiny pond and just let time float by. Soon my troubles seemed so petty that by the time I went home, something inside me had become quiet and calm too. I guess I always took a bit of the quiet and calmness home with me. I still keep some of it.

I don't think I want to go back there. Even if the city hasn't beautified My Place with pansies and gravel paths, it might seem strange. It might seem small and plain and cluttered. Anyhow, some other little kid may have made it his place now.

Now write a description of your place that will help your reader picture it and feel its importance to you.

III. WRITE A THESIS STATEMENT

The most important thing to keep in mind, no matter what you are writing, is the idea you want to get across to your reader. It doesn't matter whether you are writing a paragraph or a longer piece, you must have in mind a single idea that you want to express to your reader. In a longer paper such an idea is called a thesis statement; in a paragraph it's called a topic sentence, but they mean the same thing—an idea you want to get across.

The limited topic on page 208, "My final game in the table tennis tournament," doesn't make any point. What about that game? What did it do for you? What point about that game would you like to present to your reader? You might write

Winning that final game gave me new confidence.

or

Losing that final game made me more determined than ever.

or

Winning that final game made me decide on physical education as a major.

Now you have said something. **When you write in one sentence the point you want to present to your reader, you have written a thesis statement.**

All good writers have a thesis in mind when they begin to write. Whether they are writing articles, novels, short stories, poems, or plays, they have in mind an idea they want to present to the reader. They may develop it in various ways, but back of whatever they write is their ruling thought, their reason for writing, their thesis.

For any writing assignment, after you have done some free writing and limited your topic, your next step is to write a thesis statement. As you write your thesis statement, keep two things in mind:

1. A thesis statement must be a sentence (not merely a topic).

TOPIC	THESIS
My final game in the table tennis tournament	Winning that final game in the table tennis tournament gave me confidence.
Saving trees	We need to conserve paper to save our forests.
Speed reading	Speed reading has helped my comprehension.

2. A thesis statement must be a statement you can explain or defend
(not simply a fact that no one would deny).

FACT	THESIS
We're having a cold winter.	Three steps will successfully winterize your car.
Alaska is our largest state.	The wild lands of Alaska must be protected from developers.
Some students cheat.	Our student government should take a firm stand on cheating.

☐EXERCISE 2

Which of the following are merely topics or facts, and which are thesis statements that you could explain or defend? In front of each one that is a thesis statement, write THESIS. Check your answers with those at the back of the book.

_____ 1. Long-distance cycling

_____ 2. It was a great day when I bought my first car

_____ 3. Canada is the second largest country in the world but has a relatively small population

_____ 4. The tornado that hit our town

_____ 5. My most memorable achievement

_____ 6. Teaching my three-year-old to cross the street safely wasn't easy

_____ 7. The forests of our land should not be sold to lumber companies

_____ 8. I get a lot of satisfaction from my job

_____ 9. Most countries now use the metric system

_____ 10. Tutoring a Japanese student

_____ 11. My psychology class taught me some things about myself

_____ 12. To refinish furniture, four steps are necessary

_____ 13. The Smithsonian Institution is in Washington, D.C.

☐EXERCISE 3

Now make thesis statements from all those above that are only topics or facts. Compare your thesis statements with those suggested at the back of the book.

Suppose that in an exam you are asked to write on one of these topics. For each topic write a thesis statement that would help you write a good paper. Remember that a thesis statement must be a sentence.

1. My most valuable legacy from high school

_____

_____

2. The best summer job I ever had

_____

_____

3. My main reason for choosing this college

_____

_____

4. The place where I'd most like to live

_____

_____

5. My most satisfying moment in college

_____

_____

Now for each of the above thesis statements write a title that you think would make a reader want to read your paper.

1.

2.

3.

4.

5.

IV. SUPPORT YOUR THESIS WITH REASONS OR POINTS

Now you're ready to support your thesis with reasons or points. That is, you'll think of ways to convince your reader that your thesis is true. How could you convince your reader that winning that final table tennis game gave you confidence? You might write

> Winning that final table tennis game gave me new confidence. (because)[1]
> 1. It was the first county tournament I had ever won.
> 2. I defeated more experienced players.
> 3. I discovered I play well under pressure.

The points supporting a thesis are not always reasons. They may be examples (to make your thesis clear), steps (in a how-to paper), descriptions (in a descriptive paper), or anecdotes (in a narrative paper). Whatever they are, they should convince your reader that your thesis is true for you.

□EXERCISE 4

Add supporting points (sentences) to these thesis statements.

I've decided to change my job.

              1.

(reasons)   2.

              3.

Ours is a wasteful society.

              1.

              2.

(examples) 3.

              4.

              5.

I can change a tire in three easy steps.

              1.

(steps)   2.

              3.

---

[1](Sometimes if you imagine a "because" at the end of your thesis statement, it will help you write your reasons clearly and in parallel form.)

Learning to write a good thesis statement with supporting points is perhaps the most important thing you can learn in this course. Most writing problems are not really *writing* problems but *thinking* problems. Whether you're writing a term paper or merely an answer to a test question, working out a thesis statement is always the best way to organize your thoughts. If you take enough time to think, you'll be able to write a clear thesis statement with supporting points. And if you have a clear thesis statement with supporting points, writing a well-organized paper won't be too difficult.

Of course not all writing follows this "thesis and support" form. Experienced writers vary their writing. Using this form, however, is an excellent way to begin learning to write because it will help you think logically, and logical thinking is important for all writing.

Assignment 3 Two Thesis Statements with Supporting Points

Think of some decision you're trying to make. Are you wondering what major to choose, whether to drop out of college for a time, whether to give up smoking, whether to work as a hospital volunteer? Think of a decision that really matters to you. Only then will you be able to write something others will care to read. When you've decided on a topic, write a thesis statement for *each side*. For example, if you're wondering whether to major in music or in computer science, you would write

I've decided to major in music.
I've decided to major in computer science.

These statements now need to be supported with reasons. You might write

I've decided to major in music. (because)
1. My real love is music.
2. I'd like to help students with talent.
3. I'll be able to get either an academic or a professional job.

I've decided to major in computer science. (because)
1. I'm not sure I'm good enough in music to make it a career.
2. I'll have more job opportunities in computer science.
3. I'll make my living in computer science and keep music as a hobby.

Three reasons usually work well, but you could have two or four. Be sure your reasons are sentences.

Now write your two thesis statements for the two sides of the decision you are trying to make, and under them write your supporting reasons.

I've decided _____

    1.

    2.

    3.

I've decided _____

    1.

    2.

    3.

Eventually you'll write a paper on one of the two sides, but first we must consider how to organize a paper and how to organize a paragraph.

V. ORGANIZE YOUR PAPER FROM YOUR THESIS

Once you have worked out a good thesis with supporting points, organizing your paper will be easy.

First you need an introductory paragraph. It should catch your reader's interest and should either include or suggest your thesis statement. It may also list the supporting points, but usually it's more effective to let them unfold paragraph by paragraph rather than to give them all away in your introduction. (Your instructor may ask you to write your complete thesis statement with supporting points at the top of your paper so that it may be referred to easily.) Even if your supporting points don't appear in your introduction, your reader will easily spot them later if your paper is clearly organized.

Your second paragraph will present your first supporting point—everything about it and nothing more.

Your next paragraph will be about your second supporting point—all about it and nothing more.

Each additional paragraph will develop another supporting point.

Finally you'll need a brief concluding paragraph. In a short paper it isn't necessary to restate all your points. Even a single clincher sentence to round out the paper may be sufficient.

Paragraph 1.   Introduction arousing your reader's interest and indicating your thesis

Paragraph 2.   First supporting point

Paragraph 3.   Second supporting point

Additional paragraphs for additional supporting points

Concluding paragraph

Learning to write this kind of paper will teach you to write logically. Then when you're ready to write a longer paper, you'll be able to organize it easily. A longer paper may divide each of the supporting points into several paragraphs, and it may not present the thesis statement until later in the paper. But no matter how the material is presented, it will still have some kind of logical pattern.

Here are the introductory and concluding paragraphs from a student paper. Note that the introductory paragraph arouses the reader's interest and suggests the thesis statement. And the concluding paragraph simply wraps the paper up in two brief sentences.

Introductory paragraph	Why would anybody want to be a veterinarian? That's the question my friends keep asking me. It's taken me almost a year to get my answer down pat, but now I'm ready to tell them.
	(The paper then tells in three paragraphs the three reasons why the writer has made his choice.)
Concluding paragraph	Therefore, for the above reasons, I've decided to pursue a career in veterinary medicine. But there's still another reason—my patients will never sue me for malpractice!

VI. ORGANIZE EACH PARAGRAPH

Organizing a paragraph is easy because it's organized just the way an entire paper is. Here's the way you learned to organize a paper:

> Thesis stated or suggested in introductory paragraph
>> First supporting point
>> Second supporting point
>> Additional supporting points
> Concluding paragraph

And here's the way to organize a paragraph:

> Topic sentence
>> First supporting detail or example
>> Second supporting detail or example
>> Additional supporting details or examples
> Concluding sentence if needed

You should have at least two or three points to support your topic sentence. If you find you have little to say after writing your topic sentence, ask yourself what details or examples will make your reader see that your topic sentence is true for you.

The topic sentence doesn't have to be the first sentence in the paragraph. It may come at the end or even in the middle, but having it first is the most common way.

Each paragraph should contain only one main idea, and no detail or example should be allowed to creep into the paragraph if it doesn't support the topic sentence. Note how the following paragraph is organized.

When you look at your quiet green lawn, you wouldn't dream that perhaps a hundred animals large enough to be seen live in it. Leafhoppers, bees, and flies feed and breed among the grass blades, and birds take much of their food from lawns. Among the leaves and stems, aphids and insect larvae suck on plant juices, while on the ground you can see the slimy trails of slugs. Beetles, snails, crickets, millipedes, spiders, and ants crawl along the ground. But most of the action is underground. In some lawns moles dig for grubs, and their tunnels are reused by mice and other small animals. Bacteria, fungi, algae, molds, and yeasts break down dead animals and plants, thus providing nutrients for the grass. Earthworms plow up and aerate the ground. It's a busy world—your lawn.

Science Digest, April 1984

The topic sentence states that perhaps a hundred animals live in your lawn. Then examples are given, first of ground-level inhabitants and then of underground inhabitants. A final clincher sentence adds emphasis.

☐EXERCISE 5

Here is the topic sentence for a paragraph.

One of the most interesting places to visit in Chicago is the Oriental Institute.

Which of the following statements support that topic sentence and therefore should be included in the paragraph? Mark them S (support). Check your answers with those at the back of the book.

_____ 1. The Oriental Institute is located on the University of Chicago campus.

_____ 2. It was established in 1919 and contains artifacts brought back from expeditions to Egypt and the Near East.

_____ 3. The most striking exhibit is the Great Winged Bull, which formed one side of a gateway to the palace in Khorsabad in Iraq.

_____ 4. The Bull was carved from a single piece of stone and weighs 40 tons.

_____ 5. It was crated and brought to the Oriental Institute, where a large opening had been left in one side of the building until the Bull could be moved in.

_____ 6. Also interesting are the clay tablets and papyrus scrolls that show the development of ancient systems of writing.

_____ 7. Mummies from Egypt have survived through the centuries because of the hot, dry climate in Egypt and are now on exhibit.

_____ 8. My high school ancient history course taught me something about Egyptian history.

_____ 9. Another interesting museum in Chicago is the Field Museum.

_____ 10. Free tours are given at the Oriental Institute daily.

Transition Expressions

Transition expressions within a paragraph help the reader move from one detail or example to the next.

☐EXERCISE 6

Here are some transition expressions that would make the following paragraph read more smoothly. In each blank in the paragraph write the transition expression you think appropriate. Check your answers with those at the back of the book.

Also	Then too
Furthermore	Therefore
In the first place	

I've finally decided to look for a part-time job. It's taken me a long time to make up my mind, but now I know I really want a job. _____, I've been living off my parents too long. Since they're having some financial difficulties at the moment, this is the time for me to help. _____, my kid brother has had a job for almost a year, and I'm embarrassed that he's done more than I have. _____, most of my friends have jobs, so I'll just be joining the gang. _____, even though a job will take some time from my studies, the practical experience I'll get in my field of electronics will be valuable. _____, tomorrow morning I'm going to begin looking.

Transition expressions are also important in an entire paper. They help the reader move from one supporting point to the next. It's a good idea to start each supporting paragraph in a paper with a transition expression such as

My first reason	Another example
Second	Then too
Also	Furthermore
Equally important	Finally
Even more important	

Assignment 4   Writing a Paragraph

For practice in writing paragraphs, choose one of the following topic sentences and add support sentences. You may alter each topic sentence slightly if you wish.

1. To get ahead in a job, one needs first of all a positive attitude.
2. The first step in waxing a car is to prepare the surface.
3. For me, getting up in the morning is a slow process.
4. One way I'm changing my eating habits is saying NO to junk food.
5. Our car pool is a boon to me mainly because of the friendships I make.
6. Epcot Center is more than an amusement park.
7. The main reason I'm majoring in computer science is . . .
8. The best part of my trip last summer was . . .

Before you start your paragraph, you might like to see a paragraph one student wrote.

The best part of my trip to St. Louis last summer was seeing the Arch. I had read about it and knew it was the tallest man-made monument in this country—even taller than the Washington Monument. It was designed by the famous architect Eero Saarinen. It stands not far from the Mississippi River and looks toward the Western frontier, which was explored by Lewis and Clark and other pioneers. It's a monument to them and to Thomas Jefferson, who encouraged them. To travel to the top of the Arch I got in a little capsule that holds five people. Eight of these capsules are joined together to make a trainlike vehicle that runs on tracks up one of the hollow curving legs of the Arch. In four minutes I was at the top and able to look out over the city and on to what was once the unexplored West. I won't soon forget that Gateway Arch.

The easiest and most natural way to practice writing paragraphs is to write them as part of a paper. You'll have an opportunity to practice writing paragraphs in the assignments that follow.

Assignment 5   A Decision I Have Made

Return to the two thesis statements with supporting points about a decision you are trying to make (p. 217). Choose one of those thesis statements to write about. Even if your mind is not really made up, you must choose one side for this assignment. You may mention in your introduction the arguments on the other side, but you must focus on one side if your paper is to be effective.

Here is a student paper on this assignment. Notice how each paragraph contains only one idea. The first paragraph presents the thesis. The two middle paragraphs present the two reasons. And the final paragraph sums up the whole paper. Notice, too, how specific details are used in each paragraph to show that the topic sentence is true.

GOODBYE, COLLEGE

I'm getting out. At the end of this semester I'm leaving college. Oh, I know all the reasons for not leaving—job security later, obligation to my parents, not being a quitter, and so on. But I've decided that my reasons for leaving are stronger than those for staying.

First of all, college is interfering with my career. Music is my life. Playing my French horn with the Galesburg Symphony once last year was more satisfying to me than a whole year of college. I had a chance to solo. It was great. And now I've been offered a chair in the Tri-City Symphony for next year. It's the best thing that's ever happened to me. My parents have said I can live at home, and I'll find a part-time job to supplement my orchestra pay. So why should I let college interfere?

Second, college bores me. Oh, I've gained a lot from my music composition and theory classes, but learning the chemical formula for petroleum or the dates of the Peloponnesian War or the method of figuring compound interest is for me a waste of time. And I flunked a speech course last year simply because I wasn't interested and was spending all my time practicing my horn.

Therefore I've decided to follow my gut reaction and do what I want to do rather than what somebody else thinks I should do. I may be making a mistake. I may come back eventually. But right now I want to get out, out, out. So at the end of the semester, it's goodbye, college.

Now write a rough draft of your paper, giving enough specific details in each supporting paragraph to convince your reader that you've made the right decision.

Then take Step VII, which follows.

VII. WRITE AND REWRITE

If possible, write your paper several days before it's due. Let it cool for a day. When you reread it, you'll see ways to improve it. After rewriting it, put it away for another day, and again try to improve it.

Great writers don't just sit down and write their books in a first draft. They write and rewrite. Hemingway said, "I wrote the ending to *A Farewell to Arms,* the last page of it, 39 times before I was satisfied." And Leo Tolstoy wrote, "I can't understand how anyone can write without rewriting everything over and over again."

Don't call any paper finished until you have worked through it several times. REWRITING IS THE BEST WAY TO LEARN TO WRITE.

Assignment 6   A Hobby

Describe some hobby you enjoy. It might be playing an instrument, participating in a sport, collecting things, making something. . . . Do some free writing first. Then limit your topic. Figure out a thesis statement, listing two or three reasons why you like the hobby or two or three steps in pursuing it. Then write a first draft.

Here is a student paper about a hobby—a second draft. As soon as this second draft was finished, the writer again began to improve it by

1. crossing out unnecessary words or expressions
2. adding more specific words or details

Can you see why the writer made each change? In the right-hand margin write the number (1 or 2) showing the reason you think the writer made each change. Analyzing the reasons for the changes will help you improve your own writing.

HOOKED ON BIRDS

I'm hooked on birds. Ever since I took an ornithology course two years

ago for my biology major, I've been a bird-watcher. ~~and I'll probably always~~

~~be one.~~ There are several reasons why I like my latest hobby.

First of all, I like getting out in nature and learning more about my world.

~~but I'd probably never do it if I weren't part of a bird-watching group.~~ I like

hiking
~~the hikes~~ into the ravine to see the early warblers and to ~~the lake~~ Spring Lake to see the

~~ducks.~~ migrating wood ducks.

Also I get an ego boost from being able to identify birds. I feel pretty smart if I spot the first purple martin of the season or the first loon on the lake. I've learned to identify a lot of birds not only by their colors and markings but ~~also~~ by their songs/ and even their flights.

But the main reason I like birds is that they bring surprises. ~~The~~ my biggest surprise ~~I ever had~~ came one morning last spring, when I was setting out some plants ~~I had bought for the border of~~ in our garden, and saw ~~I dug a little trench for them, and then I stopped a minute to rest and watch~~ a baby robin ~~that was~~ hopping about ~~among~~ in the bushes, near me. I knew it was immature by the brown spots on its breast. Besides, I had watched three baby robins emerge from their nest in our poplar ~~tree~~ the day before. ~~Now this baby was trying to make it on its own.~~ I didn't watch ~~it~~ the little robin long, however, for I was in a hurry to get my plants in. I got down on my knees and bent over, setting the plants in the ~~trench~~ ground and softly patting the earth around them. I was working quietly when suddenly I felt a light tap on my stooped back. It couldn't be. It simply couldn't be! I remained motionless for about 60 seconds. Then I made a slight movement—and the baby robin hopped off my back onto the ground. I could hardly believe what had happened to me. Evidently ~~it was so young~~ the little robin ~~that it~~ hadn't yet learned to fear people. I'll never forget that soft tap as it landed on my back. I'll bet even experienced bird-watchers have never had a robin light on their backs. In fact, one could probably go a lifetime without having such an experience.

Now do you see why I'm hooked on birds?

Can you explain how each change the author made has improved the paper? And did you notice how the paper is organized—with a thesis statement, three reasons, and a one-sentence conclusion?

Once again reread your paper about a hobby and see whether you can make any more improvements before you copy it in final form.

Here's a checklist of questions to ask yourself as you rewrite any paper:

1. Will my introductory paragraph make my reader want to read further?
2. Does each paragraph support my thesis statement?
3. Does each paragraph contain only one main idea?
4. Do I have enough specific details in each paragraph to support the topic sentence, and are all the details relevant?
5. Have I used transition expressions to tie my paragraphs together?
6. Does my concluding paragraph sum up my paper in a persuasive way?
7. Are my sentences properly constructed and clear?
8. Have I avoided wordiness and clichés?
9. Have I checked all questionable spellings?
10. Is my punctuation correct?
11. Is my title interesting?

VIII. PROOFREAD ALOUD

Finally, read your finished paper ALOUD. If you read it silently, you're sure to miss some errors. Read it aloud slowly, word by word, to catch omitted words, errors in spelling and punctuation, and so on. Make it a rule to read each of your papers **aloud** before handing it in.

As you do the following assignments, be sure to take each of the EIGHT STEPS TO BETTER WRITING.

Assignment 7   My Best Class

What was the best course you had in high school? What made it the best? Give two or three reasons, including enough details so that your readers will understand why you liked it.

Assignment 8   A Process Paper

Write a process paper, a "how to" paper. For example, you could tell how to lose 20 pounds, how to make a 10-minute dinner, how to improve your vocabulary, how to repair something. . . . After stating your thesis, list the steps in your process, giving enough details to make your method clear.

Assignment 9   Most Important to Me

What is the most important thing in the world to you—your family, a good job, health, religion, achievement, self-confidence, friendship . . .? You'll need to give your decision considerable thought. Then write a paper explaining your choice. Back up your thesis statement with two or three reasons, giving specific examples to help your reader understand your choice.

Assignment 10   Someone I Admire

What person do you especially admire and why? It might be a family member, a friend, a co-worker. . . . It should be someone you know fairly well so that you'll be able to give plenty of specific details. After you have done some free writing, choose two or three characteristics of that person that seem to you most important, and write your paper.

Assignment 11   Something I've Learned

Imagine you are talking to a friend. Explain something of value that you have learned in one of your courses. It might be a concept in psychology that makes you understand yourself better, an idea in accounting that you might use, an appreciation of some aspect of music that you had been unaware of before. . . . List two or three ways in which your new knowledge has been or will be helpful to you.

Assignment 12   A Thousand Dollars to Spend

Did you learn this rhyme in kindergarten?

> If I had a hundred dollars to spend,
>   Or maybe a little more,
> I'd hurry as fast as my legs would go
>   Straight to the animal store.

Think about what you would do if someone today gave you not a hundred but a thousand dollars. After giving the problem considerable thought, write a thesis statement with two or three reasons why you'd spend your money in a certain way. Then write your paper.

Assignment 13   An Achievement I'm Proud Of

Your achievement need not be winning a trophy or a prize. It more likely will be something quite private such as handling a difficult family situation or giving help to a person who desperately needed it or making yourself work until you achieved a goal.

Your thesis statement might have for its supporting points the reasons you are proud of your achievement or the steps you took to reach your goal.

Assignment 14   A Quotation for Me

Look through the quotations on pages 186–88 and 190–91 and pick one that especially appeals to you, either because you have found it true in your life or because you know you should follow its advice. Write a thesis statement explaining your reaction to the quotation, and back up your thesis with reasons or examples. Then write your paper.

Assignment 15   Advice That Changed My Life

What bit of advice has changed your life in either a big or a small way? It might be advice someone gave you or advice you read, but it should be something of which you could say, "My life will never be quite the same again." Tell your readers about it.

Assignment 16   My Opinion on a Current Problem

Choose one of the following problems and present your arguments for one side. Write a carefully thought-out thesis statement, supported by reasons, before you begin your paper. In your introduction or conclusion, you may mention briefly the reasons you can see for the opposite side.

A. A 10-year-old boy, hurt in an accident, has been living a vegetable existence for two years, kept alive only by a life-support machine. A group of specialists have agreed that there is no possibility that the child will ever regain consciousness. His parents have begged the doctors to remove the life-support machine, which is just prolonging their agony over their son, but the doctors cannot do so without a court order. Now a bill is before the state legislature that would make such a removal possible. Plenty of safeguards are provided in the bill to make sure that such action would be taken only in extreme cases and with the approval of a panel of specialists. If you were a legislator, would you vote for the bill or not? Why?

B. A football player from a poor family is eager to come to college and has applied for a scholarship. He has just barely made it through high school and would probably have difficulty with college courses although he is eager to do his best. He would be a great asset to the college football team, which is badly in need of good players. Should the only remaining college scholarship go to him or to another student, also from a poor family, who has an excellent scholastic record but no football talent? Why?

C. Holden, Mass., was the first town in which town officials and the union drew up a contract stating that all new police officers must be nonsmokers. Their reasoning was that the last three police officers to retire did so on disability pensions arising from high blood pressure or heart disease. Two of them smoked, a habit that health studies have linked to heart disease. The smokers' pensions will cost the town $36,000 a year (a large sum for a small town with limited resources) for as long as the pensioners live. One is in his early forties and the other in his early fifties. The town feels that the new contract will help avoid such costs in the future, and they say they have a right to hire whomever they wish with any qualifications they can justify. But opponents of the contract say that although the town has the right to forbid smoking on the job, it has no right to forbid smoking at home, that what an officer does at home is his own business. If your town were considering such a contract and you were on the town or union board, how would you vote? Why?

WRITING A SUMMARY

A good way to learn to write concisely is to write 100-word summaries. Writing 100 words sounds easy, but actually it isn't. Writing 200- or 300- or 500-word summaries isn't too difficult, but condensing all the main ideas of an essay or article into 100 words is a time-consuming task—not to be undertaken the last hour before class. If you work at writing summaries conscientiously, you'll improve both your reading and your writing. You'll improve your reading by learning to spot main ideas and your writing by learning to construct a concise, clear, smooth paragraph. Furthermore, your skills will carry over into your reading and writing for other courses.

Assignment 17   A 100-Word Summary

Your aim in writing your summary should be to give someone who has not read the article a clear idea of it. First read the article, and then follow the instructions given after it. Note that difficult words are defined in the margin.

Juvenile Juries

On the theory that it takes a teen-ager to know a teen-ager, juvenile juries in Denver are deciding the sentences given to some first-time offenders at the junior and senior high school level. The student jurors, volunteers all, pass sentence only on young people who have admitted guilt and signed contracts with the district attorney's office agreeing to abide by whatever penalty their peers impose. The juries handle such crimes as assault, possession of dangerous weapons or marijuana— all but the most serious. Typical sentences include unpaid community service, obeying tight curfews, avoiding the city's high-crime Capitol Hill area, attending school, getting a job or making full restitution in cases of theft or vandalism.

peer—person of the same age

restitution—giving back stolen goods

virtually—practically
opt for—choose

Given the choice, virtually all delinquents opt for sentencing by the youthful juries. "It's a lot better than going before a judge," says a 16-year-old who stole a car at knife point and was required to accept counseling and strict curfew rules for a year. "It was good to talk to someone who understands," he says of his jury.

The volunteer juries have turned out to be sensitive and imaginative. They have handed out some less-than-draconian but effective decrees: ordering a 17-year-old to join an athletic team; rebuking a father for belittling his son and "being part of the problem"; instructing a youth to write a letter of apology to a policeman. Says Zoralee Steinberg, who heads Denver County's "diversion" (*i.e.*, from the criminal justice system) program for young offenders: "The insight these kids have is amazing."

draconian—harsh (after Draco, a harsh Athenian lawgiver)

Denver County District Attorney Dale Tooley, who with Steinberg presented the jury program to the students last spring, believes one reason for its success is that the kids get a hearing within days after their arrest, instead of brooding for two or three months while awaiting conventional trial. More important perhaps is the program's philosophy that young people are responsible for their actions, coupled with close follow-up; the district attorney's office remembers delinquents on holidays and birthdays—even after they have left the program—and makes sure that they observe whatever curfew is set. So far, only one of the 55 offenders sentenced by juvenile juries has been charged with another crime.

Reprinted by permission from *Time*, The Weekly Newsmagazine; Copyright Time Inc. 1979.

A good way to begin a summary is to figure out the author's thesis statement, the main idea the author wants to present to the reader. Take time now to figure out the thesis of the article, and write it on a piece of scratch paper BEFORE READING FURTHER.

How honest are you with yourself? Did you write that thesis statement? If you didn't, WRITE IT NOW before you read further.

You probably wrote something like this: *In Denver, volunteer juvenile juries are sentencing some junior and senior high school first-time offenders.*

Using that thesis statement as your first sentence, summarize the rest of the article by choosing the most important points. Your first draft may be 150 words or more. Now cut it down by omitting all but the most important points and by getting rid of wordiness. Keep within the 100-word limit. You may have a few words less but not a single word more. By forcing yourself to keep within the 100 words, you'll get to the kernel of the author's thought and understand the article better.

When you have written the best summary you can, then, *and only then*, compare it with the summary on page 297. If you look at the model sooner, you will cheat yourself of the opportunity to learn to write summaries because once you read the model, it will be almost impossible not to make yours similar. So do your own thinking and writing, and *then* compare.

Even though your summary is different from the model, it may be just as good. If you're not sure how yours compares, ask yourself these questions:

Did I include as many important ideas?
Did I omit all unnecessary words?
Does my summary read as smoothly?
Would someone who had not read the article get a clear idea of it from my summary?

Assignment 18 A 100-Word Summary

Summary writing is excellent practice not only for the beginning writer but for the experienced writer as well because it teaches conciseness. Keeping within the 100-word limit, write a summary of this article in which the author first describes three indignities a blind person must endure and then states his thesis statement. No model is given in the answer section of the book for this summary nor for those that follow. You're on your own now. After you finish writing, simply ask yourself whether someone who hadn't read the article would get a clear idea of it from your summary.

Darkness at Noon
Harold Krents

Blind from birth, I have never had the opportunity to see myself and have been completely dependent on the image I create in the eye of the observer. To date it has not been narcissistic.

narcissistic—causing one to admire oneself excessively

There are those who assume that since I can't see, I obviously also cannot hear. Very often people will converse with me at the top of their lungs, enunciating each word very carefully. Conversely, people will also often whisper, assuming that since my eyes don't work, my ears don't either. For example, when I go to the airport and ask the ticket agent for assistance to the plane, he or she will invariably pick up the phone, call a ground hostess and whisper, "Hi, Jane, we've got a 76 here." I have concluded that the word "blind" is not used for one of two reasons: Either they fear that if the dread word is spoken, the ticket agent's retina will immediately detach, or they are reluctant to inform me of my condition of which I may not have been previously aware.

conversely—in the opposite way

retina—the membrane lining the eyeball

On the other hand, others know that of course I can hear, but believe that I can't talk. Often, therefore, when my wife and I go out to dinner, a waiter or waitress will ask Kit if "*he* would like a drink" to which I respond that "indeed *he* would." This point was graphically driven home to me while we were in England. I had been given a year's leave of absence from my Washington law firm to study for a diploma-in-law degree at Oxford University. During the year I became ill and

graphically—clearly

© 1976 by The New York Times Company. Reprinted by permission.

was hospitalized. Immediately after admission, I was wheeled down to the X-ray room. Just at the door sat an elderly woman—elderly I would judge from the sound of her voice. "What is his name?" the woman asked the orderly who had been wheeling me.

"What's your name?" the orderly repeated to me.

"Harold Krents," I replied.

"Harold Krents," he repeated.

"When was he born?"

"When were you born?"

"November 5, 1944," I responded.

"November 5, 1944," the orderly intoned.

This procedure continued for approximately five minutes at which point even my saint-like disposition deserted me. "Look," I finally blurted out, "this is absolutely ridiculous. Okay, granted I can't see, but it's got to have become pretty clear to both of you that I don't need an interpreter."

"He says he doesn't need an interpreter," the orderly reported to the woman.

The toughest misconception of all is the view that because I can't see, I can't work. I was turned down by over forty law firms because of my blindness, even though my qualifications included a cum laude degree from Harvard College and a *cum laude*—with honor good ranking in my Harvard Law School class. The attempt to find employment, the continuous frustration of being told that it was impossible for a blind person to practice law, the rejection letters, not based on my lack of ability but rather on my disability, will always remain one of the most disillusioning experiences of my life.

Fortunately, this view of limitation and exclusion is beginning to change. On April 16, 1976, the Department of Labor issued regulations that mandate equal-employment opportunities for the *mandate*—require handicapped. By and large, the business community's response to offering employment to the disabled has been enthusiastic.

I therefore look forward to the day, with the expectation that it is certain to come, when employers will view their handicapped workers as a little child did me years ago when my family still lived in Scarsdale.

I was playing basketball with my father in our

backyard according to procedures we had developed. My father would stand beneath the hoop, shout, and I would shoot over his head at the basket attached to the garage. Our next-door neighbor, aged five, wandered over into our yard with a playmate. "He's blind," our neighbor whispered to her friend in a voice that could be heard distinctly by Dad and me. Dad shot and missed; I did the same. Dad hit the rim: I missed entirely. Dad shot and missed the garage entirely. "Which one is blind?" whispered back the little friend.

I would hope that in the near future when a plant manager is touring the factory with the foreman and comes upon a handicapped and nonhandicapped person working together, his comment after watching them work will be, "Which one is disabled?"

Assignment 19   A 100-Word Summary

Write a 100-word summary of this article in which the President of the National Geographic Society describes a change being made in the landscape of our country.

Turning Rails into Trails
Gilbert M. Grosvenor

Pick any sunny day in spring, and you'll find northern Virginians relaxing in a most unusual park. Only a hundred feet wide, it stretches 44 miles from the suburbs of Washington, D.C., to the foothills of the Blue Ridge.

Called the Washington and Old Dominion Railroad Regional Park, this narrow ribbon of open space was created in 1978 from the railway's abandoned right-of-way.

Bicyclists love the park because it provides a continuous, paved corridor through town and countryside. Equestrians appreciate its separate horse path, joggers its refreshing scenery. Cross-country skiers take to the trail after snow has driven everyone else away.

About a million people a year spend some time in the park, making it the busiest converted rail trail in the United States.

The ingenuity of the basic concept—to create a linear park from an unused railroad—has always impressed me. Only recently . . . did I discover how extensively the idea has caught on. There are now nearly 150 such rail trails in 27 states, with an equal number in planning stages.

Other nations are also getting into the act. In Great Britain, nearly a dozen railroads have been similarly converted, as has part of an old logging line near Victoria, British Columbia.

Each trail has a different character. Some, like the W&OD, are mainly suburban, serving local residents. Seattle's 12-mile-long Burke-Gilman Trail is a popular commuting route for students bicycling to the University of Washington.

Other trails are distinctly rural, such as the Elroy-Sparta Trail in Wisconsin, which runs through 32 miles of rolling hills, railroad trestles, and dark tunnels. Campgrounds, bed-and-breakfast inns, restaurants, and bike-repair shops have sprung up along the trail to serve 50,000 vacationers a year.

What makes these trails possible is the fact that for decades America's rail system has been shrinking. In 1916 there were 270,000 miles of railway. By 1986 there were only 140,000. The nation's railroads aban-

From *The National Geographic Magazine*, May 1988. Reprinted by permission.

don about 3,000 miles a year. Changing rails into trails turns these losses into gains.

And yet only a fraction of the abandoned railroads are converted to this use. Most are consumed by highways, agriculture, or unplanned development. Private groups or public agencies seeking to create trails face difficult problems, such as resolving disputes over ownership of the rights-of-way; raising money to buy the land; coordinating planning among different political jurisdictions; and winning the support of adjacent property owners. Thus far, only one of every five attempts to create rail trails has succeeded.

As with the W&OD park, however, the effort is well worth it. Property values near suburban trails are often increased by their success, and new business is generated by tourists along rural trails. I believe these trails can play an important role in the creation of a new system of parklands, a vast network of linear open spaces reaching all across the country. . . .

Assignment 20   A 100-Word Summary

This brief article should not be difficult to summarize in 100 words.

How to Keep Air Clean
Sydney J. Harris

Some months ago, while doing research on the general subject of pollution, I learned how dumb I had been all my life about something as common and familiar—and essential—as air.

In my ignorance, I had always thought that "fresh air" was infinitely available to us. I had imagined that the dirty air around us somehow escaped into the stratosphere, and that new air kept coming in—much as it does when we open a window after a party.

This, of course, is not true, and you would imagine that a grown man with a decent education would know this as a matter of course. What *is* true is that we live in a kind of spaceship called the earth, and only a limited amount of air is *forever* available to us.

The "walls" of our spaceship enclose what is called the "troposphere," which extends about seven miles up. This is all the air that is available to us. We must use it over and over again for infinity, just as if we were in a sealed room for the lifetime of the earth.

No fresh air comes in, and no polluted air escapes. Moreover, no dirt or poisons are ever "destroyed"—they remain in the air, in different forms, or settle on the earth as "particulates." And the more we burn, the more we replace good air with bad.

particulates—tiny separate particles

Once contaminated, this thin layer of air surrounding the earth cannot be cleansed again. We can clean materials, we can even clean water, but we cannot clean the air. There is nowhere else for the dirt and poisons to go—we cannot open a window in the troposphere and clear out the stale and noxious atmosphere we are creating.

noxious—extremely harmful to living beings

From *For the Time Being* by Sydney J. Harris. Copyright © 1972 by Sydney J. Harris. Copyright © 1969, 1970, 1971, 1972 by Publishers-Hall Syndicate. Reprinted by permission of Houghton Mifflin Company.

Perhaps every child in sixth grade and above knows this; but I doubt that one adult in a hundred is aware of this basic physical fact. Most of us imagine, as I did, that winds sweep away the gases and debris in the air, taking them far out into the solar system and replacing them with new air.

The United States alone is discharging *130 million tons of pollutants a year* into the atmosphere, from factories, heating systems, incinerators, automobiles and airplanes, power plants and public buildings. What is frightening is not so much the death and illness, corrosion and decay they are responsible for—as the fact that this is an *irreversible process*. The air will never be cleaner than it is now.

irreversible— impossible to turn back

And this is why *prevention*—immediate, drastic and far-reaching—is our only hope for the future. We cannot undo what we have done. We cannot restore the atmosphere to the purity it had before the Industrial Revolution. But we can, and must, halt the contamination before our spaceship suffocates from its own foul discharges.

Assignment 21   A 100-Word Summary

Summarize this editorial from the *New York Times* that gives U.S. citizens a glimpse of their neighbor to the north.

O (Backward) Canada!
Karl E. Meyer

Canada suffers from the curse of proximity. There is an abiding belief in the United States that some 18 million English-speaking Canadians are in fact closet Americans, while 6 million French Canadians are pretty much the same except that they speak French. Most Americans can probably name more Russian than Canadian leaders, and have a clearer picture in their minds of Tehran than of Ottawa or Toronto.

proximity—closeness

Yet even a fleeting visit to those cities in the populous Ontario heartland reveals an interesting truth. The surface is familiarly North American, but it bears about the same relation to the American present as a 1930s movie on some late show. The tempo is gentler; civilities flourish; the note of menace is missing.

populous—densely populated

True, Canada is in a bitter debate over the very nature of its federalism. But that argument has not poisoned personal relations and by American standards, the tone is polite. It seems, in short, as if Canada has somehow stumbled into a workable past. This is apparent in many ways, large and small. Let me count some of them:

federalism—distribution of power between central government and provinces

1. Canadians tipple differently. A popular order is "rye and coke," a concoction Americans dismiss as quaint.

tipple—drink liquor

2. With two exceptions, graffiti are unknown in Toronto, even in the subways. Exception one: the University of Toronto, where spray-paint makes an American feel at home. Exception two: a stenciled slogan, seen everywhere, that says "Post No Bills."

3. Toronto has discovered an amazingly fuel-efficient and pleasant form of urban transportation. It is called the streetcar. (Cab drivers complain that the city's public transportation is far too reliable, cheap, and pleasant.)

urban—city

From *The New York Times*, December 26, 1980. Copyright © 1980 by The New York Times Company. Reprinted by permission.

4. There is no provincial sales tax on books. The Ontario Government believes that books and reading have a positive social value.

5. In the province of Ontario, the basic college course takes three years instead of four, a timetable that is arguably 25 percent easier on schools, students and parental purses.

arguably—open to argument

6. The Canadian Broadcasting Corp. permits television commercials but does not permit commercial interruptions on the evening national news. "We don't think disasters should be used as a 'selling' environment," a CBC newscaster explained.

7. In downtown Toronto, new office buildings are required to set aside some space for apartments, so that the central city doesn't turn into a dark and lifeless canyon after work. There is a belief that commercial and residential zones should be mingled.

. . . . .

8. All handguns are subject to registration, and their sale is strictly controlled. Not once in Canada's 113-year history as a self-governing country has a prime minister, provincial premier, or pop singer been assassinated. (There have been two major political murders: Quebec's Minister of Labor, Pierre Laporte, in 1970; and D'Arcy McGee, a member of Parliament and a father of Confederation, in 1868.) In Canada as a whole, the homicide rate has been steadily declining; 631 were recorded in 1979—a third of last year's 1,733 in New York City alone.

A backward place, Canada.

WRITING AN APPLICATION

Assignment 22   A Letter of Application

You may not need to do much writing in the career you have chosen, but almost certainly you will at some time need to write a letter of application. Write a letter of application now, either for a job this coming summer or for a job you might want to apply for after you finish college. Then write a separate resume. Follow the forms given here.

000 First Street
Lansing, Michigan 48914
February 2, 1991

Mr. John Blank, Director
Chicago Park District
425 East McFetridge Drive
Chicago, Illinois 60605

Dear Mr. Blank:

I saw your ad in the Chicago Tribune for a swimming
instructor in the Park District Recreation Department
for the coming summer, and I'd like to be considered
for the position.

I am a freshman at Lansing Community College,
majoring in special education and minoring in
physical education.

I have had considerable experience teaching swimming--
first with the St. Louis Department of Parks and
Recreation, then at Camp Nesbit in Houghton, Michigan,
and finally last summer at the day camp of Harris
YWCA in Chicago.

It was in the last job that I discovered what I
really like to do. I found that teaching swimming to
physically and mentally handicapped children was most
rewarding, and I'd be happy if I could have at least
some classes of handicapped children in your swimming
program. The supervisor at Harris YWCA is going to
write you about my work.

I am enclosing a resume and will call you soon to
see whether I may come for a personal interview.

Sincerely,

Jane Doe

Jane Doe

RESUME

Jane Doe
000 Main Street
Lansing, Michigan 48914
Telephone 000-000-0000

WORK EXPERIENCE

1990 summer	Swimming instructor at day camp of Harris YWCA, Chicago. Worked with physically and mentally handicapped children.
1989 summer	Cabin counselor at Camp Nesbit, Houghton, Michigan. Also taught swimming.
1988 summer	Swimming instructor with the St. Louis Department of Parks and Recreation.

EDUCATION

1989-90	Freshman at Lansing Community College, Lansing, Michigan. Majoring in special education; minoring in physical education.
1985-89	Student at Lansing High School, Lansing, Michigan.

ACTIVITIES

Swimming	Won second place in an intercollegiate swim meet at Lansing Community College in 1989.
Bowling	

REFERENCES

Ms. Arlis Adams, Director
Harris YWCA
6200 South Drexel, Chicago, Illinois 60637

Mr. Lars Larson, Director
Camp Nesbit
Houghton, Michigan 49931

Mr. John Murphy, Director
County of St. Louis Department of Parks
    and Recreation
7900 Forsyth Boulevard
St. Louis, Missouri 63105

WRITING AN EVALUATION

Assignment 23   An Evaluation of My Performance

Do five minutes of free writing in preparation for writing a short paper on your performance in this course. Don't evaluate the course—it may have been bad or good—but simply evaluate how you performed. Although you may need to mention some weakness or strength of the course, the emphasis must be on how you reacted to that weakness or strength.

Don't be afraid to be honest. This isn't an occasion for apple-polishing. If you've gained little, you'll write a better paper by saying so than by trying to concoct phony gains. Someone who has gained little may write a better paper than someone who has gained much. How well the paper is organized and whether there are plenty of specific examples will determine the effectiveness of the paper.

Before starting your paper, write your thesis statement, listing your supporting points. If you've made gains, state the kinds—gain in writing skill, gain in confidence, gain in study habits . . . Or, if you've gained little, state the reasons why—lack of time, lack of interest, getting off to a bad start . . .

Since no one will have all gains or all losses in any course, you may want to include in your introduction or conclusion a sentence about the other side.

Answers

Answers

Words Often Confused (p. 10)

EXERCISE 1

1. new, it's, all ready
2. Its, an, it's
3. an
4. It's, forth
5. course, know, effect, our
6. hear
7. an, our
8. choose, or, our
9. Our
10. do, an, have

EXERCISE 2

1. our, new
2. chose, an
3. accept, advice
4. it's, do, desert
5. no
6. conscious, are, here
7. break, our
8. course, have
9. know, effect
10. already

EXERCISE 3

1. our
2. It's, our
3. conscious
4. an
5. hear, or
6. know
7. forth
8. Already
9. choose, do
10. course, already, know

EXERCISE 4

1. no
2. are
3. already
4. know
5. it's, accept
6. forth
7. except
8. new
9. course, an
10. an

EXERCISE 5

1. an, new
2. knew
3. our
4. course, already, knew
5. conscious
6. know
7. have
8. choose, course
9. hear, it's, does, effect
10. do

EXERCISE 6

1. course
2. knew, or
3. know, an
4. have, course, does
5. It's, clothes

6. course, conscious
7. do, know
8. desert
9. choose
10. hear, are, our

EXERCISE 7

1. an, new
2. it's, our
3. an, its
4. conscious, know
5. chose

6. It's, course
7. new
8. does
9. already
10. accepts, effect, our

EXERCISE 8

1. our, break
2. have, an
3. except, clothes
4. know, advice
5. course, knew

6. chose, our
7. No, it's
8. fourth, effect
9. accept, advice
10. already, new

EXERCISE 9

1. have, or
2. accept
3. chose, its
4. new
5. desert, have

6. It's, affect, our
7. our, knew
8. hear, advise
9. conscious, all ready
10. fourth, an

EXERCISE 10

1. choose, new
2. conscious, our
3. advice, know, courses
4. It's, fourth
5. course, have

6. already
7. feel, an
8. clothes, choose, complement
9. compliments, effect
10. does

More Words Often Confused (p. 19)

EXERCISE 1

1. an
2. knew
3. know, it's
4. There
5. course

6. past
7. here
8. are
9.
10. no, effect, here

EXERCISE 2

1. already
2. course
3. accept, advice
4. are
5. its, are

6. their
7. no
8. it's, its
9. too, too
10. already

EXERCISE 3

1. knew, there, an, than
2. write, an
3. past, threw
4. no, Then, woman
5. quite
6. where
7. there, loose
8. know, whether, or, moral
9. conscience, do, through
10. too, do, than, two

EXERCISE 4

1. our, break
2. it's, already, quite
3. chose, knew
4. There
5. principal
6. It's, weather
7. through, conscious, peace, quiet
8. effect
9. there, do, have
10. passed, too, Our, an

EXERCISE 5

1. have, our
2. were, where
3. quiet, then
4. except, too
5. woman, You're, here
6. already, their, dessert
7. woman, piece, accept
8. course, compliments
9. passed, effect, new
10. weather, through, our

EXERCISE 6

1. Our, an
2. where, there
3. to, two
4. Our, It's, does
5. its, its
6. course, its
7. Its
8. an, past
9. their, are, quite
10. knew, there

EXERCISE 7

1. led, its, fourth
2. then, morale
3. have, their
4. course, lose
5. quite, accept
6. effect, morale
7. whose, then, past
8. principal, an
9. Through, new
10. they're, to

EXERCISE 8

1. you're, advise, your
2. too, an, effect
3. lose, principal
4. you're, already, courses, then
5. advice, personal
6. too, write, passed
7. It's, do, too
8. know, choose, right
9. Whether, course
10. feel, you're

EXERCISE 9

1. new, know
2. hear, whether
3. write, then, passed, an
4. principal, personal, where
5. already, too, there
6. morale, personnel
7. advice, quite
8. course, than
9. woman
10. accept, it's

EXERCISE 10

1. an
2. know, through
3. than
4. Your
5. knew

6. there
7. are
8. Your
9. It's
10. do

Proofreading Exercise (p. 24)

. . . jagged rocks. Then I noticed . . . I knew these were hermit crabs . . . could barely fit into their shells . . . Animals that carry their homes with them . . .

Contractions (p. 26)

EXERCISE 1

1. Haven't, there's
2. Doesn't
3. It's, we've
4. wasn't, wasn't
5. it's

6. aren't, they're
7. we're
8. It's, it's
9. there's, it's, there's
10. It's

EXERCISE 2

1. Aren't, you've
2. it's, I've
3. I'm, I'll, I'm
4. won't, you've
5. don't, it's, that's

6. I've, they're
7. hadn't, didn't
8. It's, we've, isn't
9. they're, I've, can't
10. it's, you're

EXERCISE 3

1. Where's, can't, isn't
2. he's, He's
3. Doesn't, he's
4. doesn't
5. I've

6. How's
7. they're, don't, isn't
8. That's
9. Let's, He's, There's
10. I'm, he'll, he's, He's

EXERCISE 4

1. I'd
2. It's
3. It's
4. it's
5. there's

6. It's
7.
8.
9. wouldn't, hadn't
10. that's

EXERCISE 5

1. don't, that's
2. Its
3. There's
4. It's
5. isn't

6. It's
7. that's
8. wasnn't
9.
10. didn't

EXERCISE 6

1. I've
2. It's, that's, there's
3. I've
4. It's, that's
5. it's

6. there's
7. It's
8. that's, that's
9. That's
10. It's

EXERCISE 7

1. I've
2.
3. There's
4. I've, there's
5. It's

6. I've
7. can't
8. it's (first one)
9. didn't
10. I'm, what's

EXERCISE 8

1. we've
2. didn't, doesn't
3. I've
4. there's
5. didn't, can't

6. doesn't
7. it's
8. aren't, they're
9. it's
10. It's

EXERCISE 9

1. I've, there's
2. It's, I'll
3. I'm, there's, that's
4. It's
5. it's, it's

6. hadn't
7. wouldn't, hadn't
8. wasn't
9. wasn't
10. it's

EXERCISE 10

1. you'd
2. you're, you'd
3. you're, you'd
4. weren't
5. that's

6. I've
7. we're
8. I'm, that's, we're
9. Everybody's, shouldn't
10. We've, we're, it's, we'll

Possessives (p. 34)

EXERCISE 1

1. parents'
2. Wilsons'
3. Carla's
4. Carla's
5. Wilson's

6.
7. Friday's, Wilsons'
8. Wilsons'
9. men's, women's
10. Wilsons'

EXERCISE 2

1.
2. men's, women's
3. Miles'
4.
5. Julie's, Kevin's

6. Michael's, Miles'
7. Mrs. Wilson's
8. Carla's, mom's
9. dad's
10. day's

EXERCISE 3

1. Saturday's
2. men's, boys'
3. mother-in-law's
4.
5. children's

6. husband's
7. grandfathers'
8. men's
9. child's
10. money's

EXERCISE 4

1. Philip's
2. day's
3. students'
4. father's
5. mother's

6.
7. instructor's
8. semester's
9. mother's
10. Philip's

EXERCISE 5

1. students'
2. instructor's, students'
3. Sue's, child's
4. student's
5. Terry's

6. Ashley's
7. students'
8. Jason's
9. students'
10. Angela's

EXERCISE 6

1. Mike's
2.
3. Ted's
4. Tony's
5. Rudy's

6. friends'
7. father's
8. dad's
9. dad's
10. Mike's, father's

EXERCISE 7

1. winter's
2. fox's
3. squirrel's
4. cardinal's
5. winter's

6.
7. hare's
8. hare's
9. deer's
10. deer's

EXERCISE 8

1. world's
2.
3. Canada's
4. Wipper's
5. Wipper's, father's

6. Canada's
7. Rick Nash's
8. people's
9.
10. Kanawa's

EXERCISE 9

1. Men's, Women's
2. Men's, Boys', Women's, Girls'
3.
4. Women's
5. evening's

6. Keats'
7. Club's, Shakespeare's
8. Men's
9. Men's, boys'
10. College's

EXERCISE 10

1. world's, Germany's
2.
3. today's
4. architect's
5.

6. architect's, Europe's
7.
8. architect's
9. craftsmen's
10. Germany's

Review of Contractions and Possessives (p. 38)

EXERCISE 1

1. It's
2. didn't
3. wasn't, didn't
4.
5. UCRecycle's

6. year's
7. UCRecycle's
8.
9. UCRecycle's
10. Isn't

EXERCISE 2

1. I've
2. women's, men's, boys', girls'
3. men's, women's, children's
4. Someone's, else's
5. We've, baby's, toddler's, child's

6. that's
7. uncle's
8. It's
9. I've, collector's, I'm
10. I'm, it's

Rule for Doubling a Final Consonant (p. 42)

EXERCISE 1

1. putting
2. controlling
3. admitting
4. mopping
5. planning

6. hopping
7. jumping
8. knitting
9. marking
10. creeping

EXERCISE 2

1. returning
2. swimming
3. singing
4. benefiting
5. loafing

6. nailing
7. omitting
8. occurring
9. shopping
10. interrupting

EXERCISE 3

1. beginning
2. spelling
3. preferring
4. interpreting
5. hunting

6. excelling
7. wrapping
8. stopping
9. wedding
10. screaming

EXERCISE 4

1. feeling
2. murmuring
3. turning
4. weeding
5. subtracting

6. streaming
7. expelling
8. missing
9. getting
10. stabbing

EXERCISE 5

1. forgetting
2. misspelling
3. fitting
4. planting
5. pinning

6. trusting
7. sipping
8. flopping
9. reaping
10. fighting

Progress Test (p. 43)

1. B	6. A	11. A
2. A	7. B	12. B
3. A	8. B	13. B
4. B	9. B	14. A
5. B	10. A	15. B

Finding Subjects and Verbs (p. 56)

EXERCISE 1

1. bison roamed
2. Bison is
3. herds roamed
4. Herds extended
5. they blocked

6. they derailed
7. head is
8. bison is
9. It weighs
10. It travels

EXERCISE 2

1. hide furnished
2. meat furnished
3. pioneers shot
4. bison was
5. government established
6. bison roamed
7. bison roamed
8. parks developed
9. bison are
10. They roam

EXERCISE 3

1. I took
2. trees grow
3. tree is
4. tree grows
5. roots extend
6. bark is
7. wood resists
8. trees live
9. They are
10. tree is

EXERCISE 4

1. Great Wall is
2. It is
3. wall is
4. It runs
5. That is
6. road runs
7. watchtowers are
8. towers were
9. Sentries kept
10. wall was

EXERCISE 5

1. waterfall is
2. It drops
3. jungle surrounds
4. one saw
5. pilots spotted
6. explorers reached
7. Victoria Falls is
8. It is
9. Niagara Falls is
10. (You) visit

EXERCISE 6

1. people fear
2. spiders are
3. spiders are
4. They destroy
5. Spiders are
6. They calculate
7. web is
8. spider lies
9. end is
10. Dew makes

EXERCISE 7

1. crane is
2. cranes were
3. flocks dwindled
4. causes were
5. projects disturbed
6. cranes nested
7. They wintered
8. Service protected
9. Railway changed
10. cranes numbered

EXERCISE 8

1. Edison invented
2. He spoke
3. device worked
4. People marveled
5. phonograph was
6. It gave
7. Skeptics tested
8. People listened
9. they applauded
10. machine recorded

EXERCISE 9

1. phonograph played
2. Edison disapproved
3. He intended
4. Edison considered
5. phonograph is
6. grandparents had
7. They had
8. they wanted
9. they discarded
10. machine is

EXERCISE 10

1. ways are
2. One is
3. Another is
4. way is
5. families are
6. One is
7. family is
8. family includes
9. family is
10. orchestra is

Subjects Not in Prepositional Phrases (p. 62)

EXERCISE 1

1. Most ~~of my friends~~ are ~~in this English course~~.
2. All ~~of us~~ realize our need ~~for a refresher course~~.
3. ~~In high school~~ most ~~of us~~ did little writing.
4. Every one ~~of us~~ needs practice ~~in writing~~.
5. A few ~~of us~~ need help ~~with punctuation~~.
6. Many ~~of us~~ need a review ~~of sentence structure~~ too.
7. Practically all ~~of us~~ need some work ~~on spelling~~.
8. The goal ~~of the course~~ is not beautiful writing.
9. The goal ~~of the course~~ is simply clear writing.
10. ~~With a lot of practice~~ we hope to write better.

EXERCISE 2

1. ~~In the country~~, springtime is frog time.
2. ~~From ponds and puddles and ditches~~ come the calls ~~of the frogs~~.
3. Only the males sing.
4. ~~On warm evenings~~ they sing to attract their mates.
5. A frog closes his mouth ~~in calling~~.
6. He pushes air ~~from his lungs into his mouth~~ and ~~through special openings to vocal sacs or resonance chambers~~.
7. The resonance chambers give volume ~~to the call~~.
8. Each species ~~of frog~~ has its own distinctive note.
9. The spring peeper, ~~for example~~, emits a high piping note.
10. Dozens ~~of them~~ produce a noise ~~like the sound of sleigh bells~~.

EXERCISE 3

1. The largest animals ~~in the world~~ are the whales.
2. ~~Beside them~~ a 10-ton elephant is small.
3. None ~~of the ancient dinosaurs~~ were as large as whales.
4. The dimensions ~~of the blue whale, for example,~~ are enormous.
5. Many ~~of the blue whales~~ are 100 feet long.
6. Some ~~of them~~ weigh 150 tons.
7. Whales are mammals.
8. Therefore all ~~of them~~ come ~~to the surface of the water for air.~~
9. The sperm whale stays ~~under water for half an hour at a time.~~
10. Most whales, however, come ~~to the surface~~ more frequently.

EXERCISE 4

1. ~~In the Antarctic Ocean,~~ whales are numerous.
2. There they feed ~~on the abundant plankton of the Antarctic waters.~~
3. Most ~~of the time~~ they swim ~~near the surface of the water.~~
4. But sometimes they dive half a mile ~~in search of food.~~
5. The stomach ~~of a whale~~ is enormous.
6. The stomach ~~of one small orca whale~~ contained 24 seals.
7. Sometimes whales leap ~~from the water~~ just ~~for fun.~~
8. ~~In fish~~ the tail fin is vertical.
9. ~~In whales~~ the tail is horizontal.
10. Most whales make sounds ~~under water.~~

EXERCISE 5

1. Seventy percent ~~of the total surface of the earth~~ is water.
2. The Pacific is the largest ocean ~~on earth.~~
3. It represents 45 percent ~~of the world's ocean surface.~~
4. The deepest part ~~of the oceans~~ is ~~in the Marianas Trench in the Pacific.~~
5. There the water is 35,760 feet deep ~~in some places.~~
6. The average depth ~~of the Pacific~~ is 14,000 feet.
7. ~~Under the ocean~~ there are also mountains.
8. The highest ~~of the Pacific underwater mountains~~ is ~~between Samoa and New Zealand.~~
9. It rises 28,500 feet ~~from the seabed.~~
10. That underwater mountain comes ~~within 500 feet of the height of Mount Everest.~~

EXERCISE 6

1. Einstein showed
2. He did talk
3. he hated
4. He annoyed
5. family moved

6. Einstein spent
7. he decided
8. he failed
9. he was admitted
10. rebelliousnes continued
    He cut
    He tinkered
    He incurred

EXERCISE 7

1. scientists pioneer
2. farmer became
3. Wilson A. Bentley developed
4. he collected
5. He photographed

6. he learned
7. he found
8. Most are
9. Each develops
10. Several combine

EXERCISE 8

1. spokes make
2. Each contains
3. Bentley photographed
4. Bureau bought
5. Manufacturers copied

6. work used
7. People called
8. he became
9. He wrote
10. scientists made

EXERCISE 9

1. one is
2. remains are
3. burials date
4. Some are
5. Many are

6. Many contain
7. reason is
8. Dickson excavated
9. state built
10. thousands come

EXERCISE 10

1. Visitors look
2. Each is
3. loudspeaker describes
4. Visitors see
5. Archeologists determine

6. expectancy was
7. mortality lowered
8. archeologists determine
9. They had
10. exhibits span

More about Verbs and Subjects (p. 67)

EXERCISE 1

1. store was
2. Woolworth pondered
3. He had had, had worked
4. location was
5. He heard

6. inhabitants were
7. Woolworth took, explored
8. he closed, opened
9. store was
10. store was

EXERCISE 2

1. Bunky Knudson was
2. Bunky was given
3. Bunky was
4. father told
5. Bunky hurried
6. car was waiting
7. Bunky took
8. it was
9. Bunky knew
10. It had been

EXERCISE 3

1. woman phoned
2. She complained
3. piano had been banging
4. It was
5. manager was, did
6. He told
7. Paderewski would be giving, was practicing
8. woman sat, listened
9. She considered
10. nothing had changed

EXERCISE 4

1. anything can be reproduced
2. It would be
3. reason is
4. (You) imagine
5. star would be
6. vastness is
7. we can see
8. we do think
9. Milky Way was
10. We know, know

EXERCISE 5

1. Galileo was
2. He turned, realized
3. It is composed
4. sun is, is
5. I have learned
6. I can find
7. Milky Way is
8. galaxies can be counted
9. stars are
10. they are strewn

EXERCISE 6

1. Sir James Jeans made
2. (You) imagine
3. Space is crowded
4. Time is
5. sun was born
6. light started
7. That was
8. light is reaching
9. it has been traveling
10. (You) try

EXERCISE 7

1. industries were destroyed
2. Edison lost
3. record was consumed
4. Edison stood, watched
5. he walked, made
6. value is, All are destroyed, We can start
7. he did start
8. man might have surrendered
9. Edison could see
10. Adversity became

EXERCISE 8

1. Some, I, took, visited
2. One was
3. It is
4. few were
5. Many have been moved
6. hotel is
7. All are furnished
8. One is
9. one can buy
10. bottles are

EXERCISE 9

1. Many are
2. some are
3. we saw
4. we had
5. we took

6. It took
7. Riding was
8. we returned, bought
9. melodrama ended
10. (You) visit, learn

EXERCISE 10

1. Mojave Desert covers, is
2. It includes
3. Death Valley was named
4. trees, cactuses, mountains, plains, lake can be seen
5. Mojave is, attracts

6. Mojave bakes, freezes, is populated
7. rat can live, is
8. pronghorn, jackrabbit, rat live
9. wren, roadrunner are
10. Mojave has been called

Correcting Run-together Sentences (p. 74)

EXERCISE 1

1. country is, nation is
2. Joggers pound, dancers carry
3. Runners cross, Hikers scale
4. Skiers, skateboarders, jumpers, skaters add, Exercise is
5. We hiked, views were

6. We followed, it was
7. we stopped, We could climb
8. We saw, went
9. cabin was, firewood was
10. we were, spent

EXERCISE 2

1. mosquitoes. It
2. effect. Roaches
3. roaches,
4. down. Thus
5. bodies,

6. in,
7. caterpillars. Therefore
8. thatching. Then
9. happenings. The
10. nature. The

EXERCISE 3

1. lasers.
2. acronym. An
3.
4. traveling,
5. aimed. It

6. surgery,
7. century. Only
8. laser. Someday
9. weaponry. Thus
10. stages,

EXERCISE 4

1. hobby. It
2. words. Our
3. letters,
4. of letters. Thus
5. English. We

6. letters,
7. word. It
8. pyres. The
9. fire,
10.

EXERCISE 5

1. obtained,
2. money,
3. money. A
4. *trivial*. It
5. three,

6. roads. Farmers'
7.
8. trivial,
9. fun. Their
10. dictionary. It

EXERCISE 6

1. word. Its
2. Greece,
3. nude,
4. *gymnasium*. We
5. Greek,

6. words. *Moccasin*
7. Mandarin. It
8. English. It
9. today. About
10. Egyptian. Some

EXERCISE 7

1. undertaking,
2. plow,
3. people,
4. farm. By
5. Russia;

6. scarce. Every
7. money. They
8. industry,
9. worldwide,
10. five,

EXERCISE 8

1. 1920s. They
2. developed. It
3. snow. It
4. snowmobiles,
5. everywhere. Nevertheless

6. large;
7. them,
8. cattle,
9. rabbits. Foxes
10. them. Also

EXERCISE 9

1. extinction.
2. population,
3. Bible. Now
4. road,
5. foxes,

6.
7. weeks,
8. species. Only
9. food. Otherwise
10. 1970,

EXERCISE 10

The first state to honor working people was Oregon. It set aside a day for them in 1887. In 1894 Labor Day became a national legal holiday. It marks the end of summer. Of course summer really ends with the autumnal equinox about September 23. After that the nights become longer than the days. Soon leaves begin to fall, and that gives another name to autumn. It's the only season with two names; it's as often called fall as autumn. Autumn usually has pleasant weather, but surprises may occur. It was −7°F in Yellowstone National Park on September 24, 1926, and Denver got 21.3 inches of snow on September 27, 1936. The weather can also go to the other extreme. San Diego reached 111°F on September 26, 1963. Of course in the southern hemisphere the trend is the opposite, and the first signs of spring are appearing.

Correcting Fragments (p. 82)

EXERCISE 1

1. When I <u>was</u> 10, <u>we</u> <u>moved</u> to a farm.

2. Ever since <u>I</u> <u>can remember</u>, <u>I</u> <u>dreamed</u> of living on a farm.

3. <u>I</u> never <u>thought</u> that my <u>dream</u> <u>would come</u> true.

4. When <u>we</u> <u>had finished</u> unpacking, <u>we</u> <u>put</u> all the furniture in place.

5. <u>We</u> <u>worked</u> until <u>we</u> <u>were</u> exhausted, but <u>we</u> <u>were</u> happy.

6. Then <u>we</u> <u>went</u> out to the yard, <u>which</u> <u>interested</u> us most.

7. When <u>we</u> <u>saw</u> the old well, <u>we</u> immediately <u>had</u> to pump some water.

8. Then <u>we</u> <u>ran</u> out into the orchard <u>that</u> <u>was</u> behind the house.

9. Then <u>we</u> <u>picked</u> almost a bushel of apples <u>that</u> <u>had fallen</u> to the

   ground.

10. When <u>it</u> <u>began</u> to get dark, <u>we</u> <u>knew</u> that our <u>exploring</u> <u>would have</u> to

    wait for another day.

EXERCISE 2

1. Since I had always wanted to see Alaska
2. which goes through the Yukon Territory in Canada
3. which is 1,500 miles long
4. although some go by ship
5. Because Denali National Park is Alaska's main tourist attraction
6. which is the tallest mountain in North America
7.
8. that the mainland of Alaska at its most western point is only 50 miles from the mainland of Russia
9. which is 6,640 miles in length
10. which is the largest city

EXERCISE 3

1. that go more than a thousand miles into the Bering Sea
2. than it is from San Francisco to New York
3. which is more than twice the size of Texas
4. where bush pilots can land small planes
5. as their ancestors did
6. although the number of salmon has been decreasing
7. which was about two cents an acre
8. that the land was a worthless waste of ice and snow
9. which means "great land"
10. when it became the 49th state

EXERCISE 4

1. which has more than three million devotees
2. who are summer backpackers or bicyclists or joggers
3. that a few years ago had only 100 to 200 cross-country skiers
4. whereas cross-country skiing can be done anywhere
5. who enjoy cross-country skiing
6. than you might think
7. that require various kinds of waxes for different temperatures
8. that is grooved with patterns to provide both grip and glide
9. who had difficulty getting to their offices
10. which used to be a poor cousin to downhill

Only the fragments (not the sentences) are dealt with in these answers. There are several ways to change each fragment into a sentence. Your sentence may differ from the one given here and still be a good sentence.

EXERCISE 5

1.
2. He's a person whom everyone loves and admires.
3. She's a person whose leadership and experience are outstanding.
4.
5. I had to study when I could have been doing something much more exciting.
6. When I had done everything possible and felt discouraged, I turned to him.
7.
8. I went jogging, which always puts me in a better mood.
9. Whenever I want exercise, I jog.
10. I took up cross-country skiing, which I really enjoy.

EXERCISE 6

1. I decided to go home for the weekend because I hadn't been home for weeks.
2. I decided to walk because it's only about two miles.
3. Since I don't get enough exercise, walking is good for me.
4. Because I have an office job, most of my time is spent sitting.
5. As I was walking down the avenue, there in front of me I saw a gray fluffy kitten.
6. Since I can never resist a cuddly kitten, I stopped and picked it up.
7. Because I was in a hurry, I finally put it down again.
8. When I eventually got to our house, I was surprised at the new car in the driveway.
9. It was a new station wagon that my mother had been wanting for months.
10. Immediately I dashed into the house because I wanted to hear her comments.

EXERCISE 7

1. When we were driving through New Mexico last fall, someone told us about Carlsbad Caverns.
2. Although I had never heard of them before, I was immediately interested.
3. Even though I've visited several national parks, I'm always eager to see another.
4. We decided to see the park even though it meant driving several hundred miles out of our way.
5. Since the weather was good, the drive was pleasant.
6. When we finally got there, we had to wait an hour for a tour to begin.
7. Then we hiked along a trail that was more than 700 feet underground.
8. One room that is called The Big Room is the largest subterranean chamber in the world.
9. It has a ceiling that is as high as a 22-story building and floor space that would hold 14 football fields.
10. The amazingly beautiful formations that have been formed by dripping groundwater include stalactites, stalagmites, columns, and draperies.

EXERCISE 8

1. Because my courses are difficult, I need to improve my study habits.
2. Since part of my problem is lack of planning, I'm going to make a list of things to do.
3. If I'll study one subject at a time, then I won't get hopelessly bogged down.
4. If I'll turn off the stereo, then I can concentrate better.
5. When I want to concentrate, I need complete quiet.
6. Since I have a paper to write for tomorrow, I'll begin it first.
7. Then I'll put my first draft aside while I study another subject.
8. When I come back later to my first draft, I'll see ways to improve it.
9. Then I'll again put it aside while I work on something else.
10. After my paper goes through several drafts, then finally it will be finished.

More about Fragments (p. 89)

EXERCISE 1

1. I made a resolution to work four hours on my studies every night.
2. The important thing was to get every assignment in on time.
3.
4. I progressed rapidly, getting more and more ideas as I went along.
5.

6. I hoped that my paper would sound better when I read it in the morning.
7. To get an idea across, don't distract the reader with sentence errors.
8.
9.
10. Search the dictionary for the spelling of every word.

EXERCISE 2

1.
2. That is all that anybody can do.
3. There was nothing more to say.
4. There was nothing to say that had not already been said.
5. The notice on the bulletin board stated that there would be play practice that evening.
6. He kept hoping all the time that she would call him again.
7. He was a person who was always ready to help.
8. I took up sailing, which I have always enjoyed.
9. I haven't had so much fun in years.
10. I realized that our next move was important.

EXERCISE 3

I came across the little house by accident as I hiked through the green rolling hills. It sat on one side of a clearing of waving brown grass with the trees all around fencing in the little area like a yard. I looked inside the battered wooden planks that framed the opening where a door had once been. The sun shone through the one window opening and through the cracks in the walls onto the warped wooden floorboards, which did not quite keep the grass from poking through. I wondered who had built the house. I guessed an old man might have lived there alone. I imagined him hoeing his garden and wiping the sweat from his brow with an old red handkerchief. How long ago was that? And how many years had the house stood empty without him? It would stand for a few more years, but eventually the trees would retake the clearing, and the grass would grow through the old planks. Some night the boards would blow over to rejoin the earth. And new trees would grow where . . .

EXERCISE 4

No one knows who invented eyeglasses. Monks first used a magnifying glass that was laid flat on a manuscript. At the end of the thirteenth century someone put two magnifying glasses in frames, riveted the frames together, and balanced them on the bridge of the nose. But people found that keeping the glasses on the nose was difficult. Then in the sixteenth century Spanish spectacle makers attached to the frames silk ribbons that were looped over the ears. The Chinese added to the ends of the ribbons little weights that dangled on the chest and helped to hold the glasses in place. In 1730 an optician in London invented rigid sidepieces that finally kept the glasses firmly on the nose. Bifocals, which Benjamin Franklin invented in the 1780s, were the next step in the evolution of glasses. At first people were self-conscious about wearing glasses. Even in the first part of the twentieth century, Dorothy Parker wrote her famous line: "Men seldom make passes at girls who wear glasses." Only in the latter part of the twentieth century have glasses become an item of style with . . .

EXERCISE 5

"Baked Necks."
We cook 'em. . . . Then we eat 'em. . . .
What are they? Why, they're bacon and eggs, of course! They're just the right . . .

EXERCISE 6

. . . It's an experience rich in lifelong friendships and memories.
As part of International Youth Exchange, a Presidential Initiative for peace, you travel to another country, live abroad with your new host family, learn new skills, go to new schools, make new friends, and return . . .

EXERCISE 7

. . . Where else can you reach out to so many different marine animals to talk to, to touch, to laugh with, to love, to understand each other? And where else can you and your family be so entertained by your new animal friends with a whole day of fabulous shows, shows, shows? It can only happen at Sea World, where you can talk to the animals, and they can talk to you.

EXERCISE 8

Did you know that used glass bottles and aluminum cans can be transformed into new ones?
And did you know that yesterday's newspaper can be transformed into tomorrows?

EXERCISE 9

The eagle has landed in Oklahoma and Mississippi, Georgia and Alabama, where few bald eagle nests have produced young in the last 50 years. Using precious eggs and dedicated effort, the Sutton Avian Research Center is successfully raising eaglets from fuzzy to fierce and releasing . . .

Review of Run-together Sentences and Fragments (p. 94)

1. Our land is more valuable than your money. It will last forever. It will not perish as long as the sun shines and the water flows, and through all the years it will give life to men and beasts. It was . . .

2. Green is the clue to creating a garden. The most beautiful gardens in the world show few flowers. They depend . . .

3. There is a school of psychiatrists who think that "blowing one's top" is a good way to work off something bad. This view is held mostly by psychiatrists who cannot control their own tops. There is nothing to it. Blowing one's top serves no good purpose. One blowing sets the habit more firmly for the next blowing. Children blow their tops. It is a childish adult . . .

4. Who says youth can't accomplish things? Newton was 24 when he formulated the law of gravitation. Victor Hugo had taken three prizes at the French Academy before he was 20. Jefferson was 33 when he drafted the Declaration of Independence. Charles Dickens was 25 when he wrote *Oliver Twist*. McCormick was 23 when he invented the reaper.

5. But older people have done things too. Verdi at 74 produced his masterpiece *Otello* and at 85 the famous *Ave Maria*. Goethe at 80 completed *Faust*. Tennyson at 85 wrote "Crossing the Bar." Benjamin Franklin at 81 took part in the Constitutional Convention. Frank Lloyd Wright created the Guggenheim Museum in New York City when he was close to 90. Grandma Moses took up painting in her seventies and . . .

6. Some long-distance phone calls are routed through satellites that are orbiting 23,000 miles above the earth. If you make a call, for example, from the Midwest to California, your voice might travel over land lines to a satellite earth station in Illinois. Then it would travel up to a satellite. Next it would travel back down to an earth station near Los Angeles. Finally it would travel over land lines to the listening party. All . . .

7. Before the days of Shakespeare, there were no forks. A servant would bring the meat to the table on the spit or rod on which it had been impaled for cooking. The servant would hold the meat while the guest cut off chunks and laid them on a huge slab of thickly cut bread that served as a plate. Then the meat was eaten with the fingers. Toward . . .

8. Many state names come from Indian words. Wisconsin comes from a word meaning "meeting place of waters." Minnesota comes from a word meaning "sky-tinted water." Dakota comes from a word meaning "friends" or "allies." Mississippi . . .

9. Coral reefs are the largest structures in the world made by living things. They are composed of fire corals, lace corals, bead corals, bubble corals, organ-pipe corals, and many others. The largest coral reef is the Great Barrier Reef in Australia, which stretches more than a thousand miles. The chief enemy of such reefs is man. Anchors . . .

"HERE, BOY"

Early one morning I was sailing out of the harbor on my way to do some salmon fishing. I was quietly enjoying the calm water and gray mist over the distant shoreline when to my surprise I saw that I was not alone. Just a few feet away I saw a dog in the water calmly staring at me with big black eyes.

"A dog out here? This far from land? Impossible!" I thought. But there he was with big eyes, whiskers on his nose, and a sort of friendly curiosity.

I didn't know what to do. I slowed my boat and started thinking I should try to help him to shore. He just kept staring, effortlessly floating there with just his face showing above the calm water. I looked at him, and he looked at me.

"Here, boy," I said, trying to coax him closer so I could save him. He just kept watching, so I slowly swung my boat closer. But he slipped beneath the surface and didn't reappear.

"He's drowned," I thought as the minutes ticked by while I waited for him to surface.

"What was he doing out here in the early morning anyway?" I asked myself. Then I realized how silly I'd been. I turned up my motor and with a smile headed off for fishing. That was no dog with those big eyes and long whiskers. I'd been trying to save a curious harbor seal.

Using Standard English Verbs (p. 100)

EXERCISE 1

1. learn, learned
2. like, liked
3. needs, needed
4. opens, opened
5. starts, started
6. suppose, supposed
7. wants, wanted
8. has, had
9. is, was
10. do, did

EXERCISE 2

1. decided
2. work, signed
3. arrived, was
4. arrived, were
5. need, offers
6. intend, hope
7. enrolled, want
8. work, live
9. play, attend
10. hope, want

EXERCISE 3

1. do, assigns
2. discover, are
3. use, don't
4. watch, listen
5. benefits, imitate
6. talk, use
7. is, helps
8. is, intend
9. decided, expect
10. asked, agreed

EXERCISE 4

1. intend, plan
2. want, want
3. expect, is
4. were
5. practiced
6. intend, is
7. have, is
8. is, lived, moved
9. has, were
10. look, talk

EXERCISE 5

1. were
2. were, weren't
3. listened
4. were
5. talked, discussed
6. talked, attended
7. played, play
8. attended, played
9. had
10. practices, plans

EXERCISE 6

1. worked, liked
2. mowed, trimmed
3. learned
4. requires
5. was patient, helped
6. showed
7. helped
8. learned
9. worked, had
10. hope

EXERCISE 7

1. received, decided
2. realized, needs
3. had
4. intends
5. is, studied
6. plans
7. are
8. ask
9. drops
10. is

Helping Verbs and Irregular Verbs (p. 108)

EXERCISE 1

1. trying, need
2. walked, walk
3. intend, do
4. walking, walking
5. walked, walked
6. walks, walks
7. walked, does
8. started
9. walk, walk
10. know, is

EXERCISE 2

1. surprised, eat
2. known, eat
3. realized, works
4. live, eat
5. used, were
6. learned, use
7. filled, lures
8. prevented
9. is, escape
10. touches, clamp

EXERCISE 3

1. used
2. reading
3. found, helps
4. begun
5. paid
6. helped
7. noted
8. seen, used
9. noticed, used
10. did

Avoiding Dialect Expressions (p. 110)

EXERCISE 1

1. that book anywhere
2. isn't any use looking anymore
3. Maybe I never brought
4. don't have a book
5. well
6. am not going
7. I have never been . . . I did o.k.
8. says that anyone who doesn't do well just isn't
9. Anyway . . . doesn't
10. that book . . . any problem

EXERCISE 2

1. were
2. dad said . . . somewhere
3. we are doing . . . aren't
4. saw animals we had never
5. was a New . . . zoo has never
6. we have been having
7. an art . . . themselves
8. saw a Shakespeare play
9. haven't seen anything yet; there are
10. This city has

EXERCISE 3

1. had never *or* hadn't ever
2. she and **I went . . . wanted**
3. have seen him *or* saw him
4. doesn't know anything
5. anybody
6. tried . . . was doing
7. have done well . . . watched
8. said she enjoyed
9. any hits or anything
10. I ate popcorn and had

EXERCISE 4

1. were never
2. had ever gone
3. decided . . . had entered
4. worked . . . did real well
5. discovered there were . . . felt sure she had
6. saw
7. came
8. finished . . . were attached
9. gave . . . attached
10. said they sure are

Proofreading Exercise (p. 113)

IT'S THE KID IN ME

~~It's~~ hard to buy presents for friends. I hate trying to think of something clever. Of course I can always get after-shave for men and perfume for women if I can't think of anything else, but those are such usual gifts.

Now my little nephew is another matter. He's ~~he's~~ five, and I go wild getting toys for him. I walk into a toy store and get all excited about toy rockets

and building kits and battery-powered trucks. ~~last~~ *Last* Christmas I got him a
combination-lock coin bank and a water pistol and a yo-yo and a rubber-
band-powered airplane. Of ~~coarse~~ *course* I had to try them all out for hours just
to make sure that he'd like them. I suppose it's the kid in me that makes
me still enjoy playing with such things, but I hope I never grow ~~to~~ *too* old to
get a kick out of toys.

    Actually I still play. ~~Its~~ *It's* just that I have a real car now and build real
things when I play.

Progress Test (p. 114)

1. A	6. B	11. A
2. B	7. A	12. A
3. B	8. B	13. A
4. B	9. A	14. B
5. A	10. B	15. B

Making Subjects, Verbs, and Pronouns Agree (p. 117)

EXERCISE 1

1. have	6. has
2. has	7. are
3. are	8. has
4. is	9. plays, play, hope, their
5. are	10. sing, enjoys

EXERCISE 2

1. are	6. measures
2. have	7. estimate
3. has	8. wants
4. look	9. thinks, are
5. have	10. want

EXERCISE 3

1. is	6. are
2. explain	7. is
3. is	8. is
4. don't	9. is
5. are	10. help

EXERCISE 4

1. is
2. have, are
3. has
4. are, are
5. want

6. include
7. use
8. takes
9. intend
10. looks

EXERCISE 5

1. have, form
2. live
3. are
4. think
5. realize

6. puts, contributes
7. are
8. are
9. cancels
10. hope

EXERCISE 6

1. have
2. is
3. doesn't
4. have
5. have

6. was
7. has
8. doesn't
9. have
10. doesn't

Choosing the Right Pronoun (p. 122)

EXERCISE 1

1. I
2. me
3. her
4. me
5. me

6. I
7. her
8. us
9. us
10. We

EXERCISE 2

1. I
2. me
3. me
4. I
5. I

6. me
7. he nor I
8. he and I
9. us
10. He and I

EXERCISE 3

1. I
2. her
3. I
4. me
5. Debbie and I

6. me
7. I
8. I
9. me
10. I

EXERCISE 4

1. us
2. me
3. I
4. him
5. I
6. I
7. us
8. I
9. he and I
10. me

EXERCISE 5

1. us
2. me
3. I am
4. us
5. My friend and I
6. I
7. He
8. him and me
9. him and me
10. he and I

Making the Pronoun Refer to the Right Word (p. 125)

EXERCISE 1

1. The manager said, "I may be transferred to another state."
2. The instructor said, "You haven't proofread the paper carefully."
3. Although it won't be easy, I'm going to save my summer wages for college.
4.
5. Her mother said, "Why don't you wear your new suede jacket to the game?"
6. He said to the foreman, "I'm too inexperienced for the job."
7. She said to her girlfriend, "You are being too pessimistic."
8. He said to his dad, "My clothes are shabby."
9. Her daughter was having some problems when they talked that noon.
10. His lawyer said, "I don't know how the case will turn out."

EXERCISE 2

1. The salesman said, "I made an error in addition."
2. As I put the food in its dish, the canary began to sing.
3. He said to his brother, "Your tape recorder isn't working properly."
4. Diane said to Becky, "I received a letter from my boyfriend."
5. He said to his friend, "I am probably making a mistake in taking the job."
6. As soon as the mechanic changed the tire, I drove the car home.
7. Whenever I approached the high chair, the baby screamed.
8. My car swerved into a fence, but the car wasn't damaged.
9. She said to her sister, "I need a new hairstyle."
10. In that course we studied only two novels that I really enjoyed.

EXERCISE 3

1. She was in tears when her sister finally arrived.
2. I read about the famous basketball coaches and players and hope someday I'll be a coach.
3. The congressman said, "Give my bill some more thought."
4. He said to the supervisor, "My design doesn't work."
5. The manager said to the clerk, "I made an error in the day's total."
6.
7. She said to her sister, "I need to take time to think about the problem."
8. It turned out to be a good thing that I had refused to listen to my dad's advice.
9. The coach said to the captain, "I blamed the wrong player."
10. He got a scholarship because, although he is poor in chemistry, he is a whiz at math.

EXERCISE 4

1. My decision to major in business wasn't easy.
2. Since her great ambition is to be a figure skater, she spends all her time practicing figure skating.
3. His son said, "You're getting poor mileage from your old car."
4.
5. It was disappointing that the weather was cold on the trip.
6. She was underweight when she went to visit her daughter.
7. They quit spanking the child, but spanking was just what the child needed.
8. My parents disapproved of my changing jobs.
9. He said to the filling station attendant, "I've lost the cap to the gas tank."
10. When he showed his father the smashed taillight, his father was upset.

EXERCISE 5

1. The Japanese have exquisite little gardens.
2. He said, "Dad, you're a clever manager."
3. His instructor said, "I was mistaken."
4. Finally finding a job made me happy.
5. As I came near its nest, the bittern flapped its wings and flew away.
6. He was really worried when the doctor talked with him.
7. She said to her mother, "My entire wardrobe needs updating."
8.
9. The president was annoyed because only a few attended the meeting.
10. Persons experiencing chest pains and shortness of breath should be encouraged to rest, and they should be watched until their symptoms have completely disappeared.

Correcting Misplaced or Dangling Modifiers (p. 129)

EXERCISE 1

1. Because I studied . . .
2. Before leaving for vacation, I had to write . . .
3. While I was sitting . . .
4. Completely exhausted, I let my books fall . . .
5.
6. I'll eat almost anything that is . . .
7. The next day, sleepy from too many late nights, I failed to follow . . .
8.
9. Excited about my trip, I boarded the bus just before it took off.
10. After I had been away for two years . . .

EXERCISE 2

1. Last summer my parents bought a cottage with no inside plumbing.
2. Because it needed . . .
3. When I got home, I discovered Mom mopping the kitchen floor, and I decided to help her.
4.
5. As they stepped gracefully . . .
6. Then as they darted . . .
7. I watched some sparrows chirping continuously as they built . . .
8.
9. I sat and watched a blue jay boldly . . .
10. Then I put food that we had not eaten back . . .

EXERCISE 3

1. When I was . . .
2. We gave some of our old furniture that we had no use for . . .
3. Flying over Kansas, we saw all the little farms below.
4. In our new house the dining room has a buzzer under the table for . . .
5.
6. Because I was excited . . .
7. After I had mowed . . .
8. In our neighborhood a dog must be on a leash and . . .
9. Later that day a truck arrived with the cement to make . . .
10. The next day my father bought a book for $6.95 that . . .

EXERCISE 4

1. Our house, where I was born . . .
2. When I was . . .
3.
4. After I had played in . . .

5. Swimming in the shallow water, I cut . . .
6. I saw my favorite kite hanging . . .
7. When I was . . .
8. The man was obviously unnerved by the little mongrel that was barking . . .
9. While our neighbor was on a week's vacation, his . . .
10. We read in the morning paper that . . .

EXERCISE 5
1. I thought my wife looked elegant dressed . . .
2. On my tie I had . . .
3. Standing at the top of the gorge, I could see how the earth had . . .
4.
5. As I suddenly became . . .
6. Skidding on the icy pavement, my car almost hit . . .
7. By clever steering, however, I just . . .
8. Years later . . .
9. Our office intends to hire an efficient secretary after . . .
10. Because the man was obviously a crook, the banker refused him . . .

Using Parallel Construction (p. 135)
EXERCISE 1
1. and riding away into the sunset.
2. and a filling station.
3. and to get some practice . . .
4. and a large garden.
5. and reading science fiction . . .
6. never taking any responsibility.
7. and new experiences.
8. to lower taxes.
9.
10. and a supreme concern.

EXERCISE 2
1.
2. and of course had to buy . . .
3. and also gave us . . .
4.
5. and then phoned . . .
6. and would meet me . . .
7. and made sure I had . . .
8.
9. and actually made . . .
10.

EXERCISE 3

1. and carrying . . .
2. and empties . . .
3. and junked cars here and there.
4. and trying not to ram each other.
5. and granaries.
6.
7. and up-to-date fire controls.
8. 300 feet wide, 30 feet high, and 1,600 miles long.
9.
10. hawks, snapping turtles, and sometimes even deer and bald eagles can be seen.

EXERCISE 4

1. and education . . .
2. and also guided tours.
3.
4. and learned . . .
5. and then warms . . .
6.
7. and also one of the few
8. and which is just south . . .
9. and sometimes the rare trumpeter swan.
10. and that we'd save . . .

EXERCISE 5

1. and enlightening.
2. and asked . . .
3. and to get the newspapers . . .
4. and his keen intelligence.
5. and now spends . . .
6. and discuss the issues . . .
7. and handshakes . . .
8. and then write . . .
9. and even some books . . .
10. and also pretty knowledgeable.

EXERCISE 6

. . . graze on the lawns, and devour the shrubbery. . . . Visitors come to Waterton to watch the deer, to feed them, and also to photograph them.

EXERCISE 7

. . . lacked compansionship, and missed . . . waterfalls, trees, and even patches of bamboo.

EXERCISE 8

1. Getting a college education is important to me.
    1.
    2.
    3. I'll have a good time at college.
2. Knowing how to write clearly will be of value after college.
    1.
    2. It will give me a sense of satisfaction.
    3.
3. The 55 mph speed limit should be retained nationally.
    1.
    2.
    3. It has made motoring more pleasant.
4. I've decided to major in biology.
    1.
    2. Plenty of jobs are available for one trained in biology.
    3.

Correcting Shift in Time (p. 141)

EXERCISE 1

1. doesn't
2. came
3. doesn't
4. gives
5. explained
6. ended
7. asked
8. opened, took
9. came
10. gave

EXERCISE 2

. . . the fans gave him a standing ovation and began . . .

EXERCISE 3

. . . what I was talking about. He offered . . .

EXERCISE 4

. . . But when I reached for my wallet, it wasn't there. I checked. . . .
After dinner while I was sitting watching TV and trying to forget, the
phone rang, and a voice said . . .

EXERCISE 5

. . . when I finished each little project . . . gave me a feeling of satisfaction after I'd finished them.
    I learned a lot . . . I learned that every Friday . . . I learned how
long a day . . . I learned that my bike . . . I learned that the customer
. . . And I learned to drink . . .

EXERCISE 6

. . . where customers gave a list . . . The clerk then got the items from
the shelves, made out a charge slip, packaged the items, and gave . . .
where customers paid cash . . . they were carrying got too heavy . . .

Correcting Shift in Person (p. 146)

EXERCISE 1

1. but I soon got . . .
2. they can always get good jobs.
3. it will be a valuable . . .
4. you will get . . .
5. one should . . .
6. Anyone who wants to be in the next dramatic production should sign . . .
7. Students should . . . Otherwise they won't get all their . . .
8. because I should
9. To keep your figure . . .
10. gives me a feeling . . .

EXERCISE 2

1. She received lots of presents.
2. I was worried after his accident.
3. When I opened the hood of the car, I could see what was the matter.
4. A chipping sparrow lighted in front of us so close that we could see its white eye stripes.
5. Walking two miles a day is good for one's health.
6. A good garden takes constant work.
7. The ticket must be picked up half and hour before departure time.
8. His letter meant much to me.
9. When I opened the door, I could hear the commotion.
10. By the time we had gone a hundred miles, we could see the mountains.

EXERCISE 3

It can be flung farther than a Frisbee . . . Someone has said that if an Aerobie were tossed off Mt. Everest . . .

EXERCISE 4

. . . The crowd was so great that we . . . As the riders went by, we could feel . . . Just watching such a contest made us realize . . .

EXERCISE 5

. . . but it's easy to see a butterfly . . .

EXERCISE 6

There were few roads a car could be driven on . . . Also one could travel only 2 mph . . . By 1924 his Model T two-seater could be bought . . .

EXERCISE 7

. . . The first thing to do is stop . . . if one takes the trouble . . . Often there wasn't as much disagreement as there at first seemed to be.

EXERCISE 8

. . . it's shrill call can be heard everywhere . . . During their five weeks aboveground, the cicadas damage . . . After the five weeks, however, the cicadas' rasping calls are heard no more.

EXERCISE 9

. . . If one doesn't listen . . . By jerking one's mind back each time it wanders, it's possible to train it . . . Simply by recognizing the problem and working at it, one can . . .

Correcting Wordiness (p. 152)

EXERCISE 1

1. Many students are working their way through college.
2. Never before have I seen such spectacular fireworks.
3. Many of us use more words than we need in writing.
4. For 10 days in February I couldn't get my car out of my driveway because of the snow.
5. Part of her problem is that she has never had to take any responsibility.
6. Most children spend too much time watching TV.
7. The New Zealand kiwi sleeps 20 hours a day.
8 Skiing has never interested me.
9 The evening paper told about another killing.
10. We no longer carry the tape recorder you requested.

EXERCISE 2

1. My letter may not bring results.
2. All employees will meet at 11 A.M. tomorrow in the staff lounge.
3. The planning for the party was left up to Jennifer and me.
4. The supervisors may revert to the 1978 rules.
5. A strong protest followed the president's announcement.
6. Please conserve paper to save money and to save our trees.
7. He works as much on vacation as on his job.
8. I am going into law enforcement because it offers opportunities for advancement.
9. With all the cures being discovered, most fatal diseases may soon be conquered.
10. National health insurance would be valuable.

EXERCISE 3

1. I've learned from experience to watch for new investment opportunities.
2. Therefore I'm moving my savings account from the People's Bank to the Citizens' Bank.
3. Both banks have excellent reputations.
4. But the Citizens' Bank now offers a gift to anyone opening a new account.

5. For that reason I am shifting my account.
6. I happened to be in the neighborhood when that old warehouse was destroyed by fire.
7. During the fire, the building was surrounded by onlookers.
8. The firefighters did all they could to save the building.
9. Those who hope to rehabilitate the neighborhood may be glad of the loss.
10. Now they won't have to consider what to do with that old building.

EXERCISE 4

This booklet is published by the Accident Prevention Committee to alert employees to the hazards they may be exposed to. There will be fewer accidents if each employee will read this material thoroughly and take the suggested precautions.

Avoiding Clichés (p. 156)

EXERCISE 1

1. I've been trying to help my small son with his homework, but it's difficult.
2. He's smart, but he doesn't want to do his schoolwork.
3. If I do get him to sit down in front of his books, he'll work for five minutes and then bolt.
4. If I catch him, he says he hates schoolwork and that he wants some play.
5. I tell him that when I was his age I was frightened by teachers and barely made it through school.
6. I tell him that in this world he needs an education, but he won't listen.
7. I fear he'll realize his mistake one of these days.
8. Last night I got him to write out all his math problems, but soon he was sleepy, and I had to give up.
9. Of course I'm not getting very far.
10. But maybe he'll grow up to be a great success in spite of my concern.

Review of Sentence Structure (p. 157)

1. B	6. B	11. B	16. B	21. A
2. A	7. B	12. A	17. B	22. A
3. A	8. B	13. A	18. A	23. B
4. B	9. B	14. B	19. A	
5. B	10. B	15. A	20. B	

Punctuation (p. 163)

EXERCISE 1

1. game;
2. home. He
3. late. Luckily,
4. ball. Then
5. defense. Consequently

6. game. Nevertheless
7. wishbone;
8. team. Therefore
9. touchdown. Thus
10. seen.

EXERCISE 2

1. farmer. It
2. matter;
3. earthworms. Many
4. surface;
5. dark. Also

6. earthworm?
7. lost. This
8. plants:
9.
10. nature. It

EXERCISE 3

1. language?
2. inconsistencies?
3. inconsistent;
4. words:
5. *ough;*

6. words:
7. sound;
8. publications.
9. spelling. The
10. simply. It

EXERCISE 4

1. red?
2. red. Bulls
3. lived?
4. today. It's
5. length. It's

6. helicopter?
7. helicopter. It
8. envy? It's
9. easy. All
10. days. He

EXERCISE 5

1. Catalogue. The
2. prices:
3. $1.93. Their
4. defects;
5.

6. garment. Lace-trimmed
7. cents. Men's
8. following:
9. statement:
10. notice:

EXERCISE 6

1. years. During
2. mystery. They . . . eggs. Then
3. sand. Then
4. instinct;
5. water. They

6. following:
7. lot. They
8. turtles. They
9. female. They
10. go. They

EXERCISE 7

1. built:
2. Bay. The
3. Pipeline. The
4. pipeline. The
5. gravel. Furthermore

6. difficulties:
7. going. Only
8. lands. It
9. wildlife. Herds
10. dollars. Environmentalists

EXERCISE 8

1. life. Civilization
2. resources. They
3. legally. The
4. them. It
5. dams. The

6. developers. The
7. species. Most
8. helpless. Now
9. action. They
10. world. Their

EXERCISE 9

1. blue-collar. Today
2. too. The
3. efficient. Some
4. tradition;
5. way:

6. worked?
7. enthusiastic. Managers
8. ways:
9. benefits:
10. yet?

EXERCISE 10

1. coins. He
2.
3. treasury. The
4. 1864. In
5. following:

6. world. The
7. Greeks. A
8. sky. All
9. earth. Only
10. culture. Its

Commas (Rules 1, 2, and 3) (p. 170)

EXERCISE 1

1. vacation,
2. lakes, the forests,
3. Duluth, Minnesota,
4. house,
5. turns,

6. rooms, a two-car garage,
7. vegetables, enough fruit to give away,
8. jobs,
9. place,
10. there,

EXERCISE 2

1. summer,
2.
3. trees, flowers, and fountains,
4. avenue,
5. Minneapolis,

6. 43,000,
7. boundary,
8. summer,
9. floor,
10.

EXERCISE 3

1. crumbling,
2.
3. shoulder,
4. tomb,
5. sweat,

6. climbing,
7. needed,
8. $1.50,
9. needed,
10. crumble,

EXERCISE 4

1. appointment,
2. Arctic, in tropical forests, in deserts, on mountains,
3. pavements, in cornfields,
4. small,
5. seeds,
6. jaws,
7. liquids,
8. food,
9.
10. sometime,

EXERCISE 5

1. birds,
2. fly,
3. Antarctic, they did not need to fly,
4. swim,
5.
6. water,
7. sociable,
8.
9. tendency,
10. molested, but they have little fear of people, are easily trained,

EXERCISE 6

1. discovered,
2.
3. continent,
4. agriculture, timbering, mining,
5. destroyed,
6. highways, cut forests, dammed rivers,
7. century, thousands of square miles of pine, oak,
8. state,
9. remaining,
10. acres,

EXERCISE 7

1.
2. today,
3. highways, shopping centers,
4. land,
5. settled, about 500 species of plants and animals have become extinct,
6. lands,
7. awareness, to reassess national values,
8. year,
9.
10. planning,

EXERCISE 8

1. earth,
2. oil,
3. wind, weather, life, death,
4. corn, wheat, beans,
5. away,
6. people,
7. experts,
8. loss,
9. centuries,
10.

EXERCISE 9

1. nuisance,
2.
3. disease,
4. Screens, insecticides,
5. attempts,
6. time,
7. hatch,
8. lived,
9. flies,
10. week,

EXERCISE 10

1.
2. fast,
3. corners,
4. sailors,
5. us,

6. set,
7.
8.
9. seen,
10. so,

Commas (Rules 4, 5, and 6) (p. 178)

EXERCISE 1

1.
2. *Twist*, which I am reading now,
3. *Oliver*,
4. Dickens, the author,
5. Twist, the hero of the novel,

6. Sikes,
7. Oliver,
8.
9. *Copperfield*,
10. Dickens,

EXERCISE 2

1. Whales, most people assume,
2. whale, the humpback,
3.
4. birdsongs, which . . . seconds,
5. song, however,

6. following year, however,
7. compose, it seems,
8. waters, for example,
9. year, however,
10. fact, moreover,

EXERCISE 3

1. would, it seems,
2. choruses,
3. one, however,
4. Each, it seems,
5. hydrophone,

6. have, furthermore,
7.
8. whale,
9. whale,
10. song, moreover,

EXERCISE 4

1.
2. Indianapolis,
3.
4. race, which . . . 1911,
5. hour,

6. pounds,
7. stock-car race,
8. races, which . . . roads,
9. race, which . . . acceleration,
10. race, which . . . 1895,

EXERCISE 5

1.
2.
3. pines,
4. trees, it is surmised,
5.

6.
7.
8. monarchs, which are
   short-lived,
9. then, one wonders,
10. birds,

EXERCISE 6

1. was, I think,
2.
3. interior, it is reported,
4. 300, which . . . events,
5. cold, however,

6. year, though,
7. last, the
8.
9. −67°F, a level
10. Then, as we know, Max,

EXERCISE 7

1. Building, which . . . Washington,
2. L'Enfant, a French-born engineer,
3.
4. Thornton,
5. Jefferson,

6. slow, however,
7. Court, which . . . Philadelphia,
8. Latrobe,
9. 1814, however, the . . . Capitol,
10. Boston,

EXERCISE 8

1.
2. Capitol, which . . . size,
3.
4. the great new dome, which . . . masterpiece,
5. Freedom," a 19½-foot sculpture,

6. Capitol,
7. Crowds, which . . . summer,
8. Capitol, which has 540 rooms,
9.
10. Brumidi,

EXERCISE 9

1. Rock,
2. size, however,
3. "Hey,
4. mass, which . . . old,
5.

6. interesting, furthermore,
7. Indians, who . . . country,
8. remains, which . . . people,
9. important, furthermore,
10. longer, however,

Review of the Comma (p. 183)

1. in 1979 *Voyager 1* and *Voyager 2* satellites sent back to earth pictures of Jupiter,
2. The pictures showed that Jupiter is surrounded by at least 13 moons,
3. The four largest moons are named Io, Europa, Ganymede,
4. Because they were discovered by Galileo,
5. They are large enough to be called small planets,
6. Now, however, the *Voyager* cameras have shown that these four moons are all different in age, composition,
7. The surface of Callisto, the outermost of these moons,
8. Ganymede has a cracked, cratered, icy crust, which may indicate moonquakes,
9. Io, the innermost of the Galilean moons, is a brilliant orange-red and is scarred with plateaus, dry plains, highlands, fault lines,

10. Because of these colors and scars,
11. The most surprising discovery of *Voyager 1,* however,
12. Thus it is now known that Saturn, Uranus,
13. During the tense hours of the close encounters with Jupiter,
14. *Voyager 2* then went on to take pictures of Saturn in 1980, Uranus in 1986,
15. Triton, Neptune's largest moon,
16.
17.
18. For example, astronauts can someday land on Mars, but they can never land on Venus,
19. Robotic voyages began in 1989 with the launching of the spacecraft Magellan,
20. Robots will try to puzzle out the origin and evolution of the solar system,
21. Besides giving us data about our universe,

Quotation Marks (p. 186)

(Titles that are underlined in writing or typing are italicized in printing.)

EXERCISE 1

1. When James Garfield was president of Hiram College in Ohio, a father once said to him, "I want to talk to you about my son."
2. "Yes?"
3. "I want to know," said the father, "whether there is not some way my son can get through college in less than four years."
4. "Certainly," replied Garfield, "but it all depends upon what you want to make of your boy."
5. "What do you mean?"
6. "Well," said Garfield, "when God wants to make an oak tree, He takes a hundred years, but when He wants to make a squash, He takes only two months."
7.
8. "Simplify, simplify,"
9. "I wish I was as sure of anything as he is of everything,"
10. "If in the last few years," said Gelett Burgess, "you haven't discarded a major opinion or acquired a new one, check your pulse. You may be dead."

EXERCISE 2

1. "Flammable means the same as inflammable; valuable means the same as invaluable; and ravel means the same as unravel,"
2. A young man filling out a job application came to the question about marital status and wrote, "Eligible."
3. "I never understand anything," wrote Hugh Walpole, "until I have written about it."

4. In Japan, where families still arrange marriages for some young people, a young man said, "We may not marry the girl we love, but we love the girl that we marry."

5. A. A. Milne's children's books include *Winnie the Pooh, The House at Pooh Corner, When We Were Very Young,* and *Now We Are Six.*

6. "Children need love," says Harold S. Hulbert, "especially when they do not deserve it."

7. "Mozart was not an accomplished pianist at the age of eight as the result of spending his days in front of a television set,"

8. The guidebook to the Shenandoah National Park says, "The candy bar you take into the woods should provide at least the energy needed for bringing the wrapper out."

9. "You can think without writing," my instructor says, "but you can't write without thinking."

10.

EXERCISE 3

1. "Will it take you long to check the reference?"
2. "I'll do it as quick as a wink,"
3. "How quick is that?"
4. "Well, physiologists of the eye tell us it's between .3 and .4 of a second,"
5. "You do know a lot,"
6. "And if it interests you, skin deep is from ⅟₁₆ to ⅛ of an inch deep."
7. "Really! Now I wonder if you can tell me how fast a snail's pace is."
8. "Oh, that's easy," he said. "A snail travels about two inches in a minute."
9. "What you know astounds me!"
10. "Oh, I may know a few facts," he said, "but you are worth your weight in gold. And that makes you worth about $500,000."

EXERCISE 4

1. "I've discovered some word games," said Cindy. "Do you know what a palindrome word is?"
2. "Nope," said Pete. "Never heard of it. What is it?"
3. "It's a word that can be written either forward or backward. *Eye, level, radar,* and *rotator* are examples."
4. "I can think of some more," said Pete. "How about *deed* and *bob?*"
5. "Yes," said Cindy, "there are lots of them, but palindrome sentences are harder to find."
6. "Do you know any?"
7. "Yes, here's one that Adam is supposed to have said to Eve: *Madam, I'm Adam.*"
8. "How is that a palindrome sentence?"
9. "Well, try spelling it backward, and you'll see that it comes out just the same as spelling it forward."
10. "Sure enough, it does," said Pete. "Do you know any more?"

EXERCISE 5

1. "Yes, here's another palindrome sentence: *Was it a cat I saw?*"
2. "You're right. It does spell backward the same as forward,"
3. "Here's one more: *Dennis and Edna sinned.*"
4. "Amazing," said Pete. "I'll have to see if I can make one up."
5. "It's not easy."
6. When Le Baron Russel Briggs was dean of Harvard College, he once said to a student, "Why did you not finish your assignment?"
7. "I wasn't feeling very well, sir,"
8. "I think," said the dean, "that in time you may perhaps find that most of the work of the world is done by people who aren't feeling very well."
9. "Having the right to do it doesn't mean that it's right to do it,"
10. "Why is it," L. L. Levinson asks, "that goods sent by ship are called cargo while goods that go in a car are a shipment?"

EXERCISE 6

1. In our modern American literature course each student had to give a five-minute talk on the subject "My Favorite Author."
2. I chose Carl Sandburg and read his poem "Chicago" from his book *Chicago Poems.*
3. One student discussed Robert Frost's interest in the people of New Hampshire and read his poem "Mending Wall."
4. Another student told about Frost's interest in nature and read the short poem "Dust of Snow."
5. Someone talked about Hemingway and gave an analysis of the short story "The Killers,"
6. The person who talked about Vachel Lindsay gave an excellent reading of his poem "The Congo."
7. Another poem that was well read was "Patterns"
8. The only play discussed was *Our Town*
9. And the only novel presented was Mark Twain's *Tom Sawyer.*
10. The talk that interested me most, however, was one on *The Bridge of San Louis Rey* by Thornton Wilder.

EXERCISE 7

1. "Character," my dad used to say, "is the ability to eat only one salted peanut."
2. Oliver Wendell Holmes wrote, "Many people die with their music still in them."
3. "Education," said Robert Frost, "is the ability to listen to almost anything without losing your temper or your self-confidence."
4. "Golf is a good walk spoiled,"
5. "Control smoking, alcohol, handguns, overeating, and seat belts," says James Speer, a professor of biomedical history at the University of Washington, "and that would be a new world."
6. "There is at least one TV in 94 percent of U.S. homes," the lecturer said, "but there are bathtubs in only 85 percent of homes. Perhaps more brains are being washed than bodies."

7. "I never lose sight of the fact," said Katherine Hepburn, "that just being is fun."
8. "Some days the only good things on TV are the vase and the clock,"
9. "After three days fish and visitors begin to stink,"
10. In his novel *Heart of Darkness,*

EXERCISE 8

1. "Do you know who was the first American to make a flight into space?"
2. "Sure, it was Alan Shepard,"
3. "Wrong," Cheryl said. "It was a chimpanzee named Ham. He made his flight on January 31, 1961, just before Alan Shepard made his."
4. "I didn't know that,"
5. "Few people do," Cheryl responded. "And do you know who was the first American to orbit the earth?"
6. "John Glenn,"
7. "No, it was Enos, another chimp, who circled the earth two times on November 29, 1961, just before John Glenn made his orbit."
8. "Why did the chimps go first?"
9. "NASA administrators wanted to test their space technology on chimpanzees before sending human astronauts up. Both chimps survived their flights and furnished NASA with valuable information."
10. "That's interesting,"

EXERCISE 9

"What are you doing?"
The man answered, "I am cutting a piece of stone."
He asked the same question of another man and received the reply, "I am earning five shillings twopence a day."
But a third man, in answer to his inquiry, said, "I am helping Sir Christopher Wren build a beautiful cathedral."

Capital Letters (p. 194)

EXERCISE 1

1. Midwest, West
2. Dad
3. Red River
4. Mount
5. National Park
6.
7.
8. Mother, Dad, Ocean
9. County, Golden Gate Bridge
10. West Coast, East

EXERCISE 2

1.
2. State University
3. Motor Company
4. Oil Company
5.

6. Dad
7. Dad
8. "How to Buy Your First Motorcycle"
9.
10.

EXERCISE 3

1. College
2. University
3. Southwest State University
4.
5. English

6.
7.
8. Accounting Firm
9. Mother
10. Thanksgiving Day

EXERCISE 4

1.
2.
3.
4. Junior College
5. Community College

6. University
7. Dad, Mom
8.
9. Mom
10.

EXERCISE 5

1.
2.
3. Grace Lutheran Church
4. Building
5. Drama Department

6. Dad
7.
8.
9. Central Illinois Public Service Company
10. Fourth

EXERCISE 6

1.
2. Aunt, Uncle
3. Lake Superior
4. Norwegian, Finnish
5. South's

6. Buffalo Bayou
7. Bay, Gulf
8. River, River
9.
10.

EXERCISE 7

1.
2.
3. Main Street
4. Main
5. Century Museum

6. Dad
7. Professor,
8. West, Midwest
9. Roman
10. West Coast

Review of Punctuation and Capital Letters (p. 197)

EXERCISE 1

1. Should people be allowed the unrestricted use of their national parks?
2. Many say that it is their right to enjoy their parks,
3. Sailing down the Colorado River through the Grand Canyon, for example, is one of the most spectacular river trips in the world.
4. More than 16,000 people take the trip every year,
5. Strapped to rubber rafts, the riders shoot the rapids. Then they float between the canyon walls,
6. Some go in oar-rigged rafts;
7. The environmentalists say the trip should be made silently in oar-rigged rafts,
8. The voyagers used to leave behind them garbage and trampled vegetation,
9. The National Park Service has taken control,
10. The problem of park use is not new. It

EXERCISE 2

1. Rochester, New York, used to be called the Flour City because it had so many flour mills. Now it is called the Flower City
2. The most frequently sung songs in English are "Happy Birthday to You," "For He's a Jolly Good Fellow," and "Auld Lang Syne."
3. George Bernard Shaw wrote, "The test of a man's or a woman's breeding is how they behave in a quarrel."
4. Did you know that Charles Darwin and Abraham Lincoln were born on the same day—February 12, 1809?
5. In 1968 the London Bridge was sold to the McCullough Oil Corporation of Los Angeles for $2,460,000. It was transported and reassembled at Lake Havasu City,
6. A sentence containing 1,300 words appears in *Absalom, Absalom,*
7. Love is like the moon. When it doesn't increase,
8. Gandhi had this sign on the wall of his home: "When you are in the right, you can afford to keep your temper, and when you are in the wrong, you cannot afford to lose it."
9. "Love does not consist," said Antoine de Saint-Exupéry, "of gazing at each other but of looking outward together in the same direction."
10. A nickel goes a long way these days. You

EXERCISE 3

1. Many things that we consider modern were really discovered by the early Greeks. Democritus in the fifth century B.C. developed an atomic theory, spoke of a number of universes, spoke of mountains on the moon, had a theory of evolution, and knew that color is not inherent in things.

2. In the fifth century B.C., Socrates said, "Children now love luxury. They have had manners and contempt for authority. Children are now tyrants, not the servants of their households. They contradict their parents, chatter before company, gobble up dainties at the table, and tyrannize their teachers."
3. "Athletics have become professionalized,"
4. "The first of June and nothing has been done by the Senate,"
5. "I am in difficulty both summer and winter about my salary,"

EXERCISE 4

Psychologists say that how you write your name can be revealing. If you write your name clearly, you probably have nothing to hide. You are likely reasonably satisfied with yourself and sincerely want to communicate with other people. If, on the other hand, your signature is simply an unreadable scrawl, you may be ashamed of your name or of what you have written. Or you may be afraid to communicate with others or feel so inferior that you have to pretend you're a big shot with a scrawl for a signature. You should remember, however, that a big shot always has a secretary to type a name underneath the scrawl. So if you want to use a big-shot scrawl on your papers,

EXERCISE 5

The Old State House in Hartford, Connecticut, which is the nation's oldest statehouse, was in danger of being demolished to make way for office buildings. Local residents formed the Old State House Association and organized a drive to get funds for restoration. Although large corporations donated the bulk of the money, the association wanted to get more people involved. They decided upon an unusual mode of taxation. Each window with a view of the Old State House was taxed $5. The citizens responded enthusiastically, and the windows tax brought in about $8,700. The Old State House was restored, and Hartford had saved an important historic landmark.

That was in 1975. In 1989 it was decided to ask for a voluntary fee of $10 per window to help with the upkeep of the State House, which has now been turned into a museum. The companies and individuals with a view responded gladly.

Comprehensive Test on Entire Text (p. 203)

1. She ~~ask~~ *asked* my sister and me to serve the dessert. We ~~was~~ *were* glad to help.

2. ~~If~~ *A* a person *who* is serious about getting an education ~~you~~ can get one.

3. ~~Because~~ I had done the very best I could all semester in my math course.

4. ~~Its~~ *It's* not my fault that ~~hes~~ *he's* not here. ~~he~~ *He* should be coming soon.

5. While they were on ~~there~~ *their* way, they lost ~~they're~~ *their* keys.

6. I can't decide whether to study math, write my paper, or ~~whether I should~~ just watch television tonight.

7. I'll stay at home, Michelle, if you're going to be ~~hear to~~ *here too*.

8. ~~Your~~ *You're* going to the game, aren't you?

9. We girls made ~~a~~ *an* upside-down cake for ~~desert~~ *dessert*. ~~everyone~~ *Everyone* liked it.

10. I was ~~quiet~~ *quite* happy to hear about ~~Sarahs~~ *Sarah's* promotion.

11. When we reached the main road, we ~~turn~~ *turned* south and then ~~West~~ *west*.

12. ~~Which~~ *It* took us about five miles out of ~~are~~ *our* way.

13. ~~Its~~ *It's* the ~~Johnsons~~ *Johnsons'* car, but ~~there~~ *they're* letting me drive it.

14. Each of his trophies ~~are~~ *is* displayed in the entrance hall.

15. ~~Coming~~ *As the water came* quickly to the boiling point, she ~~turn~~ *turned* down the burner.

16. "That Honda belongs to my sister and me," Robin said.

17. I think ~~Kellys~~ *Kelly's* paper was more interesting then ~~Kays~~ *Kay's*.

18. I'm taking the following courses: psychology, history, ~~spanish~~ *Spanish*, and ~~english~~ *English*.

19. The Cherry Orchard, which I read last year, is a play by Chekhov.

20. He ~~told~~ *said to* his brother, "~~his~~ *your* TV ~~needed~~ *needs* a new tube."

21. Two of my friends ~~goes~~ *go* to Mt. Hood ~~community college~~ *Community College*.

22. She was supposed to memorize the poem "Birches" from Robert Frost's book Mountain Interval.

23. They invited him and ~~I~~ *me* to go with them.

24. We walked as far as we could, and then we ~~give~~ *gave* up.

25. "You are responsible for what happens in the future," my counselor said, "no matter what has ~~happen~~ *happened* in the past."

26. I would have ~~went~~ *gone* to the parade if I had ~~knowed~~ *known* you ~~was~~ *were* going.

27. Dad gave my brother and me tickets to the final baseball game.

28. Last week I ~~join~~ *joined* a lawn crew and have ~~all ready~~ *already* ~~work~~ *worked* four days.

29. My friend and I are hoping to get jobs for the summer.

30. ~~If one~~ *One who* has done all the exercises in this text, ~~you'll~~ *will* do well on this test.

31. Did you know that the octopus, of which there are about 150 species, is

    the most intelligent of all invertebrates?

Writing

EXERCISE 1 (p. 208)

1. Music as a career
   Our rock band
   Playing the drums in our rock band
2. Refinishing furniture
   Refinishing a chair
   Removing an old finish
3. My summer job
   My summer job driving a truck
   Learning to unload a cement truck
4. The house where I grew up
   Our backyard
   Our backyard skating rink
5. My elementary school
   Miss MacDonald's kindergarten
   Our kindergarten grocery store
6. Cross-country skiing
   Equipment for cross-country skiing
   Buying the right skis

EXERCISE 2 (p. 213)

2, 6, 7, 8, 11, and 12 should be marked THESIS.

EXERCISE 3 (p. 213)

1. Cycling across Arkansas showed me I have endurance.
3. Two reasons account for the relatively small population of Canada.
4. Living through a tornado was the most frightening experience of my life.

5. Building a go-cart was my greatest childhood achievement.
9. The U.S should convert more rapidly to the metric system.
10. Tutoring a Japanese student taught me things I didn't know about English.
13. A visit to the Smithsonian in Washington taught me some facts about our First Ladies.

EXERCISE 4 (p. 215)

I've decided to change my job.
1. There's no future in my job.
2. The hours are long and inconvenient.
3. My work is totally unrelated to my interests.

Ours is a wasteful society.
1. We waste electricity.
2. We waste gas.
3. We destroy our forests by wasting paper.
4. We fail to recycle garbage.
5. We encourage a "throw away and buy new" attitude.

I can change a tire in three easy steps.
1. I read my service manual.
2. I take the jack from the trunk.
3. I phone the nearest garage.

EXERCISE 5 (p. 221)

All should be marked S except 8 and 9.

EXERCISE 6 (p. 222)

In the first place
Also *or* Then too
Also *or* Then too
Furthermore
Therefore

Summary of "Juvenile Juries" (p. 231)

In Denver, volunteer juvenile juries are sentencing some junior and senior high school first-time offenders. The jurors pass sentence on students who admit guilt and agree to abide by the penalties their peers impose. Typical sentences include unpaid community service, obeying tight curfews, getting a job, making restitution in cases of theft. The delinquents prefer to face juvenile juries rather than a judge because they feel their peers understand them. Also they get a hearing within days after arrest instead of having to brood for several months. Out of 55 sentenced by juvenile juries, only one has committed another crime.

Index

a, an, 7
abbreviations, 161
accept, except, 7
addresses, commas in, 170
advise, advice, 7
affect, effect, 7
agreement
  of subject and pronoun, 116
  of subject and verb, 115
all ready, already, 8
application letter, 243
are, or, our, 8

brake, break, 8
breaking words into parts, 40

capital letters, 193
choose, chose, 8
clauses
  dependent, 80
  essential and nonessential, 177
  independent, 72–73
cliché, 155
clothes, cloths, 8
coarse, course, 8
colon, 162
comma, 169–77
comma splice (*see* run-together
  sentences)
complement, compliment, 8
conscious, conscience, 9
contractions, 25

dash, 162
dates, commas in, 170
dependent words, 80
dessert, desert, 9
dialect expressions, 110
dictionary, use of, 46–52
do, due, 9
does, dose, 9
doubling a final consonant, 41

evaluation, writing an, 246
exclamation point, 161

feel, fill, 9
fourth, forth, 9
fragments, 80–81, 88
free writing, 206

have, of, 9
hear, here, 10

interrupter, commas around, 176
introductory expression, comma after,
  170
it's, its, 10

knew, new, 10
know, no, 10

lead, led, 16
letter of application, 243
limiting the topic, 207
loose, lose, 16

modifier
  dangling or misplaced, 128
moral, morale, 16

organizing a paper, 218

paragraph writing, 220
parallel construction, 133–34
  in thesis statement, 140
passed, past, 16
past participle, 104–5
period, 161
personal, personnel, 16
piece, peace, 16
possessives, 31–33
prefixes, 40
prepositional phrases, 61
principal, principle, 17

principal parts of verbs, 104–7
progress tests, 43, 114
pronouns
   agreement of, 115
   possessive form, 32
   reference of, 124
   subject and nonsubject forms, 121
proofreading aloud, 228
proofreading exercises, 24, 39, 60, 71,
   96, 113, 132, 159, 200–202
punctuation marks, 161–86

question mark, 161
quiet, quite, 17
quotation marks, 185–86

resume, 245
rewriting, 225
right, write, 17
run-together sentences, 72–73

semicolon, 72, 162
sex bias in words, 116–17
shift
   in person, 145–46
   in time, 141
specific details, 209
spelling
   doubling a final consonant, 41
   list of frequently misspelled words,
    44
   words broken into parts, 40
   words often confused, 7–10, 16–18
standard English verbs, 97–107

subjects and verbs, 55–67
summary writing, 231–42

tests
   comprehensive, 203
   progress, 43, 114, 157
than, then, 17
their, there, they're, 17
thesis statement, 212–16
threw, through, 17
title
   for a paper, 210
   underlining of, 185
topic sentence, 220
transition expressions, 222
two, too, to, 18

usage (*see* words often confused)

verbs
   helping, 104–5
   principal parts, 106–7
   regular and irregular, 97–99

weather, whether, 18
were, where, 18
who's, whose, 18
woman, women, 18
wordiness, 151
words often confused, 7–10, 16–18
writing
   eight steps to better, 206

you're, your, 18